FINANCIAL SWAPS

New Strategies in Currency and
Coupon Risk Management

FINANCIAL SWAPS

New Strategies in Currency and Coupon Risk Management

Carl R. Beidleman
DuBois Professor of Finance
Lehigh University
Bethlehem, Pennsylvania

Dow Jones-Irwin
Homewood, Illinois

to Inge

This publication is designed to provide accurate and authoritative information in regard to the subject matter covered. It is sold with the understanding that the publisher is not engaged in rendering legal, accounting, or other professional service. If legal advice or other expert assistance is required, the services of a competent professional person should be sought.

From a Declaration of Principles jointly adopted by a Committee of the American Bar Association and a Committee of Publishers.

ISBN 0-87094-577-7
Library of Congress Catalog Card No. 84-72997
Printed in the United States of America

1 2 3 4 5 6 7 8 9 0 K 2 1 0 9 8 7 6 5

Preface

The 1970s have certainly not been dull in comparison with other recent decades. The decade experienced crises in energy, environment, and human rights; it witnessed political tensions in almost every world population center and saw military confrontations on nearly every continent. In the context of financial management, this decade gave rise to two watershed events in terms of their pervasive impact on risk and the need to manage financial positions.

The first event was the transition of the principal world currencies from fixed to floating exchange rates. This transition began in August 1971 with the initial devaluation of the U.S. dollar and ended in 1973 with the adoption of rather freely floating exchange rates among the major world currencies. Since then, exchange rates have fluctuated significantly, giving rise to increased exchange rate risk and elevating the need to manage exposed positions. Meanwhile, exposure to exchange rate risk has also increased markedly in terms of increased foreign investment, trade, and financing.

The second major event of the 1970s came near the end of the decade. In October 1979 the U.S. Federal Reserve Board announced a major policy change to target its money management operations on the monetary aggregates rather than on the level of interest rates. As a result of this change in policy, U.S. interest rates became much more volatile than they were previously. Since much of world financing and investing is tied directly or indirectly to U.S. dollar interest rates, this change has had a significant effect on the degree of coupon risk faced by financial managers. The dual impact that volatile exchange rates *and* interest rates can have on balance sheets and portfolios has led to the development of improved means to manage both exposures.

Financial Swaps: New Strategies in Currency and Coupon Risk Management begins with the basics of cash flow management. It develops a conceptual framework for the management of currency and coupon exposure, which quickly leads to more advanced material. It focuses on the underlying need for financial instruments rather than on the pricing of capital assets or macroeconomic concerns.

The book is organized to highlight the applications that arise from normal business activities that cause a currency or coupon risk exposure. It then focuses on capital market anomalies that give rise to arbitrage profit opportunities. Each set of applications is liberally illustrated with cases. The variety of these illustrations should enable most users to identify one situation that comes closest to their specific applications.

The combination of a comprehensive conceptual framework and extensive case studies can be readily used to focus on the management of currency and coupon risk. I have attempted to provide enough of the basics of risk assessment and risk management to enable readers to apply their problems to those illustrated in the book and to adapt to new situations as they arise.

The book is primarily intended for those who occupy or are preparing to occupy the position of corporate treasurer. It should also prove useful to financial managers and portfolio managers, whose function is to source or manage funds. General managers and directors should also find it useful in developing an understanding of the management of currency and coupon risk. Finally, analysts and executives of financial intermediaries should use it frequently as they seek to manage their own balance sheets or to offer advice and service in assisting their clients in asset and liability management. Hence, the book should also be useful in advanced undergraduate and MBA courses in financial management, in banking and executive development seminars, and as a resource volume for financial intermediaries and general business practitioners.

In developing the examples and case studies used to illustrate various applications of long-date cover, I made no attempt to limit them to U.S. dollar transactions. Rather, recognizing the international focus of the book, I tried to seek out illustrations and case studies in as many different currencies as practical. With the exception of public institutions, the names of all of the parties used in the actual examples and case studies have been withheld. This has been done at the request of many who offered confidential information regarding their financial management practices.

Acknowledgment of assistance in research undertakings can never be complete. This endeavor is no different in that regard. I do, however, express my appreciation to Richard W. Barsness, Dean of the College of Business and Economics at Lehigh University, for establishing an environment in which efforts such as this can be fulfilled. His ongoing encouragement and stimulating questions and conversations were most helpful. I am also grateful to many members of the community of investment and merchant bankers and to users of long-date cover for generously providing information regarding instruments, applications, and terms. In all, I contacted over one hundred firms with about an equal split between users and financial intermediaries. While it is not possible to acknowledge all of them, a number of individuals stand out based on their understanding of the concepts and their willingness to help me. Particular thanks go to Charles R. Gates, formerly of Citibank, Paul S. Efron of First Boston, Ronald W. Moore of Lehman Brothers, and

Marion Gislasson of Morgan Guaranty, all of New York. Helpful assistance from the London segment of the market came from David P. Pritchard and Victoria D. Blake, both of Citibank, John A. Price of Bankers Trust, Peter Odgen of Morgan Stanley, Allan S. Wilson of Credit Suisse–First Boston, Owen T. Mitchell of National Westminster Bank, Jeremy B. Greenhalgh of Goldman Sachs, Henry J. Mayer of Merrill Lynch, Allan Greenhalgh of the Royal Bank of Canada, J. Loughlin Callahan of S. G. Warberg, Wolfgang Moller of Commerzbank, William L. James of Hill Samuel, Geoffrey Munn of Morgan Grenfell, and Heather J. Maizels of Kidder Peabody. Significant contributions from the Toronto financial community came from Barry D. Bruce of the Canadian Imperial Bank of Commerce, Emery L. Grossland of the Royal Bank of Canada, James J. Helbronner of Wood Gundy, and Gordon K. Sherwin of Toronto Dominion Bank.

I am also especially indebted to those who read the manuscript and provided valuable suggestions during the initial and review stages. These include John W. Townsend of Goldman Sachs, New York; David F. Swensen of Shearson, Lehman, American Express, New York; and Richard H. Stevens of Independence Bancorp, Perkasie, Pennsylvania. Academic reviewers who provided useful comments include George E. Pinches of the University of Kansas and Christine R. Hekman of Duke University. In addition to reviewing the manuscript, John Townsend provided many helpful comments, applications, and contacts all along the way. Without this continuous availability of resource material, I doubt that the book would have become a reality.

I also acknowledge the generous support of a number of sources of funding that helped underwrite the costs of the effort. The Earhart Foundation of Ann Arbor, Michigan, provided a grant to assist with travel costs. The Fairchild–Martindale Center for the Study of Private Enterprise at Lehigh University provided a grant for partial summer support, and the Allen C. DuBois Professorship expense fund provided funds to augment travel and other research costs. Finally, the Union Bank of Northeastern Pennsylvania provided funds for research assistance.

I am also grateful to Samuel Weaver, who provided yeoman service as research assistant and reviewed the manuscript material. Thanks are also due to Janice Schaeffer and Judi Moran, who cheerfully typed the many drafts and assisted in the data analysis.

Finally, I thank my wife, Inge, for her confidence and encouragement during the long process that led to the preparation of this book. She alone remembers when it all began. The errors of omission or commission are mine.

Bethlehem, Pennsylvania
July 1984

Contents

List of Tables

Table
Page

Table   *Page*

List of Figures

Figure   *Page*

Introduction

THE CHARACTERISTICS OF CASH FLOWS

In its broadest and, perhaps, simplest context, finance may be thought of as a study of cash flows. Each of the myriad applications of financial management deals with the movement of funds toward or away from an entity. As we examine currency and coupon risk management, we should place them properly in context as part of a broader set of financial issues. This can be accomplished by briefly focusing on the characteristics of cash flows and evaluating the alternative means available to modify or manage an entity's (or firm's) cash flows.

Domestic activity is limited to four fundamental characteristics of cash flows. They are (*a*) the size of the flow, (*b*) its direction (in or out), (*c*) its timing, and (*d*) its quality or degree of uncertainty. These characteristics seem simplistic considering the multibillion dollar magnitude of the financial services industry; nonetheless, domestic cash flows can be defined by *size, direction, timing,* and *quality.* Whether we consider credit analysis, project finance, security valuation, capital markets, insurance, portfolio management, risk assessment, or even the current exotics (i.e., financial futures, options on securities, options on indices, and options on futures), these four attributes of cash flows form the foundation for financial analysis and decision making.

In nondomestic applications, a fifth characteristic may enter the picture—*currency* of the cash flow. The currency of cash flows warrants attention only when it differs from the currency in which the financial results are to be measured. Although questions of foreign exchange surface frequently when transactions cross national borders, many international transactions can be conducted exclusively in terms of home currency. You can, for example, denominate an international transaction in your home currency or conduct international financing or investing in the Euromarket with your home currency.

It is not possible, however, to have an international commercial transaction denominated in the home currency of both parties. Moreover, Euromarkets are not always available or appropriate for all international financial or investment transactions. Hence, many large and small transactions have been arranged in foreign currencies from the point of view of at least one of the parties to the transaction. This additional currency characteristic rounds out the fundamental components of the nature of cash flows. Since financial management is concerned with the efficient management of cash flows, examining the available ways to modify the characteristics of cash flows so as to make them more amenable to the needs or preferences of financial managers is desirable.

MODIFYING THE CHARACTERISTICS OF CASH FLOWS

Expectations for cash flows constitute the fundamental components of analytical input for all financial decisions. In developing expected cash flows for a course of action, each analyst must specify the four or five characteristics outlined above. Cash flow formulation may be extremely difficult for many financial ventures, especially those where the quality or uncertainty of the flows is sufficiently large that it precludes a great deal of accuracy in the size and timing of the flows. In extreme cases even the direction of the expected flow may be unclear. Such high risk may be associated with state-of-the-art investment projects involving new products, processes, or markets.

Despite the uncertainty of many financial decisions, a very large set of financial decisions exists for which the quality of the underlying cash flows is remarkably high and the uncertainty connected with the flows is quite low (in some cases approaching zero). Cash flows of this sort are, of course, associated with fixed income or debt securities, where highest quality flows (near-zero risk) are related to the obligations of the central government. In situations that involve high-quality cash flows, the underlying size, direction, and timing may be readily altered by implementing appropriate borrowing or investment strategies. Provided that active capital markets exist, straightforward portfolio changes can be made that shift the size, direction, and timing of expected cash flows to a revised but equivalent configuration as prescribed by the financial managers.

When evaluating the quality characteristic of expected cash flows, little can be done to alter the underlying risk profile of project, equity, or even low-grade, debt-related cash flows. However, as a result of recent innovations in financial instruments, modifications can be made, if desired, in the quality of interest payments on certain classes of debt instruments. These innovations involve the use of the newly developed financial instruments known as *coupon swaps* and *currency swaps*.

COUPON SWAPS

A *coupon swap* provides a convenient means of altering the quality characteristic of expected cash flows. Its primary objective is to exchange floating-rate interest payments for fixed-rate payments, or vice versa. In the past most contractual interest payments were fixed over the life of a debt instrument. However, as a result of innovations in financial instruments, many debt issues in recent years call for interest or coupon payments that float or are revised every three or six months. The basis for these revisions is some well-understood market rate such as the London Interbank Offer Rate (LIBOR), some short-term treasury rate, commercial paper rate, or other index of rates. Such instruments are called *floating-rate notes (FRN)*. Because the interest rate floats with market rates, floating-rate interest flows are less certain than the quality of the coupon flows of fixed-rate instruments. Using currently available documentation, this question of quality or risk of the coupon cash flows can be altered by swapping the floating-rate coupon with a borrower who may be more willing to face a floating interest cost in return for another party's servicing his fixed-rate coupon. Hence, a coupon swap may be defined as an exchange of a coupon or interest payment stream of one configuration for another coupon stream with a different configuration on essentially the same principal amount. Moreover, coupon swaps of one floating-rate instrument for another floating-rate instrument, where the interest rate floats on a different basis, are also possible. These swaps would be done to alter the quality of the coupon cash flows and to make them more compatible with the preferences of specific debt security issuers. Investors in fixed- and floating-rate securities would then be able to swap their coupon receipts as their preferences dictate.

3

CURRENCY SWAPS

The currency in which cash flows are denominated is important because it may significantly alter the ultimate cash flows to the decision makers after converting to their currencies. If the currency of the cash flows is other than the home currency of the decision makers, and if that foreign currency may be expected to fluctuate in terms of the home currency, the home currency value of the residual cash flows may be seriously altered. This condition may be more onerous the further the expected foreign currency flows are from the present. Cash flows with time horizons of 10 or 15 years can be seriously affected. Given all the forces that influence exchange rates, projecting cash flows so far out in time is extremely difficult to do with any degree of confidence. Nevertheless, long-term financial decisions where cash flows are denominated in foreign currencies over many years must still be made.

As in the case of coupon exchanges, instruments that enable participants to cover long-date foreign exchange risk have been developed. In this context, "long date" is taken to mean beyond one year, and in many cases implies periods of seven to ten years. The menu of instruments is somewhat broader than in coupon swaps, but the substance of the arrangement is essentially the same. In a currency swap, each party exchanges one currency for another on day one with an agreement to reverse the exchange at a specified time and at a specified exchange rate. Currency exchange agreements may consist of a stream of currency in each period, say year, as may be necessary to service the interest payments or receipts on an obligation in foreign currency, or they may provide for a simple one-shot or bullet transfer of funds at maturity. Many applications exist for currency exchanges, and various instruments have been devised to accommodate the intricacies of alternative applications.

Instruments and applications for long-date currency cover have been evolving since the late 1960s. In fact, because the documentation for long-date currency swaps was so highly refined, coupon swaps were able to cover the market fully since their introduction in 1982. Because the evolution of strategies for covering long-date financial exposure was initially developed to hedge currency risk, the bulk of this book is built upon currency cover concepts. Then, as appropriate, I apply these concepts to the management of the uncertain coupon payments associated with floating-rate notes and to the rigidity of fixed-rate interest obligations. Asset or liability management of this sort is termed *coupon cover*. Then, after extensive discussion of these concepts and their applications, I evaluate the nature of both currency and coupon swap markets.

The next ten chapters deal with long-date currency cover. The material of the next section offers some basic background in foreign exchange risk and places the need for currency cover in context. A similar introduction to the nature of coupon risk is presented in Chapter 12.

FOREIGN EXCHANGE RISK

Since the emergence of flexible exchange rates in the early 1970s, changes in economic fundamentals have been quickly reflected in the exchange rates of most of the actively traded currencies. As a result, recent volatility in inflation and interest rates among countries has produced wide swings in exchange rates. These fluctuations have significantly increased the exchange rate risk faced by participants in international trade and investment. This volatility in exchange rates is not expected to subside markedly in the near future. Unless properly managed, this uncertain exchange rate environment can lead to sizable gains or losses on routine foreign exchange transactions.

The high volume of short-term commercial and financial transactions has led to the development of efficient instruments and markets in forward exchange, where firms can avoid the exchange rate risk encountered in short-term international transactions. An example using actual exchange rates illustrates the management of the exchange rate risk typically encountered in short-term foreign transactions.

Short-Term Currency Exposure

An American firm wished to procure raw material parts in Canada and placed an order for parts costing 10,000 Canadian dollars (C$) on June 15, 1982. The parts were shipped on July 7 and invoiced with terms net 30 days, payment to be made in Canadian currency. On July 7 the Canadian dollar was selling for US$0.7717. The American buyer knew his cost in Canadian dollars but faced an uncertain cost in his home currency if the Canadian dollar were to appreciate or depreciate (i.e., change in value in terms of the U.S. currency). If the Canadian unit appreciated, the buyer faced a higher cost in U.S. dollars; conversely, if the Canadian dollar floated downward against the U.S. dollar, the buyer faced a windfall gain.

A number of choices were available to the American firm. It could do nothing and simply bear the risk of changes in exchange rates. It could acknowledge that adverse outcomes in exchange rates might eliminate its operating margins. Since it had insufficient expertise in forecasting changes in exchange rates, it might wish to hedge this risk in the forward currency markets. Another alternative would be to purchase the foreign exchange on July 8 at the spot rate of US$0.7717/C$ and invest the funds in Canada until the invoice was due or simply pay the bill in advance. These last two alternatives entail either incurring management costs in Canada or losing interest for the credit period. They are seldom used in practice.

The choices reduce to covering in the forward currency market or bearing the risk of exchange rate changes. Fortunately, forward markets in active currencies like the Canadian dollar have developed over the years, and the American firm could easily find forward quotes for Canadian dollars for delivery in 30 days against U.S. dollars. On July 7, a representative quote was US$0.7707/C$ for 30 days, reflecting a discount of US$0.0010/C$ or an annualized forward discount of 1.56 percent. Because of the discount implicit in the quote, the buying firm could both hedge its foreign exchange risk position *and* save 1.56 percent (annualized) on the cost of the parts. Evidently, the participants in the forward markets expected the Canadian dollar to depreciate against its U.S. equivalent and were willing to offer Canadian dollars for future delivery at a lower price than was offered for spot or current delivery.

Using the forward currency market, the American firm could lock in a fixed cost for its parts and fully side-step the risk of exchange rate changes if it chose to do so. As it turned out, the American firm would have been wise to hedge, because the Canadian dollar did not depreciate over the subsequent 30 days as expected, but, in fact, rose to US$0.8009/C$ on August 6, 1982. The appreciation in this one month was 3.78 percent over its July 7 value, and, had the firm not hedged, it would have had to pay US$0.8009/C$ times C$10,000 or US$8,009 for what it could have hedged for US$7,707. This misjudgement represented a real loss of 3.91 percent for *not* hedging. This difference in cost could have had a significant impact on the firm's final operating profits.

Availability of Forward Currency Contracts

The foreign exchange risk encountered in short-term commercial and financial transactions in major currencies can be readily hedged in the forward currency markets offered by major banks or in currency futures markets such as the International Monetary Market of the Chicago Mercantile Exchange or the London International Financial Futures Exchange. Forward currency positions have been generally available in reasonable size from commercial banks through periods of up to six months. For maturities beyond six months, however, the volume of transactions decreases markedly. Very little volume has been readily transacted based upon open quotations beyond one year.

As a result of the dearth of available forward contracts beyond one year, most long-term foreign exchange exposures either went uncovered or cover was sought by attempting to borrow the currency in which a long forward position was expected. Another seldom-used alternative entailed investing in a currency that was expected to be short in the future and using the proceeds of the investment to cover the expected foreign currency disbursement. In many cases the borrower could neither tolerate the added foreign currency debt nor find lenders. Moreover, the investment to cover expected future currency requirements required assets not normally available. Hence, long-date foreign exchange risk was frequently borne by the transactor with the hope that the trend of relative movements in price levels and interest rates between the countries would compensate for any loss suffered due to changes in exchange rates.

Such a practice resulted in extensive long-term foreign exchange exposures and thwarted many opportunities for developing trade and investment across borders. However, as multinational corporations grew in size and international diversity and as money center banks followed their multinational customers across national boundaries and developed intricate international banking networks, the recognized demand for long-date foreign exchange positions expanded. Supranational organizations such as the World Bank and the Inter-American Development Bank also found financing applications that relied on long-date foreign exchange instruments, further augmenting the demand for long-date currency cover.

ORGANIZATION OF THE BOOK

In the foregoing introductory section, I attempted to illustrate that certain fundamental characteristics of financial flows may be altered to suit the needs or preferences of financial managers. I have also briefly described how currency and coupon swaps may be used to accomplish these objectives. These tasks are elaborated upon in great detail as the book progresses. In the balance of this chapter, I provide a succinct preview of the material that lies ahead and its order of presentation.

To promptly identify the mechanisms available to procure long-date currency cover, Chapter 2 develops the instruments used for currency cover. It illustrates how they have evolved and comments on relevant applications appropriate for each type of instrument. Chapter 3 then examines the cash flow, pricing, and instrument-specific considerations of each type of long-date currency cover instrument.

Chapter 4 turns to the requisites for profitable cover of existing or planned currency exposure. It focuses on market inefficiencies and how they lead to opportunities for profit, using long-date currency and/or coupon cover. The discussion of market inefficiencies is then linked to a number of innovations in finance to show how modern financial instruments and methodology can be deployed to exploit market inefficiencies while they persist. It goes on to examine conceptual developments in asset and liability management in the context of currency and coupon cover as it shows financial decision makers the vast number of applications available. This material helps depict a contemporary financial mind-set that is able to grasp the advantages of restructuring assets and liabilities when appropriate. Developing this mind-set requires study and probation of the newly available financial swap instruments. Accepting these techniques is necessary to make optimal a larger set of available financial and operating alternatives. Several examples illustrate how portfolio and financial managers can use a newly found freedom from former rigidities and increase the risk-return trade-offs of their organizations.

Chapter 5 evaluates the comparability of a sequence or strip of renewals of short-date currency cover instruments with a single long-date instrument. It focuses on the conditions necessary to provide financial managers with a full understanding of what each strategy entails in the way of assumptions and risk.

Following the discussion of the nature of instruments and cash flows, the requisites for profitable use of long-date currency cover, and the relative attractiveness of alternative strategies, Chapter 6 summarily examines the size and scope of the potential currency risk in the United States and abroad. Here potential currency exposures are recorded using currently available summary data. (The appendix presents more detailed information on many of the data series.)

Given the grounding in the mechanics and means of covering long-date currency exposure and the size and scope of potential exposure, Chapter 7 continues with descriptions of ways in which instruments have been employed and cover obtained. Because of the often complex or unique nature of applications of currency cover and because of the value of similar applications to the eventual deployment of currency cover by inexperienced users, most typical applications are augmented with variations wherever possible. I felt that extensive material on cases and applications would be most helpful in conveying a comprehensive understanding of the full scope of uses of financial swaps.

The numerous known applications of long-date currency cover are classified into four general categories, and each group is covered in a separate chapter. Each chapter is liberally dosed with examples of long-date currency cover for each specific type of application. Thus, Chapter 7 covers foreign exchange transaction and direct investment applications; Chapter 8 treats translation, taxation, and regulation applications; Chapter 9 contains applications on hedged financing or capital market hedges; and Chapter 10 discusses hedged investing.

Chapter 11 then looks at the development of the market for long-date currency cover, the growth of intermediaries, the nature of risk related to long-date currency cover, market size, and growth prospects for the future.

Chapter 12 shifts to a discussion of coupon cover and examines the characteristics of floating-rate and fixed-rate borrowers. It examines the nature of coupon risk and assesses the access borrowers have to funds of their choice. Having benefited from many similarities contained in the previous discussions on long-date currency cover, applications and instruments for long-date coupon cover are then found in Chapter 13.

Chapter 14 considers developments in the market for coupon cover. It traces the rapid initial growth of this market and contemplates what may be in store for the future. In particular, it focuses on combined currency and coupon swaps and speculates on new applications of various types of floating versus floating-rate coupon swaps. The chapter highlights the conditions under which each may be appropriate. It also provides a description of the deepening of the market that has occurred to date together with an examination of the role of the numerous participants in the market: various financial intermediaries, brokers, and the players or principals themselves.

Finally, Chapter 15 projects what may occur in the future in markets for long-date cover. It suggests potential applications and provides a forecast for use of long-date cover. Final comments on the role of the contemporary financial mind-set necessary to use available financial methodology and the efforts necessary to achieve that mind-set conclude the book.

Chapter 2

Instruments for Long-Date Currency Cover

INTRODUCTION

The fundamental role of long-date currency cover is to create *both* a long-term liability in a currency in which an undesired actual or planned long-term asset position exists *and* a corresponding asset in an alternative currency in which denominating assets is desirable. All of the applications of long-date currency cover are the result of one party's wanting to convert the denomination of some of its planned or actual liabilities to another currency. Before delving into the cash flow, pricing, and other considerations and applications of long-date currency cover, an examination of the nature of the various instruments available to provide such cover is necessary.

A number of alternative methods have evolved to accommodate the need for long-date currency cover. Some of these are simple to understand but often difficult or impossible to implement. Our discussion of the various means available to establish long-date currency cover begins with conceptually simple methods and proceeds to the more complex, but more popular, methods currently receiving the attention of increasing numbers of international financial managers. In this process we also see how modern means of obtaining long-date cover have evolved from the earlier, more rudimentary methods and examine limitations of each.

FOREIGN CURRENCY DEBT

Recall that the essential element of long-date cover is the creation of a term liability denominated in an undesired, say foreign, currency, which is offset by a term asset in a desired home currency. Given this objective, the most straightforward means of establishing long-date currency cover is to sell foreign debt for the desired term, convert the proceeds to the home currency, and invest them in home currency debt instruments that mature on the same date as the foreign debt. A flowchart of the underlying cash flows of a foreign currency debt instrument is shown in Figure 2–1.

Figure 2–1   Cash flows associated with a foreign currency debt placement

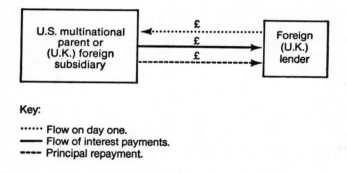

Key:

······ Flow on day one.
—— Flow of interest payments.
---- Principal repayment.

Despite its conceptual simplicity, this "do-it-yourself" method has a number of significant disadvantages in that many firms are unwilling or unable to undertake it and many foreign capital markets are not sufficiently developed to accommodate it. Firms tend to be either reluctant or unable to inflate their balance sheets by borrowing in one currency and investing in another. They are also aware that this practice generally has an adverse effect on financial ratios and that it may, in extreme cases, affect borrowing costs and lenders' willingness to extend additional credit.

The cost of obtaining long-date cover using foreign currency debt, when available, is the interest differential between the foreign loan rate and the domestic investment rate plus the transactions costs associated with borrowing, converting, and investing. The cash flow impact and limitations of each type of long-date currency cover are examined in detail in Chapter 3. Note, however, that the interest differential between the currencies is a cost common to all forms of long-date cover regardless of the nature of the instrument or its legal arrangement. Moreover, it is the interest differential that establishes the basis for negotiation of the actual pricing terms of more complex arrangements.

CURRENCY-COLLATERALIZED LOANS

Traditionally, enterprising international banks evaluate their global relationship with a customer and accommodate the customer's major needs for foreign exchange financing. Under these arrangements, a firm may be able to finance a foreign subsidiary by placing its home currency on deposit with its bank and have a foreign branch of that bank extend a credit to a subsidiary in another country and currency. In this case the bank assumes an exchange risk on the transaction as an inherent part of doing business in each country. The bank will undoubtedly offset its foreign exchange exposure against its own liability position in that currency (its so-called "book") or against other foreign exchange liabilities, or it may seek new foreign currency liabilities to restore its balanced currency position. Such currency-collateralized loans with bank participation are particularly attractive in countries where the capital markets are not well developed or where alternative sources of local finance may not be available. A flowchart of the underlying cash flows of a currency-collateralized loan is shown in Figure 2-2.

This two-step, cash-collateralized foreign exchange loan was the precursor of the *parallel loan* or *back-to-back (BTB) loans*. These more recent instruments have been developed to formalize the cash-collateralized foreign exchange bank loan and extend its use to combinations of nonbank parties, each seeking long-date cover. In a sense the cash-collateralized foreign exchange loan is a BTB loan with a bank, entered into to transfer liquidity from one currency to another. In the process the borrower also establishes a term liability in the (undesired) foreign currency. The bank either assumed this new foreign exchange asset exposure against its existing liabilities or quickly sought to lay it off against new liabilities (deposits) that its foreign branch was able to attract. In this way the bank was able to fill the global needs of its customer and price the loan and deposit to make a profit after full provision for its currency exposure. These concepts form the basic logic for parallel or BTB loans, which can be used with or without bank participation.

Figure 2-2 Cash flows associated with a currency-collateralized loan

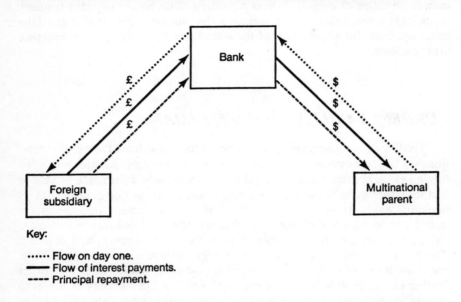

Key:

······ Flow on day one.
—— Flow of interest payments.
---- Principal repayment.

PARALLEL LOANS AND BACK-TO-BACK LOANS

Parellel and BTB loans are essentially similar economic and legal devices to which certain participants in long-date cover have attached special distinctions. Because of their great similarity, they are treated jointly here, and, subsequently, certain distinctions that have been made between them are highlighted.

Like a currency-collateralized loan, a parallel or BTB loan establishes a term liability in an undesired currency by borrowing the currency on day one from a (foreign) counterparty and promising to pay interest and principal in the (undesired) currency in which natural cash flows are generated by a foreign affiliate. However, to collateralize this arrangement, the domestic party concurrently lends available surplus liquidity in its desired (home) currency directly to its (foreign) counterparty or counterparty affiliate. The primary role of parallel or BTB loans is to transfer surplus liquidity from one currency to another. Implementation relies on a mirror-image match by two parties with excess liquidity in one currency and capital requirements in another currency for like amounts and periods. Unless a third party is prepared to assume the credit risk of each primary party, their credit standings must be similar and usually quite high. Because of their role in transferring liquidity from currency to currency, parallel or BTB loans are not useful as a primary financing strategy. They merely provide for transfer of liquidity from currency to currency while hedging the long-date exchange risk associated with an (undesired) foreign currency.

The instruments for parallel or BTB loans provide for two separate loan agreements, one for each currency, with an interest rate applicable to each. In two-party loans, the mutual agreements are between the two primary parties who may on-lend the funds to their respective foreign subsidiaries. Three- or four-party loans provide for the direct-lending of the funds to foreign subsidiaries of one or both of the parents. Flowcharts of the underlying cash flows in two-, three-, and four-party parallel loans are shown in Figures 2–3, 2–4, and 2–5, respectively.

Another variation provides for cross-lending, say, dollars by a U.S. parent to the U.S. subsidiary of a U.K. parent matched by the cross-lending of sterling by the U.K. parent to a British subsidiary of the U.S. parent. A flowchart of the underlying cash flows in a four-party cross-lending parallel loan is shown in Figure 2–6. Separate loan agreements are required with interest rates appropriate for the term and risk of each loan in its respective currency.

Figure 2–3 Cash flows associated with a two-party parallel loan

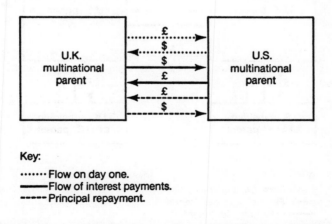

Key:
······· Flow on day one.
——— Flow of interest payments.
----- Principal repayment.

Figure 2–4 Cash flows associated with a three-party parallel loan

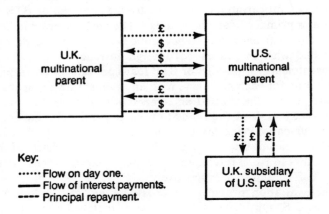

Figure 2–5 Cash flows associated with a four-party parallel loan

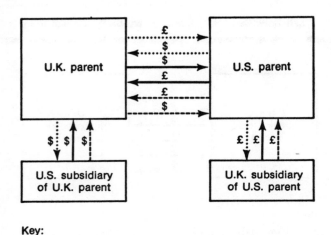

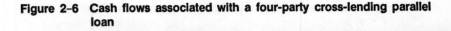

Figure 2-6 Cash flows associated with a four-party cross-lending parallel loan

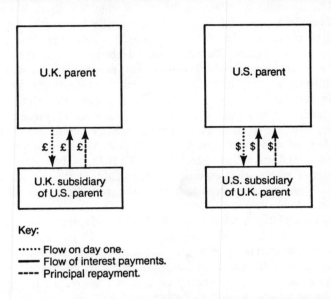

Key:

······ Flow on day one.
—— Flow of interest payments.
---- Principal repayment.

SECURITY PROVISIONS

Unlike the effective security arrangements that exist in cash-collateralized loans, the question of inadequate security in parallel or BTB loans may be significant. For one thing, cash-collateralized loans involve a bank as one party to the agreement, and banks are prepared to assess and assume reasonable credit risk for a fee. Parallel and BTB loans, on the other hand, may be done without a bank to intermediate the respective credit risks of the parties. In this case the parties are frequently ill-equipped to assess, much less assume, each other's credit risk.

At least four approaches have been employed to resolve the problem of credit risk in parallel or BTB loans.

1. The right of offset is, of course, the most obvious. It provides that if one party defaults on interest or principal, the counterparty is relieved from its obligations under the counterloan. While an offset agreement appears to resolve most of the credit exposure, it is not absolute and may not even be operational in some cases. For example, as exchange rates change with time, the security value of

the depreciating currency loan will be insufficient to offset the value of the appreciating currency loan. The result is an element of credit risk exposure even where a right of offset exists.

The operational effectiveness of the right of offset is open to question. In three- and four-party loans, the loans may have been made to subsidiaries of the counterparty rather than to the counterparty directly. Although such agreements may frequently call for the guarantee of the foreign parent, some question still arises if the subsidiary party in an unguaranteed loan goes into bankruptcy. In the case of two-party loans with additional on-lending to subsidiaries or affiliates, the question of a possible failure of a parent, with the subsidiary surviving, further clouds the legal right of offset. Moreover, recent legal precedent has been set in the United Kingdom, where parallel and BTB loans had been developing nicely, that seriously throws into doubt the prior right of setoff before other creditors of a bankrupt firm are fully satisfied.

2. "Topping up" the loan denominated in the depreciating currency whenever a currency devalues by, say, 5 or 10 percent has also resolved this vexing problem in many instances. However, topping up can cause additional problems if the receiving party has no use for the added foreign currency or if it is required to report the topping-up payment as taxable income.

3. Trying to match the credit risk of the parties (i.e., avoiding pairing an AAA-rated credit with a BBB-rated credit) is another approach to the problem of inadequate security. When this is done by AAA-rated credits, each party's concern over credit risk is diminished. However, as far as can be determined, no parallel or BTB loan has failed to date. Hence, the problem of default of a parallel or BTB loan has never been litigated, and the uncertainty associated with the right of setoff remains.

4. A safer approach to the problem of credit risk, and one that is used by many participants, is to resort to specialists in credit risk to assume this risk for the primary parties. This involves bringing in a bank, whose normal business is to evaluate and assume credit risk, to intermediate the loans for one or both parties. A flowchart that reflects the cash flows when a bank assumes the credit risk in a parallel loan is shown in Figure 2–7.

Bank compensation for assuming this risk ranges from 0.1 to 0.5 percent per annum, depending on the credit status of the parties and whether the bank, in fact, takes a principal position between them. This fee is usually lower than a bank's typical letter-of-credit fee because the availability of offset reduces the aggregate

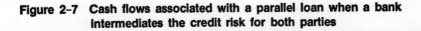

Figure 2-7 **Cash flows associated with a parallel loan when a bank intermediates the credit risk for both parties**

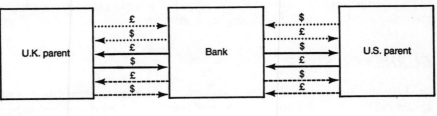

Key:
······ Flow on day one.
—— Flow of interest payments.
----- Principal repayment.

exposure to only that which may result from the devaluation of one of the currencies. Devaluations, while significant in the past, would not be expected to exceed, say, 30 percent of the value of the loan in the currencies of most developed countries. Moreover, any devaluation loss would, of course, apply to only one side of the combined loan package.

Parallel and Back-to-Back Loans Contrasted

The terms "parallel loan" and "back-to-back loan" are names for essentially the same instrument. Although certain distinctions have been made by participants in these transactions and by active intermediaries, general agreement as to the suggested variations does not exist. For example, BTB loans are regarded by some as specifically including the right of offset, whereas parallel loans are not. There is also a tendency to call a paired four-party cross-loan arrangement between parents and unrelated subsidiaries a parallel loan; and a two-party agreement, whether or not the funds are on-lent to subsidiaries, a BTB loan. It appears, however, that these distinctions have been made more for classification purposes than for conceptual reasons.

Because of the more general acceptance of alternative instruments that have recently become available, the four-party parallel loan is now more or less obsolete except where exchange controls make it imperative. As noted, in the event of default, the right of offset in a loan is unclear. Moreover, four-party loans lack flexibility and are more difficult to draft than alternative means of obtaining long-date cover. A two-party parallel or BTB loan is legally safer and more flexible because, if the subsidiary fails, its parent is normally obliged to make the loan good. However, as a result of additional innovations that occurred in 1976, the application of a long-date currency swap to commercial transactions has provided a more preferable arrangement for most applications of long-date currency cover.

CURRENCY SWAP

Like parallel and BTB loans, the currency swap is a currency exchange agreement that provides for the transfer of currencies between counterparties on day one and the reversal of the flows at the maturity of the swap, normally at the same rate of exchange. In a sense, it is a spot or current market currency transaction coupled with an agreement to reverse the transaction at maturity. Unlike a loan agreement, there is no interest payment by either side. Instead, the provider of the stronger currency normally pays a fee to the provider of the weaker currency. This fee compensates for the expected changes in exchange rates over the life of the swap. The size of the fee is negotiable by the parties; however, such negotiations invariably begin with the interest differential between interbank deposits in the two currencies of approximately the same term as that of the swap. A flowchart of the underlying cash flows in a currency swap is shown in Figure 2–8.

Figure 2–8   Cash flows associated with a currency swap

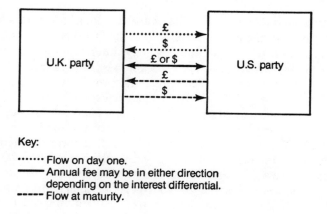

Key:

········ Flow on day one.
———— Annual fee may be in either direction
        depending on the interest differential.
----- Flow at maturity.

The introduction of the commercial swap in 1976 was a milestone in the development of long-date currency cover. It fulfilled the cover objectives of earlier instruments but removed a number of significant legal and accounting impediments. The concept itself is not new. Swaps have existed among central banks for decades. While not an economic or a financial invention, the commercial currency swap was an important legal innovation since it provided better security in the event of default than was available through the questionable right of offset employed with parallel or BTB loans.

The genius of the currency swap lies in its legal basis. Whereas the legal basis for parallel or BTB loans rests on security law and the broad question of offset is unclear, the legal basis for the currency swap is rooted in contract law where the rights of the parties are clearly understood. That is, under contract law, if one party does not perform, the contract is breached, and it is unnecessary for the other party to perform its obligation. This removes the legal question about the right of offset and vastly improves the flexibility of the available long-date currency cover. Moreover, simplified standardized documentation has been developed for the currency swap, which employs a single agreement rather than two agreements or documents as in parallel loans.

Currency swaps also have accounting and tax advantages over loans. Since they are not loans, swaps are not normally required to be included on a firm's balance sheet. Rather, they are disclosed only in the notes to the statements. Although most firms net their parallel or BTB loans on their balance sheets, this practice is dubious and subject to criticism by the strictest of public accountants. And, while the tax-deductible status of interest seems clear in the case of loans, the status of topping-up payments remains in doubt. In the case of currency swaps, firms have been successful in deducting the fees associated with the swaps, although this procedure is still untested in the tax courts.

FORWARD CONTRACTS

Forward (outright) contracts are similar to currency swaps, but they provide for no funds transfer on day one. That is, a forward contract provides only for a forward or future currency exchange at a specified future date and at a specified exchange rate. A flowchart on the underlying cash flows in a forward exchange agreement is shown in Figure 2–9.

It is, of course, quite possible to simulate a forward contract by using a currency swap and moving funds in the current or spot market to reverse the spot flow if this is desired. Normally there is no annual payment between the parties in the case of a forward contract. Instead, a forward exchange rate, which usually differs from the spot rate on day one, is negotiated. The

21

Figure 2-9 Cash flows associated with a forward exchange agreement

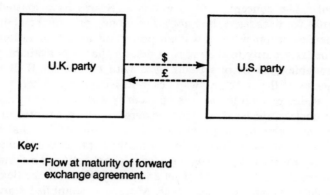

Key:
----- Flow at maturity of forward
exchange agreement.

starting basis for the long-date forward rate negotiation begins with the differential in similar term interest rates on interbank deposits in the two currencies.[1] For example, the theoretical five-year forward rate (F_5) for a forward contract for currencies A and B would be based on the spot rate on day one (S_0), where S_0 is defined in terms of units of currency A per unit of currency B, and the respective five-year interest rates on interbank deposits denominated in each currency i_{5a} and i_{5b};

$$F_5 = S_0 \left(\frac{1 + i_{5a}}{1 + i_{5b}} \right)^5 \tag{2-1}$$

or more generally for year n:

$$F_n = S_0 \left(\frac{1 + i_{na}}{1 + i_{nb}} \right)^7 \tag{2-2}$$

See Chapter 3 for additional discussion of these pricing concepts.

The calculation shown in Equations (2–1) and (2–2) provides for a downward adjustment or discount in the forward rate from the current spot rate in those currencies with a higher domestic interest rate, and vice versa. This theoretical basis for pricing long-date forward contracts is similar to that used in short-term forward contracts in that it is based on interest differentials between the two currencies. Like its short-term analog, it assumes that the market is efficient for term deposits and that forward premiums or discounts on a currency are based on interest differentials. These assumptions, while quite appropriate for short-term markets in the popular currencies, may not hold up empirically in long-date maturities or in many of the exotic currencies. Hence, there is wide latitude for negotiation of long-date forward rates.

While found most commonly in long-date forward contracts, the use of a forward discount or premium instead of an annual fee has also been employed in long-date currency swap agreements. The underlying logic and negotiating strengths that apply to long-date forward contracts are identical to those applied in long-date currency swaps.

The forward contract is, by far, the most popular of all the instruments available for long-date currency cover. Approximately 75 percent of all long-date currency cover has been implemented by forward currency contracts. This result is due to the high degree of flexibility of these swaplike agreements plus the absence of a need for fund flow requirements prior to maturity.

Even though no funds are transferred until maturity, a risk of nonperformance remains. This risk can be managed by dealing only with strong credits, or it can be passed by bringing in a bank to intermediate the credit risk. Like currency swaps, forward currency agreements need not be reflected on a firm's financial statements except for disclosure in the notes.

The simplicity of forward contracts also improves their understanding by higher levels of management and reduces the difficulty in obtaining approval from boards of directors and other supervising bodies. And the absence of funds flow prior to maturity makes it somewhat easier to find matching counterparties. Applications that require debt service in a foreign currency could be accommodated by a stream of forward contracts, further increasing their attractiveness.

Issuing contracts to highly creditworthy firms and using bank intermediation for credit risk reduces the potential loss to the parties due to nonperformance to negligible levels. Forward contracts also conform perfectly with the need for long-date cover in reducing a firm's world cost of capital or increasing an investor's all-in rate of return after the cost of hedging cash flows in an undesired currency. The suitability of forward contracts also applies with equal force to those instances where a party is hedging an existing net asset exposure or other known long-date transaction or translation exposure.

SIMULATED CURRENCY LOANS

Although simulated currency loans have limited application, they provide yet another means of creating a term liability in an undesired currency and a term asset in a desired currency. The distinguishing feature of a simulated currency loan is that it is denominated in one currency but payable in another at the spot rate of exchange between the currencies at the time of each payment. These instruments are primarily used in blocked currencies with surplus liquidity or in currencies of countries with underdeveloped capital markets. In this way, blocked or unusable funds can be deployed to earn a return for the lender, immune to exchange risk. The borrower, although bearing exchange risk, obtains access to funds not otherwise available at the lower interest rate associated with the simulated currency.

To illustrate, assume that a U.S. firm had surplus peseta liquidity that it wished to mobilize but could not effectively withdraw from Spain. A Spanish borrower needed financing but was unable to obtain it in the limited and sometimes closed Spanish capital market. A solution for both was for the U.S. firm to lend pesetas to the Spanish borrower as if they were U.S. dollars. The interest is determined based on the Eurodollar rate for credit risks similar to that of the borrower. The principal and interest were repaid in pesetas at the spot exchange rate for the dollar obligation at the time of payment. Here, the U.S. lender created a dollar asset because the interest and principal were linked to dollars. The Spanish borrower, on the other hand, bore the full exchange rate risk, but this was the price he had to pay for the availability of the capital at the lower interest rate on the dollar-

Figure 2-10 Cash flows associated with a simulated currency agreement

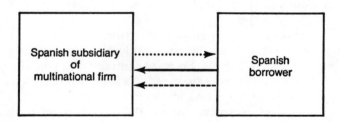

Key:

•••••••• Peseta flow on day one based on the spot rate times the dollar value of the loan.

———— Annual interest payments in pesetas sufficient to service the dollar value of the loan at the dollar interest rate.

– – – – Repayment of principal in pesetas at term exchange rate times the dollar value of the loan.

simulated loan. While this arrangement added to the exchange risk of the borrower, it afforded long-date cover to the lender whose foreign currency balances were effectively converted to his home currency. A flowchart of the underlying cash flows in this simulated currency loan is shown in Figure 2–10.

FOREIGN EXCHANGE OPTIONS

Foreign exchange options are contracts to buy or sell foreign exchange against, say, dollars at a contractual exchange rate over a specific period of time. The cost of acquiring the option is called the *option premium*. It is lost if the option expires unexercised.

Foreign exchange options began trading on the Philadelphia Stock Exchange in late 1982. Options have unique features that fit certain long-date foreign exchange applications very well. Unlike a forward foreign exchange agreement, which makes an exchange of currency mandatory at maturity at the contract exchange rate, options give their holders the choice to exchange currency at the option exercise price or not—as it suits the holders. Thus, if the future price of a currency rises above the exercise price, holders of *call options* (to buy) will exercise their options to buy the currency at the (below market) option price. On the other hand, if the price of the currency falls below the exercise price, the holders of calls will allow them to lapse and acquire the currency at the lower price available in the future spot market. The logic for *put options* (to sell) runs just the opposite (i.e., holders of puts would exercise their options to sell if the market price falls below their exercise price and allow the option to lapse if the market price rises above the exercise price).

Since put (call) currency options give their holders a choice to sell (buy) future foreign exchange at the exercise price or the then current spot price, they provide an opportunity to cover uncertain or conditional future foreign exchange cash flows if they, in fact, become real cash flows. With the use of options, this type of cover is possible without having to incur possible losses if the foreign currency cash flows do not materialize or if the foreign currency moves against the holders, as may be the case with a forward or futures foreign currency contract. The price that is paid for this flexibility is the option premium that goes to the maker of the option and is forever lost to the option purchaser.

This attractive feature of currency options provides desired protection for players with uncertain future foreign exchange cash flows. However, the general use of the currency options market, like the foreign currency futures market, loses utility for long-date applications because the longest option period currently trading is limited to nine months.

Despite the nonavailability of an organized market in long-date foreign currency options, recent innovations in finance have produced alternative instruments which may be used like long-date foreign exchange options. One example of an optionlike instrument is a particular type of dual-currency bond.[2] In 1983 a dollar bond was issued that was convertible into a sterling bond at the exchange rate on the date of issue. This conversion is at the option of the holder. Thus, if the currency, cash flow, and maturity were to fit the needs of a player wishing to hedge an uncertain cash flow, such a dual-currency bond would serve well in his long-date foreign exchange risk management plans. If more dual-currency bonds are issued and are traded in the secondary market, they can serve as effective long-date currency options to manage uncertain future foreign exchange cash flows. Given a demand for long-date options in their respective currencies, this feature could result in a somewhat lower coupon and related cost to the issuer.

Our discussion of the various instruments that have become available to implement long-date currency cover is complete. We turn next to a discussion of the cash flows, pricing, and other considerations of long-date currency instruments in Chapter 3.

Footnotes

[1]If interbank deposit rates are not available, swap pricing could also be done off the rates on government securities in each of the currencies.

[2]The term "dual-currency bond" has received multiple usage in the international bond markets. This type of dual-currency bond provided for choice of currency on the part of the investor and represents an optionlike instrument. It is not to be confused with other dual-currency bonds that became popular in 1983–84 providing for interest payments in Swiss francs and principal repayment in U.S. dollars.

Chapter 3

Cash Flows, Pricing, and Other Considerations

INTRODUCTION

Now that we have seen the evolution of instruments available for long-date currency cover, a fuller examination of the specific cash flows associated with each type of cover is in order. A more thorough perception of the financial, legal, and tax implications of each of the instruments may be seen by focusing specifically on the detailed cash flows related to each type of cover.

To clarify and ease the presentation, all examples are presented in terms of U.S. dollars (the domestic currency) and sterling (the foreign currency). Some applications lend themselves to blocked currencies or undeveloped capital markets for which pounds and dollars are not appropriate currencies; nevertheless, the illustrative use of dollar–sterling is retained throughout for purposes of simplicity and ease of comparison.

FOREIGN CURRENCY DEBT

Creating a foreign exchange term liability using foreign currency debt in a do-it-yourself fashion follows a procedure directly analogous to a covered interest arbitrage operation in the short-term forward market. Using the dollar–sterling example, term sterling is borrowed and converted to dollars at the current spot rate, and the proceeds are invested in high-quality dollar denominated term instruments (e.g., U.S. treasury bonds). The cash flows associated with this operation include:

1. The payment of sterling interest at the U.K. domestic interest rate for term debt associated with the riskiness of the borrower.
2. The receipt of dollar interest at the treasury term rate.
3. The repayment of the sterling loan at maturity.
4. The repayment of the dollar loan at maturity.

An example better illustrates these transactions. Suppose a U.S. party wished to create a sterling liability to match against its long position in sterling assets. In this case, suppose the party could borrow in the United Kingdom at 12 percent and invest in the U.S. in a treasury instrument at 15 percent. Further assume that the current exchange rate is \$1.50/£ (or £0.6667/\$). The player could borrow £66,670, convert the sterling to \$100,000, and invest the proceeds at 15 percent for one year. At the end of the year, the investor would collect 15 percent on its dollar investment (i.e., \$15,000), pay 12 percent on its sterling loan (i.e., £8,000), as well as receive and pay the principal amounts previously contracted. In this case, any rise or fall in the value of the sterling debt would be offset by a decline or rise in the value of the party's long asset position, and the party would have effectively preserved the dollar value of its sterling assets.

Additional cash flows include all transaction and legal costs connected with the operation. These costs include term debt origination costs, which may reach 1.75 to 2.25 percent of the amount borrowed for underwriting a public offering. This amount may be reduced if a bank loan is used, but bank debt is usually at higher effective interest costs and may require periodic reduction or amortization. In addition, the spot foreign currency conversion will require a transaction cost of 0.05 to 0.10 percent based on normal spreads between bid and ask prices in market quotations.

The net interest income or expense in each year on foreign currency debt cover is equal to the principal borrowed (P) times the interest differential between the two currencies ($i_{US} - i_{UK}$), with the flow being in the direction of the currency with the higher interest rate at the time the operation is put in place. Assume, for purposes of illustration, that U.S. interest rates exceed U.K. rates. However, because of possible changes in the dollar–sterling exchange rate, the effective net interest flow may rise, fall, or even reverse direction. This phenomenon is illustrated in Equation (3–1), which shows the effective net interest flow in year t to the U.S. party (I_t):

$$I_t = P i_{US} - \frac{P}{S_0} i'_{UK} S_t \qquad (3\text{–}1)$$

The net interest flow (I_t) is the difference between the higher interest income in dollars $(P \cdot i_{US})$ and the lower interest cost on the sterling equivalent of the principal converted at the spot rate (S_0), where S_0 equals dollars per pound at the beginning of the transaction. That is, the sterling interest flow would be equal to the sterling equivalent of the principal, P/S_0 times the sterling interest rate (i_{UK}) (i.e., $[P/S_0 i_{UK}]$). The sterling interest flow at the end of period (t) must then be converted back to dollars at the then prevailing future spot rate (S_t).

Thus, if U.S. interest rates exceed U.K. interest rates and the dollar–sterling spot rate decreases (i.e., the dollar strengthens), the effective net interest flow to the United States will increase. Conversely, if the dollar weakens, the effective net interest flow will fall and may turn negative if the proportionate fall in the dollar exceeds the interest differential.

Equation (3–1) may be demonstrated using the earlier example where the U.S. party could borrow sterling in the United Kingdom at 12 percent, convert the proceeds to dollars at $1.50/£, and invest in the United States at 15 percent. The annual interest flow would be:

$$I_t = Pi_{US} - \frac{P}{S_0} i_{UK} S_t$$

$$= \$100,000\,(15\%) - \frac{\$100,000}{\$1.50/£}\,(12\%)S_t$$

$$= \$100,000\,(15\%) - £66,650\,(12\%)\,S_t)$$

$$= \$15,000 - £8,000\,(S_t) \qquad\qquad (3\text{–}1A)$$

If the spot rate remained at $1.50/£, the party would realize a gain of $3,000. However, if the spot rate at the end of period t decreased, say the dollar strengthened to $1/£, or increased, say the dollar weakened to $2/£; the interest flows would increase or decrease correspondingly. In these examples the net interest flow would increase to $7,000 or decrease to a negative flow (in favor of the United Kingdom) of $1,000, respectively.

Despite the uncertainty in the effective net interest flow, the risk of the cash flows associated with foreign currency debt financing are not the major impediments to its use. Instead, questions of an inadequate borrower size or loan size, an insufficient supply of funds or some scarcity of high-quality investment opportunities, a lack of efficient spot currency markets in certain currencies, and the often onerous impact of additional borrowing on debt ratios and interest coverage, all discourage potential borrowers from using foreign currency debt to obtain long-date cover. Moreover, the inability to offset foreign withholding tax against domestic tax in countries without reciprocal tax treaties and the possible imposition of significant default risk on the related home currency investment adversely influence other potential users.

The primary opposition to the use of foreign currency debt to hedge long-date currency risk lies in the abnormal inflation of the domestic balance sheet that this method causes. This condition is compounded by a steadfast restraint on the part of lenders to allow high debt ratios to increase further to accomplish long-date cover. As a result, very few firms are able to procure do-it-yourself cover rather than resort to alternative sources of long-date currency cover.

CURRENCY-COLLATERALIZED LOANS

The cash flows associated with currency-collateralized loans follow a pattern similar to foreign currency debt. They are somewhat simpler, how-ever, because of the role and presence of an international bank. Here long-date cover is obtained by placing an interest-bearing deposit with a bank, which in turn lends to an off-shore subsidiary at a locally determined rate of interest. No public underwriting or currency transactions costs are involved. Bank fees may or may not be explicit. The latter occurs when the bank offsets its cost and exchange exposure against other compensation that it receives from its global relationship with its customer.

When bank fees are explicit they may be expected to be a 0.5 to 1 percent front-end arrangement fee plus 0.75 to 1 percent per annum service fee. The latter fee is higher than is usually charged for assuming credit risk on the amount exposed by possible exchange rate changes. This higher charge is necessitated because, in the case of currency-collateralized loans, the bank is required to include the deposit and loan on its balance sheet. Without the higher compensation, the bank would suffer dilution in its return on average assets. Thus, when banks are required to inflate their own balance sheets to accommodate long-date cover, they require compensation more comparable to a loan spread than when they are able to escape balance sheet inflation.

PARALLEL AND BACK-TO-BACK LOANS

In the case of a parallel or back-to-back (BTB) loan, the U.S. party provides dollars to the U.K. party or its U.S. subsidiary, and the U.K. party provides sterling to the U.S. party or its U.K. subsidiary. Interest payments are negotiated based on the level of interest in each currency applicable to the risk of the respective borrower. Because of possible changes in exchange rates, the net effective interest cost may vary, as indicated by Equation (3-1).

Other variations in loan interest charges have occurred in the past. For example, the Bank of England had allowed interest rates on parallel and BTB loans to ratchet downward in concert with declines in the U.K. minimum lending rate (MLR). No upward reversal had been required. With the demise of MLR, the future course of the ratchet concept is unclear. Although there is no formal provision for a downward ratchet in loans in other currencies, this concept could be incorporated in the loan agreements if the parties so elect.

Loan origination costs in the case of parallel and BTB loans are approximately 0.5 percent to each party at the time the loans are signed with a minimum of $25,000 each. Standardized documentation has been developed for these instruments, which has significantly reduced the legal cost from what would be associated with an original or de novo transaction. Nevertheless, because of the complexities, considerable legal review and cost is still incurred on each transaction. In cases where credit risk is transferred to a bank, an intermediation fee of 0.1 to 0.5 percent per annum is charged. This fee may be shared or paid by one of the parties. Where credit risk is not intermediated, topping-up payments may be required whenever exchange rates change by 5 to 10 percent as agreed in the loan documentation.

Generally, U.S. firms have been successful in obtaining approval from public accountants to net their parallel or BTB loans in their balance sheet and deduct interest expense as a tax-allowable expense. This has also been true for banks who take principal positions or intermediate credit risks. These procedures have not been thoroughly tested by legal processes, however and, if disallowed, could have a significant effect on the pricing of loans for long-date cover. Moreover, the tenuous tax position of topping-up payments and security status relative to general creditors makes bank intermediation or alternative swap or forward outright contracts advisable.

CURRENCY SWAP

The foreign currency swap is a simpler legal and administrative arrangement for the transfer of spot currency and its subsequent term repurchase than the loan arrangements already discussed. As before, the cash flows include a transfer of spot dollars by the U.S. provider to the U.K. participant or its assignee concurrent with a transfer of spot sterling from the U.K. provider to the U.S. party or its assignee. A reversal of cash flows occurs at the end of the swap period. The agreement may provide for an identical amount to be transferred at maturity of the swap or for a forward exchange premium or discount to be also transferred as agreed to by the parties.

The case of forward cash flows at the initial spot exchange rate normally also provides for an annual swap fee as negotiated between the parties. This fee is typically based on the interest differential between the currencies times the principal amount swapped and is paid by the provider of the low-interest currency to the provider of the high-interest currency. Normally, the swap fee is denominated in the currency of its recipient, and its amount remains unchanged throughout the life of the swap.

An alternative arrangement that is frequently negotiated calls for an incorporation of the interest differential between the currencies into the agreed forward rate of exchange to be used at the final settlement of the swap. The correct determination of the forward exchange rate (F_n) consistent with a specific set of term interbank deposit interest rates was given in Equation (2–2), repeated here as Equation (3–2).

$$F_n = S_0 \left(\frac{1 + i_{n\text{US}}}{1 + i_{n\text{UK}}} \right)^n \qquad (3\text{–}2)$$

where S_0 is the initial spot exchange rate (e.g., dollars per pound sterling), $i_{n\text{US}}$ is the dollar interbank deposit rate for term n, and $i_{n\text{UK}}$ is the sterling interbank deposit rate for term n. (n, of course, is the maturity of the swap agreement.)

Less correct methods, which employ simple or compound cumulation of the annual interest differential (Δi) across the years of the swap term (n), may also be considered and, perhaps, negotiated. Simple cumulation of the interest differential is illustrated in Equation (3–3) and compound cumulation is shown in Equation (3–4).

$$F_n = S_t (1 + \Delta i n) \qquad (3\text{–}3)$$

and

$$J_n = S_0 (1 + \Delta i)^n, \qquad (3\text{–}4)$$

where Δi represents the higher interest rate, say in dollars, minus the lower interest rate, say in sterling, and the exchange rates are in terms of dollars per pound. This combination would produce a forward discount on the dollar and a forward premium on the pound. Since in this formulation $(1 + \Delta i)$ is greater than unity, Equation (3–3) results in a smaller discount per premium than Equation (3–4) for multiperiod maturities. However, the discount per premium obtained by the (correct) use of Equation (3–2) is smaller still than that obtained using either of the cumulative compound approximations.

These formulations are illustrated by the following examples. Again, assume interest rates in the United States are 15 percent for a three-year note while a comparable U.K. note yields 12 percent per annum for three years. As before, assume that the current spot rate is $1.50/£. The correct formulation of the three-year forward rate [from Equation (3–2)] would be:

$$F_3 = \$1.50/\pounds \left(\frac{1 + 0.15}{1 + 0.12} \right)^3$$

$$F_3 = \$1.6238/\pounds \qquad (3\text{–}2A)$$

As noted above, under these circumstances the forward pound would be selling at a premium over the spot pound.

Equations (3–3) and (3–4) can be used as a simplifying substitute of Equation (3–2) and would yield an approximation of the three-year forward rate:

$$F_3 = \$1.50/\mathcal{L}\,(1+(0.03)^3)$$

$$F_3 = \$1.635/\mathcal{L} \tag{3–3A}$$

or

$$F_3 = \$1.50/\mathcal{L}\,(1+0.03)^3$$

$$F_3 = \$1.6391/\mathcal{L} \tag{3–4A}$$

Notice that Equation (3–2) (the correct formulation) resulted in the lowest premium, whereas Equation (3–4) produced the highest value.

The transactions cost cash flows related to currency swaps are similar to those associated with parallel and BTB loans (i.e., approximately 0.5 percent front-end arrangement fee paid by each party and 0.1 to 0.5 percent per annum bank intermediation fee when that service is provided). However, credit intermediation is required less frequently in swaps than in loans because of the improved security position available under contract law. As with long-date loans, the documentation used in long-date currency swaps has become standardized and legal costs are less than de novo swap documentation would suggest. Moreover, the swap instrument, being a single agreement rather than a pair of loans, is considerably shorter and simpler than documentation employed by predecessor instruments.

Despite its apparent advantages, the currency swap also has a few limitations. Since it is based on a forward currency agreement, it cannot be used in those countries where forward contracts are prohibited or where swaps themselves are illegal. Moreover, its general use is also precluded in countries like Australia, which bars forward contracts between residents and nonresidents, since one of the obvious parties to a swap used for long-date Australian dollar cover would be a nonresident.

FORWARD CONTRACTS

The cash flows and other provisions connected with a forward outright contract are identical to those of a long-date currency swap except for the absence of a currency exchange on day one. Transactions and intermediation costs are similar to those for swaps, and forward exchange rates are negotiated based on calculations using Equations (3–2), (3–3), or (3–4), depending upon the relative negotiating advantages of the parties.

An important advantage of the forward contract over the swap is that it employs a still simpler form of documentation. A primary reason for this is that there has been a historic and legal precedent for simplified documentation that has grown up in the foreign exchange market and has been applied to forward currency contracts. Hence, a long-date forward contract can be transacted on the basis of a simple one-page confirmation similar to that used by traders in the short-term forward foreign exchange market. Another advantage over a swap is that a forward exchange agreement removes the need for a funds transfer on day one. Finally, a forward contract reduces the loanlike characteristics of long-date cover, which further strengthens the arguments against including it on the balance sheets of the parties. The absence of a funds transfer on day one is of minor significance, since it could readily be accommodated, or undone, in the spot market by any firm of sufficient size and credit status to quality for a forward currency contract or swap.

SIMULATED-CURRENCY LOANS

The cash flows associated with a simulated-currency loan reflect its hybrid status as an instrument of long-date cover. Following our U.S.–U.K. example, the U.S. party would lend sterling to the U.K. party on day one as if it were dollars. The annual interest payment on the debt would be at the appropriate Eurodollar interest rate times the dollar equivalent of principal in pounds based on the spot rate on day one. The debt service would be in sterling of sufficient quantity to convert to the requisite dollar interest at the spot rate when each payment is made. If country specific exchange controls are not violated, this allows the lender to convert the foreign exchange interest to dollars and effectively transfers foreign currency assets to home currency assets. The borrower bears full exchange risk to access the scarce liquidity and obtain the preferential lower interest rate associated with the proxy currency. Transactions and intermediation fees are similar to swaps, forward contracts, and loans.

SYNOPSIS OF INSTRUMENTS

We have now discussed most all the financial, legal, accounting, and tax differences between the alternative means of establishing long-date cover. A few of the major cash flow differences must yet be described, and the economic similarity of each alternative must be highlighted.

The major cash flow variations implicit in the various instruments for long-date currency cover are due to frictionlike differences in transactions costs and intermediation fees. For example, the use of foreign currency debt incurs a 2 to 3 percent front-end underwriting fee and a spot transaction cost leakage. No arrangement or intermediation fees are encountered. The basic arrangement fees for parallel, BTB, and simulated-currency loans, swaps, and forward contracts are all quite similar at a negotiated rate of approximately 0.5 percent for each party with a $25,000 minimum.

Credit intermediation fees vary with the credit risk of the parties and the probability of a large devaluation in a currency. They are also similar for each instrument and vary from 0.1 to 0.5 percent per annum to be shared or negotiated by the parties. Because of their stronger security position, swaps and forward contracts have less of a need for credit intermediation than loans, and lower intermediation fees reflect this. The standardized documentation that exists for all instruments arranged by active financial intermediaries tends to make legal and administrative costs somewhat comparable across the industry. Parallel and BTB loans, because they are more complex agreements, generally require somewhat higher legal costs than do swaps and forward contracts. Forward contracts are by far the least complicated of the instruments and have received the most popular use.

In all cases the fees and interest payments between the parties are negotiated using the appropriate term interest differentials as their starting points. Hence, apart from the above differences in transaction and arrangement costs, there are no economic differences between the various instruments, other than those negotiated by the parties in terms of interest differentials or fees.

Internal Rate of Return

The internal rate of return (IRR) of the cost of obtaining long-date cover can be calculated for each type of long-date instrument. For loan or swaplike instruments where the principal is returned in the original currency, it can be couched in general terms for the annual net effective interest flow or fee (I_t), the principal or present sum of the cover obtained (P), and the term of the agreement (n). This relationship is illustrated in Equation (3–5):

$$P = \sum_{t=1}^{n} \frac{I_t}{(1+\text{IRR})^t} + \frac{P}{(1+\text{IRR})^n} \tag{3–5}$$

In Equation (3–1) I_t has been shown to depend on the interest differential and changes in spot exchange rates. Hence, these variables can be substituted into Equation (3–5) to obtain Equation (3–6):

$$P = \sum_{t=1}^{n} \frac{P(I_{US} - \frac{S_t}{S_0} i_{UK})}{(1+IRR)^t} + \frac{P}{(1+IRR)^n} \tag{3-6}$$

Since the principal *(P)* is common to all terms, it can be cancelled out of the calculation. When this is done, the internal rate of return of the cost of obtaining long-date cover (IRR) can be seen to be related to the negotiated interest differentials, the maturity of the cover, and the actual changes in spot rates over the term of the cover. The calculation of IRR based on the negotiated interest differential, the maturity of the cover, and the ratio of current to future spot rates cannot be obtained directly and must be solved for by repeated trial. The relationship is shown in Equation (3–7):

$$\sum_{t=1}^{n} \frac{(i_{US} - \frac{S_t}{S_0} i_{UK})}{(1+IRR)^t} + \frac{1}{(1+IRR)^n} = 1 \tag{3-7}$$

In cases of forward contracts or swaps whose fee is embedded in the forward exchange rate, no stream of payments is made, and the IRR calculation reduces to Equation (3–8), which has a direct solution as shown in Equation (3–9).

$$P = \frac{P(F_n/S_0)}{(1+IRR)^n} \tag{3-8}$$

$$IRR = \sqrt[n]{\frac{F_n}{S_0}} - 1 \tag{3-9}$$

If F_n is negotiated based on interest differentials in accordance with Equation (3–2), it can be substituted for *(F_n)* in Equation (3–8) to produce Equation (3–10) as shown below:

$$P = \frac{P\frac{S_0}{S_0}\left(\frac{1+i_{nUS}}{1+i_{nUK}}\right)^n}{(1+IRR)^n}$$

$$(1+IRR)^n = \left(\frac{1+i_{nUS}}{1+i_{nUK}}\right)^n$$

$$IRR = \frac{1+i_{nUS} - 1 - i_{nUK}}{1+i_{nUK}}$$

$$IRR = \frac{i_{nUS} - i_{nUK}}{1+i_{nUK}} \tag{3-10}$$

Equation (3–10) shows that the IRR of the cost of a swap or forward contract whose forward rate is negotiated based on interest differentials reduces to the discounted value of the interest differential, precisely the same as the short-term forward discount/premium consistent with interest rate parity theory.

An example will illustrate these calculations and show their mutual equivalence. Returning to the premises of our earlier examples, we continue to assume a 15 percent three-year U.S. interest rate, a 12 percent three-year U.K. interest rate, and a current spot exchange rate of $1.50/£. In our hypothetical example, a U.S. firm and a U.K. firm swap $100,000 for £66,670. The U.S. party receives 15 percent interest denominated in dollars every year and pays 12 percent in British sterling at the then current market rate. The principal is not at issue here and will be returned in its original amount (i.e., £66,670). Therefore, the principal is not necessary to the calculations. Equation (3–7) can be used directly to compute the IRR of the cost of long-date currency cover obtained using the swap.

Before using Equation (3–7), we must project the future spot rate based on our knowledge of interest differentials. Using Equation (3–2), the future spot rates at the end of each of the next three years can be estimated to be:

$$S_1 = \$1.50/£ \left(\frac{1.15}{1.12}\right) = \$1.5402/£$$

$$S_2 = \$1.50/£ \left(\frac{1.15}{1.12}\right)^2 = \$1.5814/£$$

$$S_3 = \$1.50/£ \left(\frac{1.15}{1.12}\right)^3 = \$1.6238/£$$

Equation (3–7) can now be employed to calculate the internal rate of return of the cost of obtaining long-date currency cover using a currency swap.

$$\frac{0.15 - \dfrac{1.5402}{1.50}(0.12)}{(1+\text{IRR})} + \frac{0.15 - \dfrac{1.5814}{1.50}(0.12)}{(1+\text{IRR})^2}$$

$$+ \frac{0.15 - \dfrac{1.6238}{1.50}(0.12)}{(1+\text{IRR})^3} + \frac{1}{(1+\text{IRR})^3} = 1 \qquad (3\text{–}7\text{A})$$

Solving this equation by trial and error (or via a preprogrammed computer or hand calculator) produces an IRR of the cost of cover of 2.35 percent. The cost of obtaining long-date cover using this swap transaction is 2.35 percent for the U.S. firm before any transaction costs are added.

If, on the other hand, there are no interim payments and the swap fee is embedded in the forward exchange rate, Equation (3–7) collapses to Equation (3–8). The IRR of the cost of obtaining long-date cover can then be calculated via Equation (3–8), and the previously calculated three-year forward rate ($1.6238/£):

$$\$100,000 = \frac{\$100,000\,(1.6238)/1.50}{(1+IRR)^3}$$

$$IRR = 2.68\% \qquad\qquad (3\text{--}8A)$$

The mathematical computation is simplified greatly by Equation (3–10). Notice the identical answer:

$$IRR = \frac{0.15 - 0.12}{1.12}$$

$$= 2.68\% \qquad\qquad (3\text{--}10A)$$

The IRR of the cost obtained here is the same as the IRR of the cost obtained above in the formulation of the forward rate that relies on interim interest flows [i.e., Equation (3–2A)]. The reason for this similarity is that the interim one-year forward exchange rates used in the calculation *and* the three-year forward rate used here were all based on estimates derived from the same set of interest differentials in accordance with Equation (3–2).

Notice that the IRR of the cost of the transaction using a currency swap with interim payments is lower than the IRR of the cost of the forward contract or swap without interim payments (2.35 percent versus 2.68 percent). The reason for this difference is that the interim payments were made before the depreciation of the dollar had fully progressed to the maturity date of the contract. Hence, the interim payments were made at a lower discount on the dollar than existed at maturity and resulted in a lower IRR of the swap transaction. If the same interim payments were set aside on the forward contract and invested at U.S. interest rates, the interest income would be available to reduce the dollar requirements at maturity date, and the IRRs of the two arrangements would equate.

FACTORS AFFECTING NEGOTIATING STRENGTHS

This general discussion of cash flows suggests that the economic distinction between the alternative instruments is apparently based on relatively minor differences in transactions costs and foreign exchange exposure on differences in interest payments or fees. In contrast, major differences in the IRR of the cost of obtaining long-date cover can occur because of the relative negotiating advantages of the parties. Important factors that affect respective negotiating strengths in various capital markets and at various points in time include:

1. Perceived urgency of need of each party for the long-date currency cover

2. Cost saving opportunity derived from market inefficiencies at the time of the transaction
3. Availability or need for effectively blocked currencies
4. Degree of matching of credit status
5. Degree of cash flow synchronization in terms of size and time
6. Experience in international financial management

Negotiations can, of course, take place on any of the terms or arrangements related to long-date currency cover. In most cases the negotiations are economic, but sometimes availability of cover, or willingness to accommodate cover, is the paramount factor in consummating a long-date deal. In Chapter 5 we consider the equivalence of long-date cover relative to a sequence of short-date contracts and the development of the market for currency cover. As we focus on the various ingredients in the market, additional areas of negotiation of terms will become apparent. Furthermore, as the market for long-date currency cover grows and develops, more of the items open to negotiation will become standard practice with the repetitive players in the market.

Chapter 4

Requisites for Profitable Cover

INTRODUCTION

In Chapter 3 we saw that the internal rate of return of the cost or benefit of implementing long-date currency cover was approximately equal to the differential in interest rates between the currencies. Under equilibrium conditions where efficient markets exist, incurring this cost or benefit would be necessary to obtain the desired currency cover. That is, to mitigate currency exposure, responsible parties may be inclined to enter into long-date foreign exchange transactions that effectively convert the currency of their exposed cash flows into their home currency in proximate amounts and dates. In many instances the parties would be content to pay a price for this risk reduction. However, if mutually offsetting counterparties to a long-date currency exchange can be found or if anomalies exist in the relevant currency or debt markets, both may not need to pay an exchange premium; and one, or perhaps both, may actually accrue a profit advantage from the transaction. Moreover, the size of the profit potential can be so large that long-date currency exposures may be intentionally incurred (and covered). In these cases, long-date currency cover is engaged in primarily to extract the profit advantage made possible by exploiting or arbitraging certain differences in international capital markets.

This last prospect is due to the presence of anomalies or inefficiencies across international capital markets. Market inefficiencies are the driving force behind many of the applications of long-date forward cover of currency and coupon risk. Therefore, a brief description of the general nature of such anomalies is desirable to focus on their often transient duration and observe the underlying forces that cause them to come and go. This description of market anomalies will also become the basis for many of the applications of long-date cover and is expanded in Chapters 7 through 10 when specific applications are examined in more detail.

EFFICIENT MARKETS AND ARBITRAGE

Before focusing on the means of exploiting or arbitraging certain differences between international capital markets, we must understand what an efficient market entails and what is meant by the concept of arbitrage.

In an efficient market, prices are set such that the resources traded in the market are allocated equitably or efficiently among the participants in the market. For this to occur, all relevant information would have to be available to all market participants. That is, efficient markets assume that each player has equal, costless access to all existing information upon which his market action may be predicated. In addition, highly efficient markets require that all participants agree on the implications of the equally available information and its effect on the price of the resource or commodity being traded in the market. To transmit the impact of the uniform information to the price of the asset traded, the market process should be conducted in the presence of many buyers and many sellers, each with the financial resources to implement valuation judgments.

Perfectly efficient markets are also held to be frictionless in the sense that transaction costs are zero. Moreover, in the context of an efficient world capital market, the net proceeds would have to be paid to parties so as *not* to be affected differentially by varying national taxation, regulation, or accounting impediments. Transaction costs are present in all markets to cover the cost and reward the risk inherent in the market-making function. Moreover, transaction costs as well as the effects of taxation, regulation, and accounting may differ among national markets. These differences, together with differences in the interpretation of information, the perception of risk, and the differential valuation of risk between national capital markets give rise to anomalies among them. As a result of these differences, inefficiencies or imperfections in the world capital market abound. Many of these differences may be exploited by appropriate parties to profit from the inherent discord between markets. The process by which this profit may be extracted is frequently called *arbitrage*.

Arbitrage technically involves the simultaneous purchase and sale of an identical asset in different markets. When identical assets are employed, it involves no risk. Hedged or matched transactions differ from a pure arbitrage transaction in that they involve the simultaneous purchase and sale of *similar,* but not *identical,* assets with similar maturities. Profits are possible in a pure arbitrage application because of inefficiencies or differences in alternative markets for essentially the same asset. Similarly, matched transactions give rise to profit opportunities because of anomalies among markets for assets that are close substitutes for each other. The frequency and magnitude of profit opportunities available from hedged transactions are largely accounted for by the diverse customs, specializations, norms, and objectives of the participants in each respective market.

Normally, arbitrage transactions operate to eliminate their own incentive (i.e., prices move to eradicate the initial profit opportunity). As we shall see, this effect prevails in some of the applications that employ long-date currency cover. However, certain market anomalies have been so deep-seated that repeated arbitrage transactions have had only a small impact on the underlying profit potential, with no evident prospect of full elimination.

MARKET ANOMALIES

Anomalies or inefficiencies in capital markets can create significant profit opportunities for interested players. In the most common case, market anomalies arise because of some obstacle that prevents a particular market process from operating efficiently and with equal force across world capital markets. Confronted by obstacles to normal market processes and recognizing that significant differences often exist between various national capital markets, financial intermediaries and practitioners have devised creative financial instruments and concepts to circumvent the obstacles. In the process they have been able to produce attractive returns to both the intermediaries and principals. Market anomalies frequently are associated with external impediments that thwart market efficiency. This condition provides an application of the adage: "necessity is the mother of invention," enabling creative financing techniques to arise to counter the obstacle, frequently at a profit to the participants.

Some may wonder why attention to market anomalies is warranted in a modern book on financial management. Extensive research and literature in finance has been devoted to the existence of a random behavior of changes in U.S. equity prices. Since this random behavior in changes in stock prices relies on efficient markets, allusion to market inefficiencies may sound, at first, sacrilegious. However, a major difference exists between the U.S. equity market and various national long-date currency and debt markets.

U.S. equity markets are very deep, liquid markets that suffer relatively few obstacles to efficiency; in contrast, long-date currency and debt markets are much thinner and encounter many national, international, cultural, social, and economic distortions. A few of the factors that structurally underlie these market imperfections are:

- Market segmentation
- Market saturation
- Spread compression
- Differences in financing norms
- Disintermediation
- Sluggish communication
- Inadequate market liquidity
- Credit arbitrage
- Differential taxation

These distractions make such markets ideal centers of activity for arbitrage operations by creative players. In this section we identify the nature of typical anomalies that affect long-date currency and debt markets.

Market Segmentation

Market segmentation exists within individual national capital markets on a limited scale where certain investors are statutorily or administratively limited from investing in certain instruments (e.g., limitations on life insurance firms' or banks' investments in equity). When considered on an international plane, the prospects for segmentation escalate by many orders of magnitude.

Numerous national ordinances have been established to limit the free flow of currencies in spot, short-date, and long-date forward delivery. These are usually based on protective attempts to support a currency or to prevent erosion of a country's reserves of foreign exchange. Other impediments to the free flow of currencies are rooted in cultural and nationalistic forces intended to avoid disbursement of home currencies to acquire foreign-made products. But the most severe obstructions to efficient markets in foreign exchange are governmentally imposed currency blockage or controls.

Currency blockage prevents the transfer of foreign exchange out of a country either by fiat or by excessive taxation on any attempt to repatriate foreign exchange to the offshore investors who provided the original capital funds. In such cases profitable deployment of a blocked currency for use elsewhere is nearly impossible. Alternatively, currency controls may be more limited and allow a modest transfer of currency, but only for approved purposes and often at a premium price for the foreign exchange that is expatriated. Recent examples of blocked currencies include the Brazilian cruzeiro, the Mexican and Argentinean peso, and the Spanish peseta. Currency controls prevailed on U.K. sterling until 1979 and continue to exist on the French franc and the Swedish krona.

Economic forces can also cause severe forms of forward market segmentation. This occurs when the direction of forward currency flows tend to be one-sided (i.e., a severe imbalance in the forward demand or supply for a country's currency). While this phenomenon is frequently associated with currency blockage or controls, it also occurs without them. For example, recent long-date pressures to sell forward French francs, Italian lira, and Mexican pesos have been very one-sided, as one would expect for highly inflationary currencies. Moreover, in 1982–83, the forward U.S.–Canadian dollar market had been primarily from north to south, reflecting the intense demand for forward U.S. dollars to service Yankee bond issues sold by Canadians. During the same period the forward Japanese yen–U.S. dollar market had also exhibited a strong imbalance of forward demand for yen in anticipation of appreciation of the yen, with only modest supplies of forward yen to offset the demand.

Given the segmentation that results from government controls, cultural norms, or economic motives, attractive opportunities present themselves to those who can take the opposite side of desired transactions. Such counterrequirements may take the form of a demand for a blocked currency by a player with liquidity available elsewhere. An offshore supply of a controlled currency, a naturally generated counterflow from operations of a currency suffering a severe forward supply, and an imbalance in demand represent other sources. What remains is to mobilize the counterflow to provide relief for the blocked, controlled, or imbalanced currency at a price that is satisfactory to the parties. Long-date forward players and instruments exist to facilitate these transfers at negotiated prices. Players employ the negotiating factors and the determinants of the pricing of the underlying agreements discussed in Chapter 3 in arriving at the final terms of a long-date currency transaction.

Market Saturation

An extreme form of market segmentation exists when a given national capital market is unwilling to absorb any more debt of a given issuer. In everyday jargon, the market is said to be "stuffed." The demand for additional paper of the shunned borrower is nil. If the issuer still prefers to obtain more debt denominated in the currency of that market, proxy borrowers who are acceptable to the saturated market are sought. The financing objectives can be met by exchanging or swapping the new obligations in the coveted currency for more easily salable obligations in a currency where the market has a deeper appetite for the debt of the unpopular borrower.

An example of a stuffed market is the Swiss franc long-term debt market for certain borrowers. Borrowers that have been shunned include various Austrian, French, and Italian national agencies. Others, such as the World Bank, prefer the low nominal Swiss franc interest rates but choose not to overload the Swiss franc market with their paper. Long-date currency exchange agreements have enabled certain surrogate borrowers, who have ready access to the Swiss franc market but who prefer U.S. dollar finance, to accommodate, say, the World Bank's preference for Swiss franc debt at a lower all-in cost of funds to both players. The primary impediment that facilitates these deals is the pending saturation of the Swiss franc market by certain borrowers.

Other related contributors to market inefficiency can be expressed in the concepts of spread compression and name arbitrage.

Spread Compression

Differences in the way in which default risk is perceived and monitored can affect the risk premiums required by investors in alternative national capital markets. In many markets a gradation of risk is assessed by security analysts of rating firms. In the United States a prospective borrower is given a relative qualitative rating (e.g., AAA, AA, A, ..., CCC, CC, C) by, say, Standard and Poor's or Moody's. This rating process ranks the creditworthiness of issuers along a more or less continuous scale of quality ratings using plus and minus qualifications to shade intermediate ratings. The risk premium component of the yield that investors require to invest in a rated security bears a direct relationship to the quality rating. To illustrate, a BBB-rated credit at times commands a yield of 150 to 200 basis points (i.e., 1.5 to 2.0 percent) greater than a higher-quality AAA-rated credit for term financing. The yield spread may vary somewhat based on conditions in the credit markets and the stage of the business cycle, but a significant yield spread is generally required for the lower-quality credit issues.

In contrast, continental European capital markets such as Switzerland and West Germany tend to be more liquid and require that a lower-quality acceptable credit pay a yield spread of only 40 to 60 basis points higher than the very best credits. This lower risk premium requirement is possibly related to the higher savings rates or liquidity extant in the continental countries or to their reduced concern over gradations in the credit rating process. They are more inclined to view a credit as either sound or unsound and act accordingly without serious attempts to fathom intermediate creditworthiness.

This intermarket anomaly has been called *spread compression* since the risk premium spread is lower in the continental countries than in the United States. Its effect is augmented by the fact that continental investors are very much attuned to the *name* of a borrower and its implications regarding the borrower's creditworthiness. If a lower-rated credit that has a broad international presence because it is the producer of a well-known product comes to market for capital, the everyday use and acceptance of its name tends to be a major advantage in its ability to access continental debt markets. A similar enhancement is not available in the United States where name means far less in the credit analysis and subsequent rating of a firm's securities. As a result, name borrowers with a BBB or even lower rating in New York can obtain funds in Zurich or Frankfort at significantly lower risk premiums than would be available in New York.

The ability to arbitrage market inefficiencies using one's name can lead to a lower funding cost or cost of capital for the name borrowers after the incremental transaction costs associated with financing in a foreign currency. It also leads to a liability exposure in a foreign currency, which, unless covered, could cause subsequent losses that exceed the cost-of-capital advantage. The solution, of course, is to hedge the foreign currency (Swiss franc or German mark) obligation by swapping it for a home currency or dollar liability. In this way the rather permanent market anomaly of spread compression or name arbitrage can lead to a reduced all-in cost of capital to qualified players.

Differences in Financing Norms

Differences in financing norms among nations also lead to market inefficiencies. For example, debt ratios employed by Japanese firms, while acceptable for an AAA-grade credit rating in Tokyo, are typically much higher than what would be considered sound by New York or Eurodollar term investors. Hence, Japanese multinationals seeking dollar funds to finance their U.S. subsidiaries may face unacceptably high risk premiums in their dollar borrowing. In contrast, they can borrow at prime rates in Japan. Their obvious course of action would be to borrow yen at preferred rates in Tokyo, convert to dollars to immediately satisfy the funding requirement of the U.S. subsidiary, and obtain the long-date cover necessary to service their yen debt. The requisite long-date currency agreement would provide for the sale of forward dollars for yen. Such contracts have been available because certain counterparties have been willing to take the other side. This willingness has resulted in the ability to obtain a fully hedged dollar financing cost to highly levered Japanese firms that is considerably below what would be available to them directly in dollars.

Decreased Intermediation Costs

Another contributing factor to the reduction in financing cost is possible when currency or coupon cover are employed with direct placement financing outside the bank market. This results in the elimination of the high bank spread or net interest margin from the financing process. Bank spread is the difference between the bank's cost of funds and its return on loans. It represents a transaction or frictional cost that reduces market efficiency. While it is naive to expect that transaction costs would approach zero, any excess transaction cost represents an obstacle contributing to market imperfection. Banks traditionally pay low rates on deposits and charge higher asked rates on loans to cover their costs of intermediation. When long-date cover is employed together with placement financing, the parties deal directly with each other or through an alternate intermediary process at a cost of 0.5 to 1 percent per annum. This cost of intermediation can be contrasted with the 2 to 3 percent per annum net interest margin sought by banks. This reduction in bank spread represents a source of profit to be shared by market participants, who, after the cost of obtaining long-date currency cover, can enjoy lower all-in cost-of-capital funds.

Sluggish Communication or Inadequate Market Liquidity

Near the end of our discussion of long-date cover of currency exposure we will examine the development and the prospects of the market for currency cover, and argue that trading in long-date currency cover takes place in what at best might still be called a limited market. Although market development has occurred slowly, quotations now are available in five-year forward contracts for U.S. and Canadian dollars, Swiss francs, West German marks, and U.K. sterling. Motives for the issuance of quotations run from pure advertising with no intention to trade at quoted prices to sincere offers and bids based on the presence of an existing book or inventory of counter-positions or to the desire to maintain an ongoing presence in the long-date currency market.

As we have seen in Chapter 3, long-date forward pricing is based on quotations of, or "traded off," rates in the medium-term interbank deposit market. Because of high interest rates, medium term deposit volume has tended to contract to a trickle in recent years even in many of the active currencies. This relative inactivity has caused the basis for changing long-date forward quotes to become sluggish. The result is that long-date forward quotations tend to remain unchanged for unexplainably long periods of time. Some have argued that the wide bid–ask spreads in the long-date forward quotes leave adequate room for error or negotiation. Still, the rather incomplete response of long-date currency quotations to the frequent changes in spot rates or to changes in differentials in interest rates between the respective currencies appears to be due to sluggish communication or inadequate liquidity of the market maker. This lagged response represents a market imperfection and invites arbitrage to improve market efficiency.

Such an arbitrage opportunity can be illustrated by comparing movements in the dollar–sterling five year versus spot spread in mid-1981 when sterling was in a rapid descent. One Friday in July sterling was quoted at $1.85/£ spot and $1.91/£ five-year forward. By the next Monday the spot price fell significantly to $1.81/£, but the five-year dollar did not move in tandem. Instead, it fell only to $1.89/£ resulting in slightly more than a 1 percent wider relative forward premium than before the change. In absolute terms the forward premium increased by 33 percent from $0.06/£ to $0.08/£.

Forward premiums depend on interest differentials between the appropriate term deposits in the respective currencies.[1] However, in this case there was no change in the five-year interest differential between the dollar and sterling. Only the spot exchange rate changed; the forward rate should have adjusted to reflect the same forward premium on sterling as before the spot change. This anomaly of sticky forward market quotation response gave rise to an opportunity to procure five-year sterling below the five-year U.K. treasury bond or gilt rate. The necessary strategy would entail borrowing dollars, converting them to sterling, and covering the dollar loan by selling sterling forward at an elevated premium. Although this example abstracts from transaction costs and neglects the need for cover of dollar interest flows, it clearly illustrates the inefficiencies imposed on markets by sluggish quotation responses. The arbitrage profit potential is available to players that have the needed counterpositions and are ready to react to market opportunities.

Credit Arbitrage

A market anomaly, which is related to (but different from) dissimilar risk premium requirements across capital markets, can lead to an opportunity called *credit arbitrage*. The underlying anomaly deals with the ways in which forward foreign exchange contracts are priced.

The concept of credit arbitrage is made possible by an intermarket dissimilarity in the assessment of risk and the related imposition of risk premiums. Whereas risk premium increments exist in different degrees in most capital markets, they tend to be imperceptible in spot and forward foreign exchange contracts. That is, despite whether the parties are rated AAA or BBB, the pricing of forward contracts is the same. This condition results from the fact that banks establish trading limits for each of their customers, and, provided the limits are not exceeded, the banks will deal at their quoted prices for spot or forward foreign exchange with any of their customers.

The pricing of contracts in the long-date foreign exchange market is related to interest differentials in the underlying national markets. The pricing is normally determined or traded off the term interbank deposit market. Where insufficient liquidity exists in the term interbank deposit market, forward pricing may be determined by interest differentials on term government securities. In either case, risk premiums in the underlying markets, which determine forward prices, are negligible. However, the long-date forward foreign exchange pricing *could be* determined by or traded against the securities market (e.g., bonds) where risk differentials do command incremental risk premiums. If this were done, a player would have the opportunity to arbitrage the differential risk premium across the two markets.

The concept of credit arbitrage can be illustrated by the following example. Suppose at a given time the five-year interbank West German mark deposit offer rate was 7 percent and the five-year interbank U.S. dollar offer rate was 10 percent. This 3 percent interest differential could be used to form a five-year forward rate of 0.87 times the current German mark price for the dollar[2] (i.e., a premium of 13 percent on the forward mark or a discount of 13 percent on the forward dollar). Continuing our example, suppose that on the same date an AAA-rated firm could float West German mark bonds at a 7.5 percent coupon and a BBB-rated credit could float them at 8 percent. If the five-year forward contract were traded against the BBB-rated bond on the mark side rather than off the interbank deposit rate, the forward premium on the mark would be reduced from 13 percent to 8.8 percent.[3] This results in a reduced forward premium of 4.2 percent, which would give rise to an arbitrage opportunity. We will say more regarding the details of this opportunity in the discussion of credit arbitrage applications of long-date forward currency cover in Chapter 9.

Taxation Differentials

Although some similarity occurs in taxation patterns across countries, numerous differences continue to prevail. To the extent that differential taxation rates apply to cash flows in various currencies, careful management of the currency of the flows can be helpful in minimizing a player's world tax bill. Stated differently, tax savings, based on the country and currency in which expenses are incurred or income is earned, provide incentives for use of long-date forward currency transactions.

A record of most of the prevailing tax differentials across nations, which may introduce market inefficiencies and lead to arbitrage opportunities, is provided elsewhere.[4] We shall not attempt to reproduce it here. However, it may be helpful to cite a few examples of the more popular tax anomalies at this point. More of the details will be covered in the taxation applications of long-date currency cover discussed in Chapter 8.

To stimulate capital investment, the tax rules of a number of European countries provide for exceptionally large capital consumption allowances (i.e., very short allowable depreciation lives on fixed assets). Some countries also have inventory revaluation allowances that provide for the write down of inventory values below cost or market levels. These tax practices often produce very low or zero taxable income with the result that interest expense may obtain little or no tax-shield effect in these countries. Given such tax rules, a tax-reducing course of action would be to borrow in a high-tax country, convert the currency, and make an equity investment in the untaxed subsidiary. This strategy would transfer interest expense to a country where it can shield taxes. To cover the currency risk that the strategy introduced, selling a sufficient amount of the untaxed subsidiary's currency forward to cover the debt in the high tax currency would be prudent. Repatriation risk can be reduced by making the equity investment a callable preferred stock with call flexibility tied to the timing of the swapped debt service flows.

Another tax-driven illustration, which quickly became very popular, was related to leases of fixed assets. Until 1982 a double depreciation write-off of fixed asset costs including an instant capital recovery in one currency could be obtained. This was possible because of differential tax treatments between the United States and the United Kingdom. The underlying strategy entailed having a U.K. leasor lease a long-lived fixed asset to a foreign, say U.S., user. The one-year allowable depreciation life in the United Kingdom provided a tax shield, the benefit of which could be built into the periodic rental payment. Such a lease provided for a terminal buy-out and was, therefore, treated as an installment purchase in the United States with its own depreciation provisions. Despite their popularity, these deals incurred a currency exposure because, if the rent were denominated in dollars, the U.K. leasor would have to sell the dollars forward using a series of long-date forward currency contracts. If the rent were in sterling, the dollar-based leasee would have to purchase a sequence of sterling forward contracts to cover its exchange risk.

As frequently occurs, not all market anomalies are a long-standing phenomenon. This particular situation illustrates that point. In 1982 the Inland Revenue Office disallowed a one-year tax life on assets in the hands of foreign users making it no longer an attractive arbitrage strategy.

Other tax factors prompt market inefficiencies. For example, in the United Kingdom interest can be deducted against regular income taxed at 50 percent, whereas any gain on forward cover of funds borrowed in a currency where interest rates exceed U.K. interest rates is taxed at capital gains rates of 30 percent. Another example of asymmetric tax treatment applicable in many countries involves repatriation of dividends. In this case, a distribution of dividends normally increases the parent's tax bill, but tax liability to the parent may be deferred at the time of the cash flow if the cash flow is implemented by a parallel loan with the right of offset. Another favorite way to avoid withholding tax on interest is to set up a subsidiary in a zero or low-tax country and have the subsidiary undertake financing on behalf of the parent or other subsidiaries. This strategy would entail on-lending the funds using upstream loans to the parent or cross-stream loans to sister subsidiaries to transfer funds to other members of the multinational firm in their own currencies. In these cases long-date forward currency instruments would be appropriate to hedge the underlying currency risk to the subsidiary doing the original financing.

In still another illustration, the West German tax authority extracts a tax on the long-term capital of its firms. Intercompany transfers are counted here as long-term capital. The use of a short-term parallel or cash-collateralized loans with a bank between the parent and subsidiary effectively reduces the subsidiary's long-term capital and its related tax.

CASE STUDY

In Chapter 3 we presented the necessary formulation and calculations to determine the internal rate of return of the cost of procuring long-date currency cover. The various formulae and calculations were based on interest differentials between the respective currencies obtained from more-or-less efficient capital markets. At that time no one paid attention to the prospect of market anomalies, and no one attempted to reduce the cost of currency cover below that based solely in interest differentials. Now, however, with the benefit of information regarding various anomalies that exist between national capital markets, we attempt to provide a comprehensive case study to illustrate the way in which both parties to a long-date currency cover transaction can profit from its use.

Each party can extract an advantage because of the arbitrage of prevailing market anomalies. When both sides of a representative transaction are considered, multiple market anomalies have occasionally contributed to the forces that drive the transaction. The following comprehensive example illustrates this point by drawing on the foregoing concepts of market saturation, spread compression, and name arbitrage.

The case study took place in the summer of 1981 between the World Bank and a weaker credit BBB-rated U.S. rubber firm. Because precise data on the transaction are not totally available, the following terms and cash flows are approximations of what occurred based on market rates at the time.

At the time of the transaction, the BBB-rated firm, which was scarcely investment grade in New York, faced a five-year term borrowing cost of 17 percent per annum plus a 2 percent front-end placement cost. The combined effect of these costs would be a 17.63 percent all-in cost of direct dollar financing. At the same time, the World Bank, being a higher-rated credit, was able to borrow dollars directly in New York at a cost of 16 percent per annum plus a front-end placement cost of 1.75 percent. This produced a total effective cost of 16.53 percent, or 1.10 percent lower than what was available to the BBB-rated credit.

Meanwhile, the risk premium faced by the rubber firm in Switzerland was considerably less. Because it was well-known and because of the risk assessment process there, Swiss lenders were willing to offer five-year francs at a rate of 7.35 percent per annum. When the 1.5 percent one-time placement cost was added, this resulted in an effective financing cost of 7.72 percent. This cost was slightly below the World Bank's objective cost of 8 percent based upon what it felt it could obtain in the Swiss franc market. Thus, the rubber firm had an effective negative spread over the World Bank target cost of 0.28 percent. When this was added to the preferential cost advantage over the BBB-rated firm obtainable by the Bank in New York of 1.10 percent, an aggregate differential of 1.38 percent resulted. This differential in borrowing costs represents an arbitrage profit potential available for covering the transaction costs associated with the long-date currency cover necessary to protect the parties. The balance of the saving can then be negotiated by the parties in accordance with the factors discussed in Chapter 3.

To implement this arbitrage opportunity, the World Bank borrowed $50 million and the BBB-rated firm borrowed SF100 million. They exchanged respective obligations for interest and principal (i.e., assumed by each other using a series of long-date currency contracts). The approximate size of the cash flows that resulted from this currency swap after front-end transaction costs is shown in Table 4–1.

Note that the BBB-rated firm was able to reduce its financing costs by 1.10 percent and the World Bank was able to obtain funds at a cost of 0.28 percent below its cost objective. Some of these savings would be lost to the

Table 4-1 World bank versus BBB-rated firm cash flows

Year	BBB-Rated Firm Receives (Pays) ($ million)	World Bank Receives (Pays) (SF million)
0	49.125	98.5
1	(8.0)	(7.35)
2	(8.0)	(7.35)
3	(8.0)	(7.35)
4	(8.0)	(7.35)
5	(58.0)	(107.35)
Indirect cost of funds (%)	16.53	7.72
Direct cost of funds (%)	17.63	8.00
Savings (%)	1.10	0.28

cost of arranging the necessary long-date currency cover and credit intermediation. Nevertheless, this case study clearly illustrates how interested players can obtain profit advantages if they are willing to participate in world capital markets to reduce their cost of funds or to increase the availability of funds in a preferred currency. The exchange rate risk that these strategies incur can be readily covered by long-date currency contracts, and all parties benefit from the arbitrage transaction.

IMPACT OF PROFESSIONAL ARBITRAGEURS

Having seen examples of market anomalies that operate to produce profitable arbitrage opportunities using long-date foreign exchange, we might ask why professional arbitrageurs do not fully exploit the profit opportunities that are available. After all, foreign exchange markets abound with up-to-date communication capabilities, and professional arbitrageurs can detect market anomalies as readily as other market participants. The problem is that the size of the requisite currency flows is so large and the duration so long that professional arbitrageurs are not sufficient to the task. As generally practiced, arbitrage relies on short-term movements of funds to exploit short-term market anomalies in modest size. However, considering the billions of dollars, or foreign currency equivalent, for periods of from five to ten years that are required to remove or even diminish some of the market rigidities, professional arbitrageurs across the world cannot be expected to be sufficient to remove all arbitrage opportunities.

As a result of the insufficient supply of professional arbitrageurs, the gains that arise from many market anomalies continue to persist. In effect, it is the users of the long-date currency and coupon cover markets that perform the arbitrage function. They are not professional arbitrageurs, but they employ arbitragelike transactions to increase their rates of return, reduce their cost of capital, or move funds from one currency to another. In some cases the natural flows that give rise to an arbitrage opportunity may be diminished or become satisfied by economic and/or arbitrage flows so that the opportunities cease to prevail. In fact, it is possible at times to see a reversal in currency flows so strong as to produce an arbitrage opportunity in the opposite direction. In other cases the underlying market anomaly is so deep-rooted and permanent that it is not satisfied by the arbitrage actions of available participants, and the opportunity continues indefinitely.

CONCEPTUALIZED LIABILITY MANAGEMENT

Since its inception as a profession, informed portfolio management has considered shifting assets and asset categories to best fit the objectives of their portfolio consistent with the range of market opportunities at any particular time. Feeling comfortable with asset shifts that improved the risk–return complexion of their portfolio, money managers have developed complex analytical techniques to prompt changes in portfolio composition and to specify the characteristics of desired or undesired portfolio components. This kind of flexibility has gone on in financial portfolios for decades. More recently, with the advent of strategic planning, many of the concepts of the management of a portfolio of financial assets have been applied to portfolios of real assets (i.e., industrial firms have sought to manage their various businesses along the risk–return lines long applied to financial assets). This practice has resulted in the divestiture of entire divisions of product lines the characteristics of which did not fit the strategic objectives of a firm and in the acquisition of other product areas that had strategic fit.

The concepts of portfolio management remained largely confined to the asset side of balance sheets until the early 1960s. At that time progressive banks and other financial intermediaries discovered that their liquidity needs as well as their risk–return calculus could be better addressed by actively managing their liabilities. Hence, trading liabilities became an acceptable practice among the funds managers of many financial institutions. Given that the institution was well-managed overall, fluctuations in funding needs became a relatively simple matter of purchasing or selling liabilities. Although conceptually simple and similar to asset management, managing an institution's liabilities to produce an optimum return–risk relationship caught on more slowly. Today, however, it is practiced by virtually all progressive financial intermediaries.

To adequately develop the use and full potential of long-date currency and coupon cover, modern liability management as practiced by banks and other financial institutions needs to be applied to the currency and coupon needs of long-date players. Such players would include industrial companies, financial organizations including banks, investment managers, supranational organizations, and others for whom trading liabilities may be appropriate to the realization of their strategic objectives. However, to deploy modern liability management across a broad spectrum of players, many of which are reluctant to use it, a new way of thinking regarding the liability side of the balance sheet must be developed. Instruments and methodology now exist to enable players to structure economic transactions to best suit their financial needs. This was illustrated by the New York Federal Reserve Bank in its discussion of the evolution and growth of the U.S. foreign exchange market: "Indeed, the location of economic activity no longer indicates where associated financial transactions will be executed or in what currency they will be denominated."[5]

Indeed, financial managers now have the opportunity to modify the entire structure of their liabilities. If certain debt markets in one currency are more developed and thus preferable to those in another currency, the financial manager is now free to borrow the currency in the preferred market, enjoy any cost or other advantage, and swap the undesired currency exposure for the currency of his choice. Similarly, portfolio managers can unbundle the choice of issuers from the currency of their investment. This can be accomplished by selling the future proceeds in any undesired currency offered by preferred issuers of securities for the currency desired by the portfolio manager. Moreover, now both investors and borrowers can have access to the variety of floating- or fixed-rate debt markets that are most available to them, with the assurance that they can swap the debt service income or cost into the currency or coupon configuration of their choice. This represents a very important step forward in the practice of asset and liability management.

Financial Flexibility

The currency, pricing, and rate flexibility made available by long-date currency and coupon cover significantly widens the horizon for choice in many financial and operating decisions. Financial managers can now seek out those financial markets that are most developed in deciding which currency or market will help to carry out their borrowing most efficiently. Long-date cover allows users of capital markets to separate the markets they use from the currency of their choice. Examples of this choice include the well-developed Eurodollar market and domestic U.S. dollar commercial paper market. Borrowers with natural cash flows that occur in nondollar currencies may not prefer to bear the currency risk associated with dollar debt. However, if they can obtain an all-in cost of financing in the Eurodollar market that is lower than in their preferred currency, they should tap the Eurodollar market and convert to their desired currency for investment. To maintain their position free from exchange risk, it would be necessary to sell simultaneously sufficient home currency forward against dollars across the life of the Eurodollar debt to service it. In many instances, this strategy can result in a lower overall (all-in) cost to the borrower.

The well-developed U.S. commercial paper market illustrates how financing can be shifted to more efficient, developed markets somewhat independent of the currency of the market. In the case of short-term financing by non-U.S. borrowers, an underlying obstruction is the absence of a commercial paper market in West Germany, the United Kingdom, or Japan. Hence, U.S. multinational firms with need for short-term finance in these countries cannot tap a low-cost equivalent of commercial paper in foreign currencies. Nevertheless, a creditworthy U.S. firm could borrow short-term funds at 75 to 100 basis points below the London Interbank Offer Rate (LIBOR) by using the U.S. commercial paper market. The financing alternative faced by its offshore subsidiaries would be approximately LIBOR plus 0.375 percent. A potential strategy is for the parent to sell commercial paper, convert to the subsidiary's currency, transfer the funding to the subsidiary using a downstream intercompany loan, and cover the dollar exposure by selling sufficient foreign currency forward to repay the paper when due. The highly efficient short-term forward market in major currencies can accommodate the required transactions with ease and produce a funding cost about 1 percent less than if dollar funding occurred in London, with perhaps an even larger saving when compared to short-term financing in other local financial markets.

Similar savings would not be available to foreign borrowers in the U.S. commercial paper market because foreign names are either denied access or must pay a rate about equal to LIBOR in the U.S. commercial paper market, significantly reducing the saving over London funding. This situation occurs because many U.S. investors in commercial paper have been reluctant to buy paper from foreign issuers due to their lack of understanding of the underlying creditworthiness of the foreign names. Other investors, such as insurance companies, are limited in their purchase of foreign obligations. Those investors that are willing to purchase foreign-issued commercial paper require a higher return for doing so, thus eliminating much of the advantage for foreign issuers in the United States. Although not universally applicable to all borrowers, the U.S. commercial paper market illustrates how the location of the market and the currency of the borrower can be uncoupled using forward cover. To the extent that this financing technique is recurrent, long-date currency cover using a long-date forward contract would be appropriate to manage the exchange rate risk.

Another important concept that can now be implemented using forward coupon cover is that of separating the risk of interest payments from the risk of principal payment. This concept is illustrated in detail in Chapter 12, which deals with applications of coupon cover. It is also significant at this stage because of its conceptual content. Essentially, a coupon swap exchanges the obligation to service an interest expense depicted by one cash flow configuration through time with an interest expense that has a different configuration through time (i.e., a series of fixed-rate interest payments versus a series of floating-rate interest payments). In a one-currency coupon swap, no principal is at risk because the principal is precisely the same on each side of the coupon swap. What is being traded is the interest obligation only. This type of transaction effectively separates the interest rate risk from the risk associated with the principal of the loan and significantly adds to the flexibility enjoyed by a financial manager or portfolio manager.

Asset Arrangement

The flexibility made available by currency and coupon cover is useful to both managers of portfolios of financial assets and managers of portfolios of liabilities. In highlighting the underlying application concepts of currency and coupon cover, we have traveled from asset management to liability management. Now we come full circle and return to asset management for a more complete understanding of the role of long-date currency and coupon cover. With currently available financial instruments and methodology, an institutional investor can assume country risk without assuming its related currency risk. That is, by swapping the proceeds of an investment, a Swiss or Japanese investor could participate in the expected growth of the U.S. or Australian security markets without having to incur either U.S. or Australian dollar risk. Or a British investor could invest in the expected cash flows of the Canadian economy but have its currency flows denominated in, say, Swiss francs to obtain a preferred level of stability. The combinations are nearly limitless and can be accommodated wherever counterparties to the long-date agreements can be arranged. Long-date currency transactions are known to have been done in all of the major currencies plus Austrian schillings; Australian dollars; Belgian francs; Danish, Norwegian, and Swedish kronor; Greek drachma; Italian lira; Malaysian ringgits; Mexican pesos; New Zealand dollars; South African rand; and Spanish pesetas. Hence, the flexibility available is far broader than most would expect.

To take full advantage of the opportunities made available by long-date currency and coupon cover, financial and portfolio managers and their superiors need to develop a way of thinking that is less rigid than in the past. A new contemporary financial mind-set is needed—one that builds on the flexibilities available in modern asset and liability management. Considering that liabilities can now be traded as assets were formerly traded, we are freed from many of the rigidities that previously constrained business and financial decisions. Questions such as: In what currency should I sell my product?, Can I take advantage of subsidized export financing?, Can I participate in the development of a country without fear of losses in its currency?, Can I finance in a currency without being locked into that currency over the life of the loan?, Can I assure my home currency value of a stream of dividends, royalties, license fees, or the like? can now be evaluated before decisions are made to undertake a course of action. Managers are free to examine the structure of their assets and liabilities from a currency, coupon, and maturity point of view; reach appropriate decisions for a structure that is currently optimal; and move to implement the desired structure. The flexibility to move assets and liabilities has arrived. The contemporary financial mind-set to adapt to preferred structures still has inherent inertia to overcome. But substantial progress is being made and will become evident as the forces that underlie the use of long-date currency and coupon cover are examined. Next we consider the limiting assumptions inherent in the use of a strip or sequence of short-date forward currency contracts to substitute for a long-date contract in providing long-date currency cover.

Footnotes

[1]J. L. Hilley, C. R. Beidleman, and J. A. Greenleaf, "Does Covered Interest Arbitrage Dominate in Foreign Exchange Markets?" *The Columbia Journal of World Business* (Winter 1979), vol. xiv, no. 4, pp. 99–107.

[2]Calculated using Equation (2–1) in Chapter 2.

[3]Ibid.

[4]See "1983 International Tax Summaries," *Coopers and Lybrand International Tax Network,* ed. Alexander Berger (New York: John Wiley & Sons, 1983).

[5]"Evolution and Growth of the United States Foreign Exchange Market," *Federal Reserve Bank of New York Quarterly Review* (Autumn 1981), vol. 6, no. 3, p. 33.

Chapter 5

Comparison of a Series of Short-Date Forward Currency Contracts with a Long-Date Contract

INTRODUCTION

Financial managers faced with a long-term foreign exchange exposure can attempt to hedge this exposure by using either a single long-date forward currency contract or a series (strip) of contiguous short-date forward currency contracts. By hedging the exposure using a long-date forward currency contract, they fully eliminate the risk of unfavorable currency exchange movements. On the other hand, a strip of short-date forward currency contracts does not totally eliminate this risk but may prove more flexible over the hedge period. In this chapter we examine the interrelationship of a long-date forward currency contract and a strip of short-date forward currency contracts. Specific discussion revolves around the pricing of a long-date forward currency contract and a strip of short-date contracts. Emphasis is placed on the role of implied interest rates and the underlying assumptions necessary for a long-date forward currency contract to equate to a strip of short-date forwards. We present detailed illustrations of the role of implied interest rates, and examine the plausibility of the assumptions required for equivalence.

Short-Date versus Long-Date Currency Contracts

The pricing of a long-date forward contract between a U.S. and a West German concern was given in Equation (2-1) and is repeated here as Equation (5-1)

$$F_n = S_0 \left[\frac{(1 + i_{n\text{US}})}{(1 + i_{n\text{WG}})} \right]^n \tag{5-1}$$

where F_n = Forward exchange rate in time period n ($/DM)

S_0 = Spot exchange rate on day one ($/DM)

$i_{n\text{U.S.}}$ = n-year interest rate in the United States

$i_{n\text{W.G.}}$ = n-year interest rate in West Germany

n = Number of years of exposed position (i.e., the maturity of the forward contract).

If the U.S. firm wishes to hedge a position for a five-year period and the current spot exchange rate is $.3886/DM, while the five-year U.S. and West German interest rates are 11.27 and 8.35 percent, respectively, it should expect to see a five-year forward rate of approximately $0.4438/DM. This calculation is based on Equation (5-1) as presented below.

$$F_5 = \$.3886/\text{DM} \left[\frac{(1 + 0.1127)}{(1 + 0.0835)} \right]^5$$

$$F_5 = \$.4438/\text{DM}$$

This forward rate could be locked into on day one with absolute certainty. The U.S. firm would know that the exchange rate facing it in five years will be $0.4438/DM. Capital budgeting decisions, hedged financing operations, or long-range planning processes could be initiated based on this future exchange rate.

On the other hand, the financial managers might prefer the added flexibility associated with shorter forward rate commitments. Recognizing that there is a much more active market in short-date forward contracts, they might consider a strategy of hedging their positions with five sequential annual forward contracts. In this case, they would enter into a forward contract for one year. At the end of that year, they would roll over their forward contracts for another one-year period. This process would continue for n-years (five years in this illustration). The determination of each of the five forward exchange rates (F_n) is summarized below:

Annual Roll-Overs

(year zero to year one) $F_1 = S_0 \left[\dfrac{(1 + i_{0\text{-1US}})}{(1 + i_{0\text{-1WG}})} \right]$

$$\text{(year one to year two)}\ F_2 = S_1 \left[\frac{(1+i_{1\text{-}2US})}{(1+i_{1\text{-}2WG})}\right]$$

$$\text{(year two to year three)}\ F_3 = S_2 \left[\frac{(1+i_{2\text{-}3US})}{(1+i_{2\text{-}3WG})}\right]$$

$$\text{(year three to year four)}\ F_4 = S_3 \left[\frac{(1+i_{3\text{-}4US})}{(1+i_{3\text{-}4WG})}\right]$$

$$\text{(year four to year five)}\ F_5 = S_4 \left[\frac{(1+i_{4\text{-}5US})}{(1+i_{4\text{-}5WG})}\right]$$

where F_n = Forward exchange rate at the end of year n

i_{m-n} = One-year interest rate at the end of year m and the beginning of year n $(n = m + 1)$

S_0 = Spot exchange rate at the end of year zero and the beginning of year one

S_m = Expected future spot exchange rate at the end of year m and the beginning of year n

If, at the beginning of a strip of forwards, the forward rate for each one-year period is equal to the expected spot rate at the end of that one-year period (i.e., $F_1 = S_1$, $F_2 = S_2$), substitutions and simplifications lead to the following:

$$F_5 = S_0 \left[\frac{(1+i_{0\text{-}1US})}{(1+i_{0\text{-}1WG})} \frac{(1+i_{1\text{-}2US})}{(1+i_{1\text{-}2WG})} \frac{(1+i_{2\text{-}3US})}{(1+i_{2\text{-}3WG})}\right.$$

$$\left. \times \frac{(1+i_{3\text{-}4US})}{(1+i_{3\text{-}4WG})} \frac{(1+i_{4\text{-}5US})}{(1+i_{4\text{-}5WG})}\right] \quad (5\text{-}2)$$

Although the forward rate (F_1) may not be an accurate predictor of the actual future spot rate (S_1), it is an unbiased predictor of the future spot rate. Numerous studies have shown that, given certain assumptions, the forward rate as calculated above does *not* produce a systematically biased estimate of the future spot rate.[1] The necessary assumptions are that purchasing power parity, the Fisher effect, and interest rate parity prevail uniformly throughout the hedge period.[2] If these assumptions are upheld, inflation differentials between countries will be reflected in changes in both foreign exchange rates and in differential nominal domestic interest rates; and forward exchange rate premiums will equate to nominal domestic interest differentials.[3] From Equation (5-2), given that the requisite assumptions hold, we see the future exchange rate using a strip of forward annual contracts is a function of the expected forward annual interest rates for a succession of sequential one-year periods. This relationship provides a groundwork for equating a long-date forward currency contract with a strip of short-date forwards. Before exploring this relationship further, we must examine the underlying long-term interest rates and implied interest rates.

Implied Interest Rates

Implied interest rates are the forward one-period, say annual, interest rates implicit in an observed multiperiod or intermediate-term interest rate. That is, a two-year rate can be separated into a one-year rate and an implied forward rate from the end of year one to the end of year two. This specification of implied forward rates is similar to that employed in connection with the expectations theory of the term structure of interest rates. It is also quite helpful here in focusing on the relationship between short-date and long-date forward currency contracts.

To place the concept of implied rates in context, suppose that an investor wants to invest for two years and has numerous investment alternatives. Specifically, in our case, suppose that the investor has an alternative to invest for two years in, say, a zero coupon instrument that returns an annual interest rate of 12 percent or in a bank deposit for one year at 10 percent and at the end of the year reinvest for the second year at the then prevailing one-year interest rate.

If the first alternative is accepted so that $1,000 is invested for two years at 12 percent, the investor will have $1,254 at the end of the second year based on annual compounding as follows:

$$FV = PV(1+i)^n \qquad (5-3)$$

where FV = Future value at the end of period n
PV = Present value at the beginning of the investment process
i = Stated interest rate
n = Number of years of investment

or, specifically,

$$\$1,254 = \$1,000(1+0.12)^2$$

On the other hand, rolling over the money in sequential one-year commitments assures the investor of nothing more than that at the end of one year the money will have increased by 10 percent to $1,100 in accordance with Equation (5–3). The question that the investor must face is: What will be the annual interest rate from the end of the first year to the end of the second year (or in previous notation i_{1-2})? To answer this question, rearrange Equation (5–3) to provide for dissimilar annual reinvestment rates as follows:

$$FV = PV(1+i_{0-1})(1+i_{1-2})\cdots(1+i_{(n-1)-n}) \qquad (5-4)$$

or, specifically,

$$FV = \$1,000(1+0.10)(1+i_{1-2})$$

Table 5–1 presents the results of three different reinvestment rates (i_{1-2}) and

Table 5-1 Future values and reinvestment rates

Annual Reinvestment Rate (I_{1-2})	Value at the End of Year Two
10%	$1,210
14%	$1,254
18%	$1,298

the associated future values of the initial $1,000 assuming a 10 percent return in the first year of the two-year investment.

Clearly, with the given structure of interest rates (one year, 10 percent; two years, 12 percent), the investor would be indifferent between an investment of two years or an investment of one year with another one-year roll-over if that roll-over took place at 14 percent annual interest. Given the assumed rates, the market would be expecting that the second year's one-year interest rate would be 14 percent. This result can be seen more clearly by equating the future value at the end of the long-term investment [Equation (5–3)] with the future value of the roll-over strategy [Equation (5–4)] and solving for the implied annual interest rate from the end of year one to the end of the investor's holding period *(n)*. This is shown in Equation (5–5).

$$PV(1+i_n)^n = PV(1+i_{0-1})(1+i'_{1-2})\cdots(1+i_{n-1)-n})$$

$$(1+i_n)^n = (1+i_{0-1})(1+i_{1-2})\cdots(1+i_{(n-1)-n}) \qquad (5-5)$$

or, specifically, for a two-year holding period:

$$(1+0.12)^2 = (1+0.10)(1+i'_{1-2})$$
$$1.254 = 1.10(1+i'_{1-2})$$
$$1.14 = 1+i'_{1-2}$$
$$0.14 = i'_{1-2}$$

If the investment community thought that the one-year interest rate at the end of the first year would be only 10 percent, everyone with a two-year investment horizon would invest in a two-year investment rather than rolling over a one-year investment at an expected 10 percent reinvestment rate. This would put upward pressure on two-year security prices and downward pressure on one-year security prices, which would alter the stated interest rate relationship of 10 percent for a one-year investment and 12 percent for a two-year investment. Conversely, if the market expected annual interest rates to increase next year to, say, 18 percent, the roll-over alternative would appear to be more attractive. Again, buying and selling pressure would alter the stated interest rate relationships.

The foregoing example suggests that discerning what the market expects

67

interest rates to be in subsequent years (i.e., determining implied forward interest rates) is possible, based on today's stated short- and long-term interest rates. This derivation of implied forward rates coupled with the roll-over relationship of Equation (5-2) provides an insight into the forces that underlie the equivalence of a long-date forward currency contract with a strip of short-date currency forwards.

Reliance of a Strip of Short-Date Forward Contracts on Implied Interest Rates and Differentials

Implied interest rates can be derived from the yield curves of West Germany as well as from those of the United States. Table 5-2 presents actual interest rates and their associated implied annual interest rates for the United States and West Germany as of July 1983 for a five-year period. The

Table 5-2   Actual and implied interest rates for the United States and West Germany

Year to Maturity	U.S. Interest Rates (%) Actual*	Implied**	West German Interest Rates (%) Actual*	Implied**
1	10.01	10.01	6.45	6.45
2	10.60	11.19	7.45	8.46
3	10.86	11.38	7.80	8.50
4	11.07	11.70	8.00	8.60
5	11.27	12.07	8.35	9.76

*Observed multiperiod interest rate on day one.

**The implied rate of interest is the one-year rate of interest implicit in the actual interest rate structure. The implied rates are for the one-year period ending at the year shown as the year of maturity. For example, the 11.19 percent implied U.S. rate is the implied annual rate from the end of year one to the end of year two. Similarly, the 11.38 percent implied U.S. interest rate is the annual interest rate implied for the period from the end of year two to the end of year three, and so forth.

implied rates were calculated using Equation (5-5) for a five-year period. As before, a roll-over strategy in the United States that earned the implied interest rates (i.e., 10.01 percent return from the end of year zero [the beginning of year one] to the end of year one, 11.19 percent return from the end of year one to the end of year two, etc.) would earn exactly what a five-year investment would earn at a compound interest rate of 11.27 percent.

If the financial managers decided to hedge an exposed long-term position with a strip of forwards, they could calculate the expected exchange rate at the end of the fifth year by employing Equation (5-2) and the implied U.S. and West German interest rates as follows:

$$F_5 = \$0.3886/\text{DM} \left[\frac{(1+0.1001)(1+0.1119)(1+0.1138)}{(1+0.0645)(1+0.0846)(1+0.0850)} \right.$$

$$\left. \times \frac{(1+0.1170)(1+0.1207)}{(1+0.0860)(1+0.0976)} \right]$$

$$F_5 = \$0.4438/\text{DM}$$

Notice that the expected five-year forward exchange rate calculated in this example using a strip of short-date forwards is the same forward exchange rate calculated previously using Equation (5–1) for determining long-date forward exchange rates. This occurs because the limiting assumptions that underlie Equation (5–2) provide that forward rates are accurate predictors of future spot rates (i.e., $F_1 = S_1$, $F_2 = S_2$). Under these conditions we have a mathematical identity as shown:

$$\left[\frac{(1+0.1127)}{(1+0.0835)} \right]^2 = \left[\frac{(1+0.1001)(1+0.1119)(1+0.1138)}{(1+0.0645)(1+0.0846)(1+0.0850)} \right.$$

$$\left. \times \frac{(1+0.1170)(1+0.1207)}{(1+0.0860)(1+0.0976)} \right]$$

and which can be generalized as Equation (5–6):

$$\left[\frac{(1+i_{n\text{US}})}{(1+i_{n\text{WG}})} \right]^n = \left[\frac{(1+i_{0-1\text{US}})}{(1+i_{0-1\text{WG}})} \frac{(1+i_{1-2\text{US}})}{(1+i_{1-2\text{WG}})} \cdots \frac{(1+i_{(n-1)-n\text{US}})}{(1+i_{(n-1)-n\text{WG}})} \right] \quad (5\text{–}6)$$

A similar relationship for a single country was also evidenced in Equation (5–5), where an actual long-date interest rate was shown to be equivalent to a series of implied one-year forward interest rates.

At the outset of a hedge decision, it is not at all clear that exchange rate expectations implicit in market interest rates would favor either the long-date forward strategy or a strategy employing a strip of short-term forwards. From the calculations above, it appears that the market's expectations are for a $0.4438/DM exchange rate in five years. Whether a strip of short-date forwards would actually produce the same ex-post five-year exchange rate as a long-date contract depends upon whether the actual one-year interest rates turn out to be equal to the implied annual interest rates.

The problem (the decision) that faces the financial managers arises from the fact that market and economic factors underlying implied interest rates are infrequently realized. Hindsight will show that implied interest rates seldom turn out to be accurate predictors of actual future interest rates. Despite the fact that forward exchange rates are unbiased predictors of future spot rates, the same forecasting quality does not clearly apply to interest rates.

The burden that implied interest rates equate to actual future interest rates is mitigated in part by a (perhaps) less onerous requirement. As we shall see shortly, it is not necessary that implied interest rates in each currency be precise predictors of actual future interest rates for a strip of short-date forwards to equate to a long-date forward currency contract. Instead, it is only essential that the interest differential between currencies conform to the differential predicted by the implied forward interest rates. The following section both analyzes and illustrates the results that occur when actual annual interest rates differ from implied interest rates. Appropriate generalizations are then drawn from these illustrations to assist in the comparison of short-date versus long-date strategies.

Differing Actual versus Implied Annual Interest Rates and Forward Foreign Exchange Rates

As previously stated, a strip of short-date forward currency contracts would equate to a long-date forward contract if all actual future annual interest rates were equal to implied annual interest rates. Even if actual future annual interest rates differ from implied annual interest rates, the future exchange rate derived from a strip of short-term forward currency contracts could equate to the future exchange rate from a long-date swap if the current relationship between foreign and domestic interest rates were maintained. For example, the five-year exchange rate ($0.4438/DM) would be maintained even if the realized interest rates were not equal to the implied rate, provided that the ratio of

$$\frac{1 + \text{Implied U.S. Interest Rate}}{1 + \text{Implied West German Interest Rate}}$$

were equal to the ratio of

$$\frac{1 + \text{Realized U.S. Interest Rate}}{1 + \text{Realized West German Interest Rate}}$$

In essence, despite differences between implied rates and future realized rates, as long as the difference between U.S. and West German interest rates remains constant, the five-year exchange rate encountered in a strip of short-date forward contracts will approximate the five-year forward exchange rate. This result is illustrated in Table 5–3, which presents the implied interest rates of the base scenario discussed above and a 200 basis point increase or decrease in the realized annual interest rates of both countries over the implied annual interest rates. Using Equation (5–2) and the realized annual interest rates with the interest rate difference between the countries held constant, the five-year exchange rate turns out to be approximately the same as in the case where realized interest rates equaled implied interest rates. Thus, as indicated in the calculations in Table 5–3, if realized interest

Table 5-3 Constant differential between U.S. and West German realized and implied annual interest rates

Year	Realized Rates* = Implied Rates† (%)			Realized Rates* > Implied Rates† (%)			Realized Rates* < Implied Rates† (%)		
	United States	Germany	Interest Differential‡	United States	Germany	Interest Differential‡	United States	Germany	Interest Differential‡
1	10.01	6.45	3.56	10.01	6.45	3.56	10.01	6.45	3.56
2	11.19	8.46	2.73	13.19	10.46	2.73	9.19	6.46	2.73
3	11.38	8.50	2.88	13.38	10.50	2.88	9.38	6.50	2.88
4	11.70	8.60	3.10	13.70	10.60	3.10	9.70	6.60	3.10
5	12.07	9.76	2.31	14.07	11.76	2.31	10.07	7.76	2.31
Effective five-year forward exchange rate using a strip of short-date forward contracts	$0.4438/DM			$0.4431/DM			$0.4447/DM		

*Realized rates represent the actual annual interest rate incurred from the beginning of the year to the end of the year shown.

† Implied rates represent the forward annual interest rates from the beginning of the year to the end of the year that were implicit in the observed multiperiod interest rates on day one.

‡ Interest differential (i.e., U.S. rate minus German rate).

rates were equal to the implied interest rates, the five-year exchange rate as calculated before would be $0.4438/DM. And if the realized interest rates increased or decreased by 200 basis points in each country with respect to the implied interest rates and the rate difference between countries remained constant, the five-year foreign currency exchange rates would be $0.4431/DM and $0.4447/DM, respectively.

Many factors influence the behavior of interest rates and cause realized interest rates to deviate from implied rates. These factors include unexpected changes in:

- Fiscal policy
- Future inflation rates
- Monetary policy
- Money supply
- Balance of payments
- Political developments and uncertainties

While actual deviations from implied rates may run in parallel between two countries, even the implied interest rate difference is not likely to be fully realized in actual interest rates.

Figure 5–1 presents the actual interest rate difference or spread between U.S. and West German ten-year government bonds. This spread has been quite volatile over the past four years and, as shown, has ranged between 263 and 563 basis points in the year ending in May 1984.

If the interest rate difference between the United States and West Germany narrows due to either a decrease in realized U.S. interest rates, an increase in realized West German interest rates, or some combination of each, the five-year foreign exchange rate will be less than if realized annual interest rates were the same as implied annual interest rates. Table 5–4 presents two scenarios to illustrate this point: (1) where U.S.-realized interest rates are less than implied interest rates and (2) where West German-realized rates are more than implied rates (i.e., a narrowing of the interest rate difference or spread). In both cases the spread was decreased by 200 basis points between the realized and implied interest rates.

The results of these scenarios can be compared with our base case. In the base case, if the realized annual interest rates equal the implied annual interest rates, a five-year exchange rate of $0.4438/DM would prevail. However, if the spread narrowed as shown on Table 5–4, the realized five-year exchange rate would be only approximately $0.4128/DM as illustrated in both cases.

Similarly, if the realized interest rate spread increased over the implied interest rate spread, the five-year mark would be more expensive. This result is shown on Table 5–5. In this instance the additional 200 basis point spread results in a five-year mark, which would cost over $0.4765/DM.

In summary if realized annual interest rates in both countries were equal

Figure 5–1   Yields and yield spreads: West German government's versus U.S. government's ten-year maturities

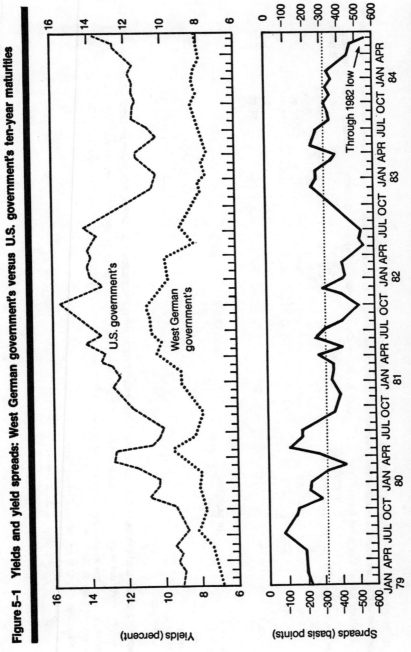

Source: "International Relative Values," Salomon Brothers, Inc., June 12, 1984, p. 16.

73

Table 5-4 Narrowing differential between U.S. and West German realized and implied annual interest rates

	Realized Rates* = Implied Rates† (%)			U.S. Realized*<U.S. Implied† (%)			German Realized*>German Implied† (%)		
Year	United States	Germany	Interest Differential‡	United States	Germany	Interest Differential‡	United States	Germany	Interest Differential‡
1	10.01	6.45	3.56	10.01	6.45	3.56	10.01	6.45	3.56
2	11.19	8.46	2.73	9.19	8.46	0.73	11.19	10.46	0.73
3	11.38	8.50	2.88	9.38	8.50	0.88	11.38	10.50	0.88
4	11.70	8.60	3.10	9.70	8.60	1.10	11.70	10.60	1.10
5	12.07	9.76	2.31	10.07	9.76	0.31	12.07	11.76	0.31
Effective five-year forward foreign exchange rate using a strip of short-date forward contracts	$0.4438/DM			$0.4129/DM			$0.4127/DM		

*Realized rates represent the actual annual interest rate incurred from the beginning of the year to the end of the year shown.

†Implied rates represent the forward annual interest rates from the beginning of the year to the end of the year that were implicit in the observed multiperiod interest rates on day one.

‡ Interest differential (i.e., U.S. rate minus German rate).

Table 5–5 Increasing differential between U.S. and West German realized and implied annual interest rates

	Realized Rates* = Implied Rates† (%)			U.S. Realized*>U.S. Implied† (%)			German Realized*<German Implied† (%)		
Year	United States	Germany	Interest Differential‡	United States	Germany	Interest Differential‡	United States	Germany	Interest Differential‡
1	10.01	6.45	3.56	10.01	6.45	3.56	10.01	6.45	3.56
2	11.19	8.46	2.73	13.19	8.46	4.73	11.19	6.46	4.73
3	11.38	8.50	2.88	13.38	8.50	4.88	11.38	6.50	4.88
4	11.70	8.60	3.10	13.70	8.60	5.10	11.70	6.60	5.10
5	12.07	9.76	2.31	14.07	9.76	4.31	12.07	7.76	4.31
Effective five-year forward foreign exchange rate using a strip of short-date forward contracts	$0.4438/DM			$0.4765/DM			$0.4780/DM		

*Realized rates represent the actual annual interest rate incurred from the beginning of the year to the end of the year shown.

† Implied rates represent the forward annual interest rates from the beginning of the year to the end of the year that were implicit in the observed multiperiod interest rates on day one.

‡ Interest differential (i.e., U.S. rate minus German rate).

75

to implied annual interest rates or if their ratios are maintained, the future currency exchange rate of a strip of short-date forward contracts would be equivalent to the future currency exchange rate of a long-date forward contract. On the other hand, in the more likely case where realized annual interest rates differ from implied annual rates, the following possibilities exist:

• Interest rate spread remains constant between realized and implied interest rates	Five-year forward currency exchange rate is approximately the same under a strip or a single long-date forward contract
• Interest rate spread narrows between realized and implied interest rates	Five-year forward currency exchange rate is lower under a strip than a single long-date forward contract
• Interest rate spread widens between realized and implied interest rates	Five-year forward currency exchange rate is higher under a strip than a single long-date forward contract

COMPARISON OF COVER STRATEGIES USING STRIPS OF SHORT-DATE VERSUS LONG-DATE FORWARD CURRENCY CONTRACTS

Now that we have seen how forward exchange rates depend upon implied interest rates in each of the countries and how implied interest rates depend on term interest rates, what financial managers can really accomplish when short-date or long-date forward currency cover are considered becomes clearer. Ever since the advent of floating exchange rates, the future course of exchange rates has been extremely difficult to predict. Moreover, bearing the full risk of changes in exchange rates may be intolerable for those players who never really know where the exchange rates may go and who cannot afford the cost of excessive adverse exchange rate movements.

As we have seen, financial managers may partly mitigate their exposure to exchange rate risk by employing a strip of short-date forward currency cover. Such a strategy essentially changes the risk determinant from that of the future course of exchange rates to the risk of the future course of differentials between interest rates in the two currencies. Some may argue that interest differentials can be predicted with a higher degree of accuracy than foreign exchange rates. In such cases using a strip of short-date currency cover may be partially justified for them. That is, if financial managers have the view that interest differentials will be stable or move in their favor over the duration of their foreign exchange exposure, then a strip of short-date contracts would be the preferred currency hedge. However, as indicated in Figure 5-1, even long-term interest differentials tend to fluctuate significantly in contemporary capital markets. Continuing such volatility would make a strip of short-date currency contracts a questionable choice over a long-date instrument except where the issue of flexibility is paramount.

Advantage of Short-Date Forward Currency Cover

The major advantage of a strip of short-date forward currency contracts is the flexibility that it provides to financial managers. If they can succeed in riding the long-term trend in the course of spot exchange rates, the use of a strip of short-date forward currency contracts may provide nearly all of the advantages of a long-date forward contract and still preserve the flexibility that is so coveted whenever long-date instruments are contemplated.

The concept of flexibility as applied here is multidimensioned. Flexibility is usually sought with regard to both size and maturity. The ability to forecast the size and timing of foreign currency flows accurately is important to the deployment of forward cover. For example, one U.S. oil firm expected to be short sterling by £10 million in 1981 and wound up the year £5 million long. This degree of imprecision makes long-date cover of operating foreign currency flows inappropriate and strengthens the need for the flexibility associated with short-date forward contracts. Similarly the accuracy of the timing of the expected foreign currency flows is important to the choice of cover. For firms that are unsure when profits would be repatriated, perhaps short-date forward cover would be preferred. However, there are many foreign currency flows that are contractual, or nearly so, and do not impose problems of unknown size or timing. These currency flows lend themselves ideally to long-date forward cover.

Advantage of Long-Date Forward Currency Cover

In cases where foreign currency flows can be forecast with a high degree of confidence, and in others where financial managers prefer to manage uncertain future currency flows to the risk of uncertain interest differentials across their exposure horizon, long-date currency cover may be desirable. Riding the time trend of exchange rates or banking on stability in interest differentials may sound appealing to some, but in the recent period of volatile inflation and interest rates, fluctuating inflation and interest differentials can easily disrupt the trend and be very costly. That is, if financial managers have to roll over short-date forward contracts at much higher costs in terms of local currency than the trend of exchange rates would suggest, they would have been better off with long-date currency hedges.

Another significant disadvantage of using a strip of short-date forwards to secure long-date currency cover is the adverse impact on current cash flows. A current cash flow problem can be illustrated by a roll-over of a dollar–sterling short-date forward where, if sterling were to fall, the player would require additional sterling at the end of year one to buy the dollars forward before rolling the contract. Suppose that on day one the one-year forward exchange rate was \$2.20/£ and the player bought \$2.2 million to cover the, say, ten-year dollar exposure. If, by the end of year one the one-year forward rate were \$1.80/£, the U.K. hedger would be able to get only \$1.8 million/£1 million and would need additional current sterling cash flow to cover the dollar exposure.

A related factor that may be a disadvantage to a strip versus a long-date forward currency contract is the multiple transaction costs incurred with the former. Actually, because the short-date bid–ask spreads tend to be much narrower than their long-date counterparts, transaction costs could be higher, lower, or approximately the same regardless of the choice of strategy. In most cases, the question of differential transaction costs will not be significant to the choice.

Disadvantages of Long-Date Forward Currency Cover

Having examined the disadvantages of a strip of short-date forward contracts and applauded the merits of long-date forward cover, fairness requires an examination and evaluation of the disadvantages of a strategy of long-date forward currency cover over a strip of short-date contracts. The most potentially serious disadvantage has already been discussed at length (viz, the loss of flexibility associated with a long-date instrument). When foreign exchange flows differ from those expected, a long-date instrument may leave a player locked-in and unable to avoid unintended exposure. We shall see examples of this in Chapter 7. However, with the development of the long-date market in currency cover, it is not unusual to unwind a hedge and manage a long-date currency position as required. To illustrate the feasibility of this approach to risk management, a U.S. soft drink producer considered using a ten-year long-date single payment or bullet contract for \$20 million to cover a German mark net asset position exposure. The parent was not quite sure of the size and timing of the future flows to be repatriated.

However, if repatriation took place as planned, the parent expected to reduce the hedge in year six by $4 million. In this way it would accomplish its primary objective of covering its aggregate foreign exchange exposure and leave the fine-tuning of its hedge until after it had determined how the exposure was playing out through time.

Another of the disadvantages of long-date forward cover is the fact that a long-date contract done with a bank uses up much more of a player's line of credit than a short-date contract. Because the bank has more at risk due to larger potential changes in exchange rates in a long-date forward contract than in a short-date forward and because multinational banks impose borrowing limits on each of their clients, long-date contracts can place an undesired constraint on players who deal primarily with banks. Thus, using long-date forward cover may be an opportunity cost to a firm in that it uses up its credit limit and may reduce its other borrowing possibilities from the bank. This potential disadvantage may have become somewhat more acute due to the liquidity squeeze experienced by banks that was associated with the Poland, Argentina, Mexico, Brazil, Drysdale, and Penn Square experiences and the silver losses of the German banks. As a result of these factors interbank credit lines have been reduced and have had an adverse impact on the size of the credit lines extended to their clients.

Two other disadvantages of long-date forward cover warrant limited attention. Long-date swaps have been viewed by some British and American lawyers as a form of gambling that, if this view prevailed, may result in the swaps being unenforceable in courts. To date this view has not been tested; hence, its potential threat cannot easily be quantified. Little concern has been given to its overhanging implications in the practice of covering long-date currency exposure.

Another impediment to the deployment of long-date forward cover lies in the inertia and lack of understanding of the nature of long-date currency cover instruments by boards of directors. Because of their lack of understanding and the apprehensiveness that this engenders, some boards have been reluctant to grant their approval to long-date forward currency instruments. This is a matter that can be overcome only by continuing to study the subject and recognizing the satisfactory results that other users have experienced.

MONETARY RELATIONSHIPS AND FORWARD EXCHANGE RATES

Now that we have progressed through the interrelationships between inflation rates, interest rates, implied forward interest rates, exchange rates, and forward exchange rates, we should integrate these terms and draw some conclusions that will be helpful in our later discussion of markets in long-date currency cover. A flowchart of the basic monetary relationships that underlie these variables is shown in Figure 5–2. Actually, all deposits, bonds,

Figure 5–2   Monetary relationships that affect forward foreign exchange rates

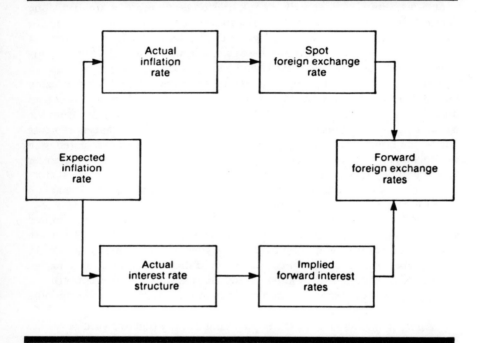

and forward foreign exchange contracts are interest related and depend on the level and structure of interest rates. Moreover, both foreign exchange rates and the level and structure of interest rates are deeply influenced by expected and actual rates of inflation. For this reason we find common ground for fixed income instruments and spot and forward foreign exchange transactions within the banking system.

We shall next examine the potential currency exposure throughout the world and its related demand for long-date currency cover in Chapter 6. Numerous applications of long-date currency cover are discussed in Chapters 7 through 10. Then we shall review the development of the market for long-date cover in Chapter 11. At that point the gradual lengthening of the maturity of long-date foreign exchange contracts will become clear. Note that in recent years the term of fixed income instruments (e.g., deposits, loans, and bonds) has become considerably shorter because of the high level and volatility of interest rates. Apparently, both of these courses are about to merge so that a relatively fluid market in term debt instruments and term forward foreign exchange contracts in five- to ten-year maturities may evolve. If this occurs, it would provide adequate liquidity in the long-term instruments that will be required by international financial managers.

Footnotes

[1]See, for example, I.H. Giddy and G. Duffy, "The Random Behavior of Flexible Exchange Rates," *Journal of International Business Studies* (Spring 1975), vol. 6, no. 1, pp. 1–32; and D.E. Logue, R.J. Sweeney, and T.D. Willett, "The Speculative Behavior of Exchange Rates During the Current Float," *Journal of Business Research,* (May 1978), vol. 6, no. 2, pp. 159–174.

[2]Purchasing power parity holds that spot exchange rates will adjust to reflect differences in the rate of inflation between countries; the Fisher effect states that the nominal level of interest rates in country are equal to the required rate of return plus a factor that reflects the expected rate of inflation in the country; and interest rate parity asserts that discounts or premiums on forward exchange rates equate to the differential in interest rates between the two countries but with opposite sign. See D.K. Eiteman and A.I. Stonehill, *Multinational Business Finance,* 3d ed. (New York: Addison Wesley), Chapter 4, for a full description of these concepts and their interrelationships.

[3]See I.H. Giddy, "An Integrated Theory of Exchange Rate Equilibrium," *Journal of Financial and Quantitative Analysis* (Dec. 1976), vol. 11, no. 6, pp. 883–92.

Chapter 6

Potential Long-Date Currency Exposure

INTRODUCTION

The magnitude of potentially exposed currency positions worldwide is immense and continues to grow. In this chapter we gain insight into the size and direction of potentially exposed foreign currency positions as we examine the size of representative measures of international trade, direct and portfolio investment, currency flows that arise from investment, royalties, fees, and subsidized export financing.

The tables that follow present striking evidence of the potential size of foreign exchange exposures throughout the world. The available data tend to be limited to U.S. transactions, and focus primarily on foreign investment by the United States in foreign countries and direct investment within the United States by foreigners. The data on international loans are also limited to the major currencies used in international finance. Despite the fact that data availability constraints restrict the data to only a subset of the total worldwide potential foreign exchange exposure, the figures represent a major subset of global currency exposure and provide convincing affirmation of the massive size of the latent vulnerability that exists throughout the world to changes in foreign exchange rates.

The historical data presented in this chapter summarize a proximate assessment of the potential exposure to foreign exchange risk in representative countries of the world. When available, additional supportive data provide more detail to these summary tables. These supplementary data can be found in the appendix.

TRADE FLOWS

Table 6-1 presents the aggregate worldwide trade flows from 1977 to 1982 and their trend rate of growth. To the extent that these exports and imports are sustained year over year or grow from year to year, they represent recurrent transactions and, hence, reflect the need for long-date currency cover to protect their users from the ongoing risk of changes in exchange rates.

As is evident from Table 6-1, world trade has contracted slightly from 1980 to 1982 due primarily to the worldwide recession. However, the more rapid growth in the three earlier years still produced a trend rate of growth of 11.6 percent over the period 1977-82. With the world economic recovery that began in 1983, growth in world trade should resume its modest course. Table 6-2 contains similar data for U.S. exports and imports of merchandise and services. The sizes of the flows speak for themselves. The decline in 1982 also reflects the worldwide recession in that year and should be reversed in the near term.

INVESTMENT FLOWS

Table 6-3 presents the international investment position of the United States in private assets abroad for the period 1977-82 by categories of investment. Relevant growth rates are shown for each category. The overall growth of 16.9 percent to a level of $726.3 billion suggests extensive exposure of asset positions unless these investments have been financed abroad or otherwise hedged for foreign exchange risk. Table 6-4 presents parallel data for the foreign investment position in the United States for the same period. Note from these data that foreign investment has been growing at a higher rate of 21.2 percent during this period, reaching a level of $476.3 billion in 1982.

Data that present the U.S. direct investment and provide detail by trading area and industry, respectively, for each of the years back to 1979 are presented in the appendix as Tables A-1 through A-3. The slight decrease in 1982 in U.S. direct investment abroad was partly recession related but may

Table 6-1 World trade flows—export and imports ($ billions)

	1977	1978	1979	1980	1981	1982	Trend Rate of Growth* (%)
Exports							
Industrial countries	$ 718.5	$ 857.9	$1,052.7	$1,239.4	$1,218.2	$1,155.5	10.3
Oil-exporting developing countries	149.0	142.3	211.0	295.0	274.4	213.1	11.7
Non-oil-exporting developing countries	164.8	193.7	251.6	320.1	333.8	315.2	14.6
Total †	$1,041.6	$1,206.3	$1,531.4	$1,875.6	$1,848.8	$1,703.6	11.3
Imports							
Industrial countries	$ 770.6	$ 891.0	$1,143.0	$1,369.6	$1,298.6	$1,219.9	10.3
Oil-exporting developing countries	84.4	94.8	97.6	131.4	153.5	153.8	13.6
Non-oil-exporting developing countries	203.0	247.1	310.8	406.4	435.8	385.6	14.8
Total †	$1,066.9	$1,244.1	$1,566.4	$1,927.3	$1,909.6	$1,778.9	11.6

Source: *International Financial Statistics*, International Monetary Fund, November 1982 and 1983.

*The trend rate of growth is obtained from a time series regression of the natural logarithms of the growth series using observations for each year of the data span.

† Totals contain statistical discrepancies.

Table 6-2 Trade flows—U.S. exports and imports of merchandise and services by year ($ billions)

	1977	1978	1979	1980	1981	1982	Trend Rate of Growth* (%)
Exports							
Merchandise	$120.8	$142.1	$184.5	$224.2	$236.3	$211.0	12.9
Services	63.5	78.1	2102.3	117.9	136.7	139.1	16.4
Total	$184.3	$220.2	$286.8	$342.1	$373.0	$350.1	14.2
Imports							
Merchandise	$151.7	$175.8	$211.8	$249.6	$264.1	$247.3	10.9
Services	42.1	54.1	69.9	84.2	97.7	103.0	18.4
Total	$193.8	$229.9	$281.7	$333.8	$361.8	$350.3	12.8

Source: *International Economic Conditions*, Annual Survey, St. Louis Federal Reserve Bank, 1983, p. 4.

*The trend rate of growth is obtained from a time series regression of the natural logarithms of the growth series using observations for each year of the data span.

Table 6-3 International investment position of U.S. private assets abroad at year-end 1982 ($ billions)

U.S. Private Assets Abroad	1977	1978	1979	1980	1981	1982	Trend Rate of Growth* (%)
Direct investment abroad	$146.0	$162.7	$187.9	$215.4	$226.4	$221.3	9.2
Foreign securities	49.4	53.4	56.8	62.5	63.1	75.3	7.7
U.S. claims on unaffiliated foreigners reported by U.S. nonbanking concerns	22.3	28.1	31.5	34.7	35.9	27.3	5.3
U.S. claims reported by U.S. banks (not reported elsewhere)	92.5	130.8	157.0	203.8	293.0	402.4	28.7
Total	$310.2	$375.0	$433.2	$516.4	$618.4	$726.3	16.9

Source: *Survey of Current Business*, August 1983, Table 3, p. 44.

*The trend rate of growth is obtained from a time series regression of the natural logarithms of the growth series using observations for each year of the data span.

Table 6-4 Foreign investment position in U.S. foreign private assets at year-end 1982 ($ billions)

	1977	1978	1979	1980	1981	1982	Trend Rate of Growth* (%)
Direct investment in U.S.	$ 34.6	$ 42.5	$ 54.5	$ 68.4	$ 90.4	$101.8	22.5
U.S. securities other than U.S. treasury	51.2	53.6	58.6	74.1	75.3	93.3	12.2
U.S. liabilities to unaffiliated foreigners reported by nonbanking concerns	11.9	16.0	18.7	30.4	29.9	25.8	17.8
U.S. treasury securities and other liabilities reported by U.S. banks	67.7	86.6	124.5	137.2	183.9	255.4	25.7
Total	$165.4	$198.7	$256.3	$310.1	$379.5	$476.3	21.2

Source: *Survey of Current Business*, August 1983, Table 3, p. 44.

*The trend rate of growth is obtained from a time series regression of the natural logarithms of the growth series using observations for each year of the data span.

also represent a measure of decreased attractiveness to U.S. firms of relative investment opportunities abroad.

The U.S. long-term security position abroad at year-end 1982 by trading area and type of investment is detailed in Table A–4 in the appendix. Table A–5 follows with a running summary by security type back to 1977. These data reflect a 7.7 percent trend rate of growth and indicate the persistent continuation of long-term portfolio investment abroad by U.S. investors. Unless otherwise hedged, the need for long-date currency cover of these investments is palpable.

Table 6–5 presents income on U.S. direct investment abroad for the period 1977–82. These income data are then detailed by trading area, industry, and year in Tables A–6 and A–7 in the appendix. Note that despite the minor declines in income in 1980 and 1981 and the larger decline in 1982, the trend growth rate for income on U.S. direct investment was a positive 4.1 percent per year. It is also possible that future growth in income on direct investment may be constrained by the declining relative attractiveness of U.S. direct investment abroad.

Data on fees and royalties earned in various areas of the world by U.S. parties are shown on Table 6–6 for the period 1977–82. Again a respectable growth rate of 7.4 percent is evident. The data on fees and royalties are sorted out by major industry and presented in Table A–8 in the appendix. Table A–9 adds to the data of Tables 6–6 and A–8 and presents figures for all recurrent international cash flows on U.S. investment abroad by type of income for 1977–82. These results reflect a similar five-year growth rate of 7.4 percent per year.

Similar data for foreign investment and related flows into the U.S. are presented in the appendix in Tables A–10 through A–19. These data are directly parallel to that shown in Tables 6–5 and 6–6 and A–1 through A–9 for U.S. investment abroad. Note that, with the exception of the low level of fees and royalties, all other forms of foreign investment by foreigners into the United States and investment-related income flows back to the investors have been growing at higher trend rates of growth than have the equivalent series for U.S. direct investment abroad. This finding is summarized in Table 6–7.

These results reaffirm the current incremental attractiveness of foreign investment in the United States relative to current U.S. investment abroad. From the point of view of long-date cover of currency exposure, however, it does not matter whose boundaries are crossed in making an international investment decision. Whenever an asset is denominated in a currency other than the currency of its owner, a potential exchange exposure arises, which, unless covered, can impose the risk of loss to the owner if the currency in which the asset is denominated devalues relative to the owner's home currency. The size of the potential exposures by U.S. parties abroad and by foreign

Table 6-5 Income on U.S. direct investment abroad by year by area ($ billions)

Area	1977	1978	1979	1980	1981	1982	Trend Rate of Growth* (%)
Canada	$ 3.3	$ 3.5	$ 5.5	$ 5.9	$ 4.2	$ 2.9	(0.1)
Europe	7.2	10.4	17.1	16.0	11.8	9.2	4.4
Other developed countries	1.4	2.4	2.3	2.8	2.8	1.4	1.9
Latin America	3.7	4.8	6.5	7.0	6.1	2.9	(1.2)
Other	4.1	4.4	6.8	5.4	7.5	6.5	10.5
Total	$19.7	$25.5	$38.2	$37.1	$32.4	$22.9	4.1

Source: *Survey of Current Business*, August 1983, Table 10, p. 22.

*The trend rate of growth is obtained from a time series regression of the natural logarithms of the growth series using observations for each year of the data span.

Table 6-6   U.S. fees and royalties earned abroad by year by area ($ billions)

Area	1977	1978	1979	1980	1981	1982	Trend Rate of Growth* (%)
Canada	$0.8	$0.8	$0.9	$0.9	$1.0	$1.0	5.1
Europe	2.2	2.5	2.6	3.2	3.0	3.0	6.6
Other developed countries	0.5	0.7	0.7	0.7	0.7	0.6	2.6
Latin America	0.3	0.4	0.4	0.6	0.7	0.6	15.9
Other	0.1	0.3	0.4	0.4	0.4	0.4	22.3
Total	$3.9	$4.7	$5.0	$5.8	$5.8	$5.6	7.4

Source: *Survey of Current Business*, August 1983, Table 10, p. 22.

*The trend rate of growth is obtained from a time series regression of the natural logarithms of the growth series using observations for each year of the data span.

Table 6-7 Comparative trend rates of growth, 1977-82

	Abroad by United States (%)	In United States by Foreigners (%)
International investment position of private assets	16.9	21.2
Direct investment	9.2	22.5
Long-term securities	7.7	12.2
Income on direct investment	4.1	13.8
Fees and royalties	7.4	(24.7)
Recurrent cash flow on foreign investment	7.4	25.4

parties in the United States which are contained in Tables 6-3 and 6-4, totaled $1.2 trillion in 1982, which was nearly 40 percent the size of the U.S. gross national product that year. Non-U.S. investment in other countries adds substantially to this figure.

The foreign exchange exposure inherent in the sum of worldwide foreign direct investment naturally would have to be reduced by offsetting strategies to manage foreign exchange risk. This would include strategies such as financing in foreign currencies, natural cash flows available within multinational firms to offset foreign currency requirements or sources, or other long-date hedges already put into place. Nevertheless, the sheer size of the numbers contained in these tables suggests ample opportunities and occasions where long-date currency hedge strategies could be applied to manage foreign exchange risk throughout the world.

FINANCIAL FLOWS

Another application for long-date currency cover is found in the financing by borrowers in a currency other than the currency of the issuer. To focus on the magnitude of these transactions, we look at the size of the international financing that has taken place outside the domestic markets. Before moving to the data, however, there are a few terms used in international finance that should be defined. The relevance of each of these terms to foreign currency exposure will immediately become apparent.

We look first at the Eurocurrency market size. Eurocurrencies are currencies on deposit in banks outside of the country of the currency. The most popular example of a Eurocurrency would be a dollar deposit in a bank in London. This Eurodollar balance in a London bank could then be loaned to a borrower of dollars. If that borrower were other than a U.S. party, a currency exposure may result. The magnitude of that potential exposure in terms of bank deposits of all currencies by nonbanks outside of their national markets and its trend rate of growth is shown on Table 6–8. The data shown in Table 6–8 are net Eurocurrency deposits and could be loaned out to create a currency exposure.

Absolute data on Eurocurrency loans are not as easily accessible. Most of the loans made in Eurocurrencies by the Eurobanks are held confidential and are not publicly disclosed. Nevertheless, those Eurocurrency bank credits that have been made public since 1977 are shown in Table 6–9. The overall level of publicly announced Eurocurrency bank credits has grown at a trend rate of 15.5 percent per year since 1977 and credits to industrial countries have seen a trend growth rate of 23.4 percent per year over the same period.

Eurobonds are bonds issued by foreign entities in a currency different from the currency of the market in which they are issued. An example would be a dollar bond issued by an Italian governmental agency in London. A strong potential for foreign exchange exposure is inherent in such a combination of nationalities. The historical record of outstanding Eurobond issues in each of the major currencies and their trend rates of growth can be seen in Table 6–10. Notice the rapid growth rates in Japanese yen and U.K. sterling Eurobonds at 48.6 and 45.5 percent per year, respectively, and the less rapid but still remarkable trend growth rates for U.S. dollar and French franc Eurobonds at 28.8 and 20.9 percent per year, respectively. While some of this nonnative currency financing may have foreign exchange hedging as its objective, a sizable fraction is more likely to occur because of the attractiveness of specific offshore debt markets for which long-date currency cover would be an appropriate collateral strategy.

Parallel data are presented for foreign bonds in Table 6–11. Foreign bonds differ from Eurobonds in that the former are issued in the currency of the market of issue but by nonnationals. For instance, a U.S. dollar bond issued in New York by a Canadian firm is an example of a "Yankee" foreign bond. Other popular names associated with sterling and yen foreign bonds are "Bulldog" bonds and "Samurai" bonds. Notice the rapid growth rates in such Bulldog and Samurai bonds at 77.3 and 29.6 percent per year, respectively. Growth in French franc foreign bonds ran close behind yen issues at 26.1 percent per year. A primary reason that foreign issuers are attracted to a specific market rests in its depth and liquidity. In many cases the issuers quickly convert the funds to their home currency, immediately incurring a foreign exchange exposure on the debt service requirements and establishing a need for long-date currency cover.

Both Eurobonds and foreign bonds are subsets of a broader classification of debt instruments called *international bonds*. Table 6–12 lists the volumes of international bonds newly issued by various areas of the world from 1977 to 1982. The trend rate of compound growth for this series was also a rapid

Table 6-8 Net Eurocurrency market size exclusive of Interbank claims ($ billions)

	1977	1978	1979	1980	1981	1982	Trend Rate of Growth* (%)
Claims on nonbanks	$210	$265	$330	$425	$530	$595	21.5
Claims on central banks and banks outside of market area	150	185	200	230	275	270	12.2
Conversion of Eurofunds into domestic currency by banks in Europe	30	45	60	75	85	95	22.6
Total	$390	$495	$590	$730	$890	$960	18.5
Eurodollars as a percent of gross liabilities in all Eurocurrencies	76%	74%	72%	75%	78%	79%	

Source: "World Financial Markets," Morgan Guaranty Trust Company.

*The trend rate of growth is obtained from a time series regression of the natural logarithms of the growth series using observations for each year of the data span.

Table 6-9 Publicly announced Eurocurrency bank credits by year of announcement and area ($ billions)

Area	1977	1978	1979	1980	1981	1982	Trend Rate of Growth* (%)
Industrial countries	$ 17.2	$ 28.9	$ 27.2	$ 39.1	$ 86.0	$ 42.8	23.4
Developing non-OPEC countries	13.5	26.9	35.4	24.0	33.4	28.7	11.5
Developing OPEC countries	7.5	10.4	12.6	11.1	11.9	12.7	8.3
Communist countries	3.4	3.8	7.3	2.8	1.8	0.8	(29.8)
International organizations	0.2	0.2	0.3	0.4	0.3	0.1	(5.6)
Total	$ 41.8	$ 70.2	$ 82.8	$ 77.4	$133.4	$ 85.1	15.5

Source: "World Financial Markets," Morgan Guaranty Trust Company.

*The trend rate of growth is obtained from a time series regression of the natural logarithms of the growth series using observations for each year of the data span.

Table 6-10 Eurobonds outstanding at year-end 1982 (billions of local currency units)

Eurobond	1977	1978	1979	1980	1981	1982	Trend Rate of Growth* (%)
U.S. dollar	—	—	—	63.8	80.3	113.4	28.8
Japanese yen	30.0	45.0	70.0	125.0	205.0	322.0	48.6
West German mark †	52.9	63.2	70.1	79.2	80.3	83.6	8.9
U.K. sterling	0.1	0.3	0.4	0.7	0.8	1.2	45.5
French franc	4.4	4.7	6.0	8.7	11.1	10.5	20.9
Canadian dollar	2.7	2.7	3.2	3.3	3.2	3.9	6.8
Dutch guilder	5.5	5.7	5.1	5.4	5.5	5.9	0.9

Source: "How Big Is the World Bond Market?—1983 Update," Salomon Brothers, August 1, 1983.

*The trend rate of growth is obtained from a time series regression of the natural logarithms of the growth series using observations from the source cited for each year of the data span.

† West German foreign and Eurobonds are combined.

Table 6-11 Foreign bonds outstanding at year-end 1982 (billions of local currency units)

Foreign Bonds	1977	1978	1979	1980	1981	1982	Trend Rate of Growth* (%)
U.S. dollar	38.9	43.1	47.0	47.8	53.4	58.4	7.7
Japanese yen	534.0	1,240.0	1,553.0	1,784.0	2,251.0	2,874.0	29.6
West German mark †	52.9	63.2	70.1	79.2	80.3	83.6	8.9
U.K. sterling	—	—	—	—	0.6	1.3	77.3
French franc	1.4	2.1	2.4	3.9	4.1	5.3	26.1
Canadian dollar	0.2	0.2	0.1	0.3	0.3	0.4	16.5
Swiss franc	18.5	19.9	21.4	26.0	31.1	42.6	16.3
Dutch guilder	2.3	2.5	2.7	3.1	3.7	5.4	15.9

Source: "How Big Is the World Bond Market?—1983 Update," Salomon Brothers, August 1, 1983.

*The trend rate of growth is obtained from a time series regression of the natural logarithms of the growth series using observations from the source cited for each year of the data span.

†West German foreign and Eurobonds are combined.

Table 6-12 New International bond issues by area ($ billions)

Borrower	1977	1978	1979	1980	1981	1982	Trend Rate of Growth* (%)
Industrial countries	$23.9	$25.0	$31.9	$32.7	$41.0	$61.5	17.8
Developing non-OPEC countries	2.7	2.7	2.7	2.0	4.3	3.8	8.0
Developing OPEC countries	0.7	1.5	0.4	0.5	0.4	1.0	(5.6)
Communist countries	0.2	—	0.1	0.1	0.1	0.1	(13.9)
International organizations	6.5	5.1	5.9	6.6	7.2	9.7	9.0
Total	$34.0	$34.3	$41.0	$41.9	$53.0	$76.1	15.3

Source: "World Financial Markets," Morgan Guaranty Trust Company.

*The trend rate of growth is obtained from a time series regression of the natural logarithms of the growth series using observations for each year of the data span.

15.3 percent per year. Table A–20 in the appendix breaks down the newly issued international bonds into Eurobonds, as well as foreign bonds issued within and without the United States. Notice that the trend rates of growth on Eurobonds of 22.5 percent per year and on foreign bonds issued outside the United States at 10.7 percent per year far outpaced the trend rate of growth on Yankee bonds. This reflects the development of foreign capital markets and the increasingly liberal attitudes of foreign monetary authorities in more of the developed countries in making their markets accessible to international borrowers.

The new issues of Eurobonds in each year are detailed by category of borrower and by currency of issue in Tables A–21 and A–22. The high trend rates of growth by U.S. companies and U.S. dollar bonds reflect the rate advantages in the Eurodollar market over the domestic dollar market in 1981 and 1982. Little or no forward currency cover would be needed for these issues because there is no currency risk. Note from Tables A–21 and A–22 that the U.S. dollar segment of the Eurocurrency bond issues represented from 70 to 85 percent of total issues in recent years, far more than the fraction floated by U.S. companies, suggesting that much of the dollar bonds were issued by non-U.S. entities with a strong prospect that currency cover would be prudent.

Tables A–23 and A–24 provide parallel data on new issues of foreign bonds outside the United States. Here the dominant issuers were national and supranational agencies and national governments. Major nondollar currencies of issue were Swiss francs and yen.

Details of new issues of Yankee bonds are presented in Table A–25. Note that the largest class of issuers were Canadian entities, which issued a total of $18.2 billion in the period 1977–82. Most of this finance was converted to Canadian dollars and represented a significant demand for long-date purchase of U.S. dollars to service the debt. The other significant issuer group was international organizations such as the World Bank, which in turn employed currency swaps to convert much of the dollar debt for Swiss franc- and German mark-denominated debt.

EXPORT CREDITS

A final source of demand for long-date currency cover rests with subsidized export financing. The rationale and motivation for this application and case studies are provided in Chapter 7. Table 6–13 summarizes aggregate export financing outstanding in 1980 and 1981; more detailed data are provided in Tables A–26 and A–27. Together these data illustrate the significance of export credits in international trade. Because these credits frequently finance large engineering projects where repayment covers many years, they lend themselves readily to long-date currency cover as a risk management

Table 6-13 Long-term and medium-term export financing outstanding ($ billions)

Country	1980	1981
Belgium	$ 2.7	$ 2.3
Canada	3.5	3.8
France	30.4	28.1
West Germany	3.2	5.1
Italy	4.3	5.1
Japan	22.5	25.1
United Kingdom	12.7	12.4
United States	15.8	16.6
Total	$95.1	$98.5

Source: Report to the U.S. Congress on Export Credit Competition and the Export-Import Bank of the United States, December 1982.

strategy. Table 6–13 shows that the large volume of export credits outstanding in 1981 and 1982 was approaching $100 billion. Table A–26 presents the amounts of new export credits issued during these years. The data illustrate how France and Japan have aggressively used export credits to stimulate their capital goods industries. Finally, Table A–27 provides data on the share of exports from each of the industrialized countries receiving official export credit support. The aggressive roles of Japan, France, and the United Kingdom are evident in these data. The extent of the subsidy has not been obtainable from available data; however, any credit subsidy obtained by purchasers represents a potential incentive to use long-date currency cover to hedge the exchange rate risk inherent in many of the alternative types of export financing.

This completes the review of the international transactions, investment, and financing data that demonstrate the extensive potential demand for long-date currency cover. These data place the size of the potential foreign exchange exposure into perspective. Because of the enormous size of the potential worldwide currency exposure (i.e., aggregate volumes that may approach 30 to 40 percent of a country's gross national product), the magnitude of the potential exposure to foreign exchange risk continues to endure. The fraction of the potential exposure that is covered by natural or managed positions is unknown. However large this fraction may be, the sheer size of the potential exposure suggests that the latent demand for long-date currency cover is far from being fully satisfied. In the next four chapters we examine applications and case studies where long-date currency cover has been employed to manage existing or planned foreign exchange exposure.

Chapter 7

Foreign Currency Transactions and Direct Investment Applications

INTRODUCTION TO LONG-DATE CURRENCY APPLICATIONS

Long-date currency cover is needed when a party presently has a net long or short position in a foreign currency resulting from current or capital transactions or when it plans to be long or short to accommodate a planned financial or operational course of action. Long-date foreign exchange contracts are used to cover unwanted liabilities in any currency or to cover assets in a weak currency.

Transactions and direct investment currency exposure occurs for many reasons:

1. Current or recurrent international transactions give rise to cash flows in an undesired currency.
2. Recurrent cash flows associated with transnational royalties, license fees, dividends, rent, long-term performance contracts or subsidized export financing often warrant long-date cover.
3. A firm may have a protracted currency exposure because of the form of financing of its foreign assets.

4. When a firm's direct investment assets and its liabilities in a given currency are imperfectly matched, it has a currency exposure that may justify covering actions. In most cases, net asset positions in a foreign currency are positive because of the presence of parent equity capital. Among the solutions available to address this problem is an asset hedge using long-date forward cover to bring the currency of both sides of the balance sheet into balance.

Certain accounting conventions for currency translation can also give rise to a foreign exchange exposure in reported income or on the balance sheets of firms. Despite the fact that these accounting translation techniques do not involve foreign currency cash flows, some firms have seen fit to hedge their effect on financial statements. Other factors that prompt long-date currency cover are related to sovereign-imposed taxes and regulations that introduce obstacles to free market processes. These include dissimilar tax provisions from country to country and various degrees of interference in the free flow of currencies such as currency controls and blockage.

A very significant set of applications of long-date currency cover deals with its role in obtaining a lower cost of financing using a liability, or financial hedge. These capital market applications have been responsible for much of the growth in the demand for long-date cover. Liability hedges are used as devices to facilitate the separation of the currency of the sourcing of funds from the currency of the ultimate deployment of funds. This separation enables borrowers to turn to capital markets in currencies different from the currency in which they plan to use the funds. Thus, liability hedges broaden the financing opportunities available to users of funds and enable them to take advantage of worldwide financing opportunities that occur from time to time. Such opportunities result from the presence of market anomalies and may be transient or more permanent as discussed in Chapter 4. The presence of anomalies, of however long duration, often facilitates cost savings in the procurement of funds and enables borrowers to obtain lower all-in cost of capital than otherwise would be available in conventionally accessed capital markets.

One solution to an unmatched foreign direct investment position is the use of an asset hedge, which employs long-date forward cover to bring the currency of both sides of the balance sheet into balance. A variety of asset hedge can also be used to exploit market anomalies to increase investment returns. In this process a portfolio investment alternative can be designed that produces a higher all-in rate of return than otherwise would be available in equivalent risk instruments. This latter variety of an asset hedge is called a *portfolio hedge*. Its applications rest largely on concepts that will become more clear after we discuss liability hedges; hence, its location in our applications framework is separated from direct investment asset hedges by extensive discussion and illustrations of liability hedges.

In this chapter, we focus on many of the specific applications of long-date currency cover that relate to recurrent transaction and direct investment by multinational parties. Here, examples illustrate the use of specific instruments to implement the desired cover. Some of the applications and illustrations are very simple and straightforward. Others involve more complex cash flows to accommodate the requisite supply or demand of desired currencies in appropriate size and date. Multiple examples illustrate various aspects of a given application. Chapter 8 provides a similar presentation of translation, taxation, and regulation applications and examples.

Applications involving hedged financing and hedged investing have been reserved for Chapters 9 and 10. Because of the importance of long-date currency cover to the arrangement and rearrangement of the liabilities and assets of international players, separate chapters are warranted for each of these applications. These types of capital market applications have accounted for much of the vigorous growth in the market for long-date currency cover and have led directly to the application of swap techniques to the problems of coupon cover. Chapters 9 and 10 generously supply examples of long-date currency cover of specific applications.

As will shortly become evident, all of the applications of long-date cover are the result of one party's wanting to convert the denomination of some of its planned or actual long-term assets to another currency. Hence, a review of applications of long-date currency cover also entails an understanding of why a party would have, or plan to have, long-term asset positions in an undesired currency. In each application discussed, a basic understanding of the underlying rationale that drives the application is provided.

RECURRENT FOREIGN EXCHANGE TRANSACTIONS

Short-term foreign currency transactions in major currencies can be readily hedged in the foreign currency forward or futures markets. However, recurrent transactions or other determinants of an ongoing stream of foreign currency cash flows warrant consideration of long-date currency cover. The alternative is to employ a series of short-date cover as a substitute for long-date cover with its inherent risks and disadvantages, as discussed in Chapter 5.

Size and Timing of the Currency Flows

A major difficulty in hedging foreign currency cash flows that arise from offshore transactions is the concern that the hedger may have about the precision of the amount and timing of the flows. Therefore, in addition to forecasting the timing, amount, and direction of foreign currency flows, both focusing on the quality or riskiness of the flows and attempting to quantify this risk to the extent possible are necessary. Factors such as pricing and quantity changes and deviations in shipping, receiving, inspection, and payment practices can significantly influence the accuracy of a foreign currency flow forecast. And in the longer term, the level of demand or supply can fluctuate significantly, giving rise to material variations from originally expected foreign currency flows.

Whatever the underlying forces that impinge on a foreign exchange forecast, classifying each forecast at some confidence level is usually possible. Those foreign currency flows that are firm, or for which the forecaster has a high degree of confidence, make excellent candidates for hedging. On the other hand, less precise forecasts should not be hedged in full but may be appropriate for partial hedging.

An example will illustrate this point. In 1980 when the demand for the products of Canadian natural resource firms was strong, many of these firms used a declining formula in selling forward their expected U.S. dollar cash flows from the sale of their products. Recognizing the potential inaccuracy of their foreign exchange forecasts, some firms adopted a policy of selling forward, say, 75 percent of their projected first-year U.S. dollar receivables, 50 percent of their projected second-year collections, and 25 percent of anticipated receivables beyond two years. As it turned out, the world recession curtailed the subsequent demand for forest and mineral products, and the conservativism employed in the declining formula had proven wise indeed. As illustrated, the reason for hedging transactions-oriented foreign currency flows is that hedge protection can be obtained in part and is appropriate even for fairly imprecise forecasts. While it may not be prudent to hedge an inexact projection fully, one can be reasonably secure in hedging some fraction of it and still obtain much of the protection of the hedging process.

As we have seen, imprecise projections in the timing or amount of transaction-generated foreign currency flows represent an obstacle to perfect hedging. However, as in most risk management practices, attempts can be made to manage large exposures and sacrifice full protection in the absolute size and timing of the currency flows. Thus, an appropriate hedge operation would be considered successful if it significantly reduced exposed currency flows, despite the fact that it did not perfectly synchronize the timing or the amount of the hedged flows. It is usually possible to dispose of small amounts of excess cover in the short-term, or spot, foreign exchange markets. Furthermore, slightly imperfect hedges can seldom be criticized when the bulk of the currency cover has been obtained.

Repetitive Foreign Trade

A typical arrangement in the pricing of international transactions is to denominate them in the currency of the exporters. A notable exception is the pricing of international oil contracts and other agricultural and natural resources, which are normally denominated in U.S. dollars. In either case, it very frequently becomes necessary for importers to obtain specified amounts of foreign exchange to fulfill their part of international transactions.

If the amounts involved are irregular or small, hedging them in the short-term forward market or simply bearing the risk of adverse exchange rate movements as the party perceives them may be sufficient. However, if the transactions are large, recurrent, and reasonably predictable, the importer may prefer to procure a long-term source of foreign exchange, which provides a stream of foreign currency tailored to his needs. In this application, importers would sell forward their long-term planned acquisition of (undesired) domestic currency that results from the sale of the imported products (or finished goods that contain the imported products) in favor of the foreign exchange needed to pay for their imports.

Transaction motives for long-date currency cover take forms other than that of a repetitive importer. The most apparent is its converse (i.e., a repetitive exporter who chooses to sell forward the undesired currency of the importer in which the sales contracts were denominated). Another example is that of a foreign subsidiary of an international firm that prefers to have its profits and return cash flows denominated in the currency of the parent. In these cases, repetitive trade transactions produce a stream of cash flows (assets) in an undesired currency. A stream of long-date currency cover would be ideal to establish a liability in the undesired currency in exchange for an asset in the desired currency at a predetermined rate of exchange.

A few examples will illustrate how a stream of long-date currency cover can be used to hedge recurrent transactions related to foreign exchange exposure. Consider a large U.S. international oil company that receives monthly payments for crude oil from its foreign subsidiaries. Since crude is priced in international markets in U.S. dollars, the parent requires payment from its subsidiaries in dollars. The subsidiaries, of course, receive payment from the sale of refined petroleum products in their local currencies. Since these currency flows are relatively stable, the parent firm, or the subsidiaries (if financial control is decentralized), should consider a strategy to sell forward a stream of local currency for U.S. dollars to obtain the dollars necessary to compensate the parent for the crude. This forward sale of local currency could be handled by using a series of long-date forward outright

105

agreements to provide for the transfer of currencies across a multiyear horizon.

Another example of a recurrent transaction-generated long-date currency cover application can be found in an Australian affiliate of a U.S. aluminum company that produced alumina and sold it in many companies. Alumina, an internationally traded natural resource, is also priced in U.S. dollars. Contracts for its sale are often long-term and run from 5 to 15 years. This situation created a stream of long-term currency exposure for the Australian subsidiary because it faced U.S. dollar revenue and Australian dollar costs. Since both streams were relatively assured, the Australian company elected to hedge its currency mismatch exposure. It did this in a number of ways, paramount of which was to sell a stream of U.S. dollars forward against Australian dollars. Counterparties to these forward contracts were Australian affiliates of U.S. dollar-based firms that wanted to hedge their dividend payments to their parents or Australian firms or subsidiaries that had U.S. dollar loans and no other source of U.S. dollars to service them. Another risk management strategy by this parent firm entailed the borrowing of U.S. dollars and subsequent conversion and investment in Australia to generate Australian dollar cash flows. During this time the U.S. dollar debt was serviced with the proceeds from the sale of the alumina. In addition, some of the U.S. dollar flows were earmarked for dividend service to the U.S. owners.

Similar transaction-motivated hedges have been employed by Canadian natural resource firms as discussed in the previous section. In these cases, each firm's expected sales of forest or mineral products were denominated in U.S. dollars, and its costs were incurred primarily in Canadian dollars. As in the Australian example, the hedge consisted of the sale of a stream of U.S. dollars forward for foreign currency, in this case Canadian dollars. To the extent that long-term contracts can be expected to provide assurance of the U.S. dollars flows, a large proportion of the expected flow may be sold forward. If, however, the uncertainty of the U.S. dollar flow is high, a decreasing fraction should be sold using some form of declining formula. Also, as in the Australian example, sale of U.S. dollar debt, conversion to Canadian dollars, and investment in Canada could be used to hedge the stream of expected cash flows.

LONG-TERM PERFORMANCE CONTRACTS AND SUBSIDIZED EXPORT FINANCING

International long-term performance contracts represent other transaction-generated applications of long-date currency cover. In each of these cases a stream of foreign exchange is required by the buyer or the seller to perform on the contract. Contracts for nuclear installations, subways, oil exploration and recovery, ocean vessels, and aircraft are notable examples. Similarly, subsidized export financing may generate financing cash flows for a capital project in a currency different from that in which the project will generate operating cash flows. In subsidized export-financing applications, government or quasigovernment institutions frequently provide low-cost financing to stimulate a country's export of capital goods. Unless the project directors sell enough undesired currency forward to provide the foreign currency needed to service their performance obligations or export financing requirements, they incur foreign exchange exposure. Such exposure may be severely damaging to the ultimate profitability of the project.

In many cases large-scale international construction contracts are priced in U.S. dollars. Nevertheless, negotiating concessions may require pricing in local currencies, or subsidized export financing may dictate that the financing, and hence the financing flows and requisite debt service, be in alternative currencies. Countries currently active in providing subsidized export financing include the United States, United Kingdom, France, West Germany, Japan, Sweden, Spain, and Australia. Specific data on the level and recent rate of subsidized export financing are presented in Chapter 6 and the appendix.

The following examples describe applications of long-date currency cover to both long-term performance contracts and subsidized export financing. In the case of the former, the cash flow payments occur in a currency not fancied by the performer of the contract. In the latter the currency of the financing of the contract is different from that preferred by the purchaser of the contract but at such subsidized rates that it cannot be rejected. Both imply currency mismatches that can be resolved by a stream of long-date currency cover.

Long-Term Performance Contracts

Long-term performance contracts are frequently used to cover the sale, manufacture, and installation of capital equipment. In one example, a U.S. manufacturer agreed to supply container-making machinery on a long-term contract to a Canadian customer. The contract was priced in Canadian dollars and provided for a uniform stream of Canadian dollar flows over three years, beginning in early 1982. These flows were sold using forward currency contracts and produced sizable gains to the hedger because of the concomitant decline in value of the Canadian dollar.

In another example, a U.S. firm sold gas turbines to a Saudi Arabian customer. The contract was denominated in riyals and provided for a stream of riyals over a 2.5- to 4-year period. At the time that it was done in the late

1970s, there was a modestly active, or deep, market in forward riyals, and the U.S. manufacturer was able to sell the stream forward for dollars using 2.5- and 4-year forward contracts. The other side of the contracts was taken by sellers of oil who wanted to sell forward dollars for riyals to invest or expense the riyals in domestic development. At the time of the transaction, the forward riyal was at a premium over the spot market price. It subsequently moved to a forward discount with much less market depth and only a 2-year maximum forward period available because of increases in country risk. These changes reflect the sensitivity of forward markets in some currencies and the wisdom of obtaining forward cover when it is available.

Risk Management of Potential Currency Flows

Long-term performance contracts, where cash flows are expected in an undesired currency, present a difficult problem in foreign exchange risk management during the bid stage of the contract. The problem is caused by the uncertainty attached to the potential currency flows. During the bid stage, it is not certain whether the proposal will be successful and a contract will ultimately be awarded. If the project manager hedged the expected contract cash flows and if the contract were lost, the manager would not have the ability to deliver the foreign currency necessary to perform on the hedge and might incur a foreign exchange gain or loss. On the other hand, if the future foreign currency flows were not hedged and the contract were won, the flows would be uncovered and the contractor might incur a cost to cover.

The only absolute solution to this problem is the use of a foreign currency option to purchase or sell the foreign currency *if* the contract is awarded. In this scenario the option cost could be built into the proposal price, and the conditional foreign exchange exposure would be covered if incurred. However, finding the other side for a long-date foreign currency option is difficult, and little has been done to identify option counterparties. There is a developing market in foreign currency options with maturities out of nine months in major currencies at the Philadelphia Stock Exchange. However, this market does not go out far enough in time to provide long-date cover, and there is little prospect at this writing that its longest contract will be lengthened.

Other solutions used by proposal project managers to deal with this exposure include:

1. Bearing the exposure through the bid period and covering if the contract were won (with the cost of cover included in the proposal price based on current forward rates).

2. Forecasting the spot and forward exchanges rates on the date of award and pricing the proposal based on these forecasts.
3. Incorporating a price readjustment provision in the contract based on changes in exchange rates.

It may be difficult to negotiate the provisions of either the second or third point into a competitive contract. Because of this difficulty, bearing of the currency exposure during the bid period has been the most popular approach. However, the moment that the contract is awarded, the currency flows are known and should be hedged in order not to extend the exposed period.

Subsidized Export Financing

A large number of applications of long-date currency cover result from subsidized export financing arrangements. This is not surprising considering the volume of subsidized export financing shown in Table 6–13. The presence of a financing subsidy introduces a market inefficiency that quickly invites players seeking a lower cost of capital. A few of the subsidized export financing deals illustrate the general nature of the arrangements and their complexity.

A well-known example of a subsidized export financing arrangement was the Caracas subway project undertaken in the late 1970s. The foreign exchange exposure created by this project occurred when Venezuela contracted with a French engineering firm to build the Caracas metropolitan subway. As part of the contract, the French export authority, Coface, provided Venezuela with a subsidized French franc loan. The amount of the loan was 1.3 billion francs, with debt service extending through 13.5 years.

The currency exposure problem occurred because Venezuela planned to use its oil revenue, which was denominated in U.S. dollars, to pay for the subway. If the franc were to rise against the dollar, it would take more dollars to service the franc loan, and the project would be more costly to Venezuela than planned. Hence, Venezuela wanted a dollar liability rather than a franc liability. To accomplish this, they went to a large French bank and a large U.S. bank to seek the necessary long-date currency cover. The result was a series of forward outright contracts to buy forward francs for dollars. The sellers of the forward francs included U.S. corporations with assets in France, which wanted to create French franc liabilities to match their franc assets. Other sellers were parties with franc dividends or royalties that they planned to repatriate. Still other motives for selling forward francs against dollars were predicated on the profit potential occasioned by a liability hedge. In this way, lower-cost franc financing could be obtained by borrowing dollars, converting to spot francs, investing, and selling forward francs to provide the dollars necessary to service the dollar debt. We will say more regarding liability hedges in Chapter 9. In all, 26 counterparties participated in the Caracas subway forward cover.

In a similar application, the central bank of an African republic engaged a U.S. investment banker to find counterparties to hedge their need to service another French franc Coface loan. The central bank of the African country offered a menu of dollar–franc forward contracts in nominal amounts from two- to nine-years' maturity.

Another interesting export finance-driven application was based on the financing of the construction of a synthetic fuels plant in New Zealand. To encourage the use of Japanese goods in the project, the export–import bank of Japan agreed to finance Japanese sales plus offshore sales of up to half the amount purchased from Japan. As a result, the contractor arranged a $260 million financing in yen at a below-market rate with a three-year grace period before payments were due.

Generally, international construction contracts are priced in U.S. dollars, and much of the cost is incurred in dollars. When export credits are denominated in nondollars, the contractor has to determine how it wants to treat any residual foreign exchange exposure. In this case, the contractor was a U.S. firm, and it wanted to manage its currency exposure from a dollar point of view. Hence, it needed to arrange for the purchase of long-date forward yen against dollars to service the yen loan. A Japanese trading company agreed to take the foreign exchange risk by selling forward yen in exchange for U.S. dollars. The trading company charged a 2.6 percent fee on the amount of the forward yen–dollar contract, and this cost had to be recovered in the construction contract. The trading company may have obtained the offsetting forward yen flows by selling dollar flows obtained from the sale of Indonesian natural resources against yen throughout the contract period. If so, an attractive fee was earned by matching nearly mirror-image long-date currency requirements.

Numerous other examples of export finance-driven foreign currency hedges have been identified. Many of them have been difficult to arrange because of the inertia of some of the foreign bureaucracies involved. All operate in a similar manner. Their counterparties may be motivated by almost any of the other applications for long-date currency risk management discussed in each of the applications chapters. We turn next to other rather predictable, recurrent sources of foreign exchange that give rise to the sale or purchase of streams of forward currency flows.

DIVIDENDS, ROYALTIES, AND FEES

Earlier we saw that the reliability or precision with which foreign currency flows can be expected to occur is a paramount determinant of a player's willingness to hedge its currency exposure. Moreover, as the timing of an expected foreign currency flow lengthens, the confidence level in its expectation diminishes. The problem of reliability or precision is easily sidestepped in the case of asset, liability, and portfolio hedges by the contractual nature of the cash flows, making them primary candidates for the use of long-date currency cover. There are also a significant number of foreign currency flows that are expected to occur with sufficient regularity, often due to contractual considerations, which makes them amenable to long-date currency cover to avoid foreign exchange exposure. Among these currency flows are (*a*) dividends from a foreign subsidiary to a parent, (*b*) royalties, (*c*) license fees, and (*d*) installment payment sales contracts.

Examples of this use of long-date currency cover generally entail straightforward financial applications and lend themselves well to the variety of motives and hedging techniques that are frequently used in obtaining long-date cover. Since we are dealing here with streams of approximately equal foreign currency flows, the examples also represent natural counterparties for the hedge of interest payments in a liability or portfolio hedge, as discussed in Chapters 9 and 10.

Note that holders of a stream of expected foreign currency flows have a choice of hedging the stream for a long period at one time or hedging in the short-term forward market for a year and sequentially hedge for one-year periods as each short-term hedge expires. We discussed the implications of this decision and their effects on the currency exposure of the firm in Chapter 5.

Dividends

An example of a stream of long-date forward contracts to hedge an expected dividend stream can be found in a U.S. food company that became concerned that its net asset position in sterling was becoming too high. The parent had been following a policy of being banker to its foreign subsidiaries by financing in the United States and advancing funds to its offshore subsidiaries. As a result of this policy and the expectation for earnings by the U.K. subsidiary, its exposure in sterling rose above acceptable levels. This condition, coupled with an unusually strong pound at the time, prompted the firm to sell forward a stream of sterling that approximated its expected dividend payments. Despite the fact that it did not know the exact foreign currency flows with certainty, this firm was able to hedge the bulk of its sterling exposure at a propitious time. It was then able to balance any small mismatches between actual and contractual cash flows in the future spot market without significant profit impact.

A second dividend hedge took a different course. In this case, a U.S. industrial products firm with a Belgian subsidiary was offered a Belgian franc loan at a very attractive interest rate. The firm's Belgian subsidiary borrowed the $20 million worth of financial francs that were offered and converted them to dollars for repatriation to its parent. The hedge strategy relied on the expectation that the stream of Belgian franc dividends from the subsidiary to the parent would service the franc debt. In this case the parent obtained attractive financing for redeployment elsewhere and locked in a fixed exchange rate on the franc dividend payments.

In another case a drug and personal products firm was unwilling to hedge a long-term expected stream of dividends from its foreign subsidiaries; instead, it elected to use one-year forward contracts to sell the estimated amount of the next year's dividend each year. The parent argued that it preferred the flexibility to determine each year where it wanted its values to grow or shrink and was unwilling to give up the loss of payout flexibility implicit in a long-date currency contract.

Royalties and Fees

The forward sale of license fees or royalties can be illustrated by a U.S. manufacturer of desalinization plants, nuclear reactors, and other major capital equipment. This firm had future license fees and royalties under contract in Canadian dollars, yen, French francs, and Saudi Arabian riyals for varying periods up to eight years. Its policy was to cover its foreign exchange exposure wherever possible. Hence, it sold French francs and yen forward as its commitments developed. In the past, the strengthening of the dollar against the franc and the yen has caused them to do well with their hedges. Should this trend reverse, however, some of the book gains could be reversed.

In a similar vein a U.S. investment banker arranged a pair of deals whereby a ten-year stream of Kuwaiti dinars was swapped for Swiss francs. The dinars were being paid to a Japanese capital equipment manufacturer to service the installation and maintenance of a sewage disposal plant. In turn, the francs were swapped for yen, the preferred currency of the seller of the capital equipment. The source of the Swiss francs may have been the return on prior investment of oil funds in franc assets to Kuwaiti investors for use at home.

A final example of a transaction-related contractual stream of foreign exchange arises in a U.S. manufacturer of office equipment. This firm sold copiers to foreign subsidiaries, which in turn leased them to users. The parent set up a five-year installment payment contract in foreign currencies to pay for the sale of the copiers. The foreign currency proceeds of these installment payment contracts were then sold using a series of forward contracts out through five years. The payments were made quarterly and involved 20 forward contracts. These deals have been arranged in Canadian dollars and in the major European currencies, counterparties have been more difficult to locate in some of the less-active European currencies, such as the Italian lira and Spanish peseta.

In many cases, the application that motivates long-date currency cover varies from one side of the contract to the other. Hence, transaction-oriented applications are often coupled with deals that are driven by other motives, and vice versa. As we shall see in the applications that follow, transaction applications will appear again, often in indirect ways. We turn now to foreign direct investment applications of long-date currency cover. Since in most cases the direct investment currency mismatch results in an asset exposure, these applications are called an *asset hedge*.

ASSET HEDGES

Asset hedges of a net foreign direct investment position were among the earliest applications of long-date forward cover. They result from the need to counteract a mismatch of assets and liabilities denominated in a foreign currency. Such a mismatch or gap in assets and liabilities denominated in a foreign currency is generally termed the *net asset position* (NAP) of a foreign subsidiary. Thus, the NAP equals the aggregate value of assets denominated in a foreign currency less the value of all liabilities denominated in the foreign currency. Since almost all foreign subsidiaries rely on some parent equity or intercompany financing, the NAP is usually positive, indicating a net asset exposure. Abstracting from distortions introduced by alternative translation methods, a net asset exposure would produce an exchange loss if the foreign currency devalued against the home currency and an exchange gain if the home currency devalued against the relevant foreign monetary unit. Hence, even before foreign currency translation methods became a major issue of debate, firms with overseas subsidiaries faced exchange rate risk and were concerned with managing their exposure to changes in exchange rates. This concern has become much more acute following the demise of fixed exchange rates and the transition to floating exchange rates in 1971–73.

The obvious way to hedge a net asset position is, of course, to make a loan denominated in the foreign currency. However, in those instances where capital markets are not well developed, this method has not always been available. In other cases, the credit status of the foreign borrower may not be adequate to qualify for a loan. This condition may force the multinational parent to increase its contribution of risk capital to the subsidiary, which naturally increases its net asset exposure in the foreign currency.

Given that a currency mismatch may occur because of a parent's financing of a foreign subsidiary, another alternative sometimes available to hedge

113

the long-term asset exposure is to sell forward the foreign currency value of the exposed assets. This procedure involves the use of long-date instruments, which range from parallel loans to currency swaps and long-date forward contracts, to obtain currency cover. Numerous examples of asset hedges exist in a large number of currencies. The following examples illustrate the principal applications of asset hedges in various currencies using alternative instruments.

Sterling Applications

To reduce an impending asset exposure in sterling that would have resulted from a major expansion and relocation of its administrative facilities, a major U.S. chemical manufacturer entered into a 10-year, $12 million swap agreement with the London branch of a U.S. investment bank. The U.K. counterparty was unknown to the U.S. multinational firm and a commercial bank assumed the credit risk. Two years earlier, the same firm obtained a 10-year asset hedge in sterling for a similar fixed asset application using parallel loans; a financial intermediary assumed the credit risk. The currency swap was used in the later case because of its increased flexibility and simplicity. This multinational parent also hedged a DM10 million net asset position in 1979 using a German mark–dollar swap.

In a slight adaptation of a straight asset hedge, an AA-rated U.S. foods multinational used a five-year dollar–sterling forward contract to hedge its sterling exposure in 1982. In this case the parent borrowed dollars, converted them to sterling to finance its U.K. subsidiary, and then sold the sterling forward for dollars to service its dollar loan. The alternative to this strategy would have been a sterling loan, which, at the time, would have been more costly. Here we have an example of a hedged financing to obtain a lower capital cost serving also as an asset hedge to cover foreign currency exposure.

A similar application was undertaken by a health care products company in 1980. This firm employed back-to-back loans to obtain £2.5 million to finance its U.K. subsidiary. The parent provided dollar liquidity and received sterling at $1.82/£. It did not know the other principal to the loan and used bank intermediation for credit risk. At the time the interest differential was a 2.5 percent premium on sterling. This company's strategy provided the lowest-cost financing available for the U.K. subsidiary while protecting the parent against foreign currency exposure.

Canadian Dollar Applications

A major U.S. consumer finance company with numerous foreign subsidiaries provides a variety of examples of asset hedges, some of which also qualify as translation hedges. This multinational enterprise had adopted a firm policy that required matching assets and liabilities by currency worldwide to the extent possible. It had subsidiaries in Canada, West Germany, the United Kingdom, and Japan.

This firm had previously used long-date currency swaps to hedge its NAP. As its retained earnings accumulated in sterling, it swapped them forward using a $20 million single payment or bullet swap. It also hedged its significant investment in Canada by borrowing Canadian dollars in the early and mid-1970s. It borrowed C$115 million using four public issues with maturites from five to seven years at interest rates from 9 to 10 percent. The spot conversion of the Canadian dollars to U.S. dollars at US$0.98/C$ proved to be fortuitous indeed, given the subsequent decline of the Canadian dollar to below US$0.77/C$.

In an application related to recurrent currency flows, a U.S. paper and forest products multinational with large operations in Canada hedged its NAP exposure by having its Canadian subsidiary borrow U.S. dollars. The intent was to service this U.S. dollar debt with the sales proceeds of pulp and paper that were produced in Canada but priced in U.S. dollars. Thus, in the late 1970s and early 1980s the Canadian dollar earnings of the subsidiary increased as the C$ devalued against the US$; the parent's consolidated earnings were protected from Canadian dollar currency exposure.

French Franc Applications

A U.S. personal products firm with a subsidiary in France covered its net asset position in francs by borrowing $35 million worth of French francs in November 1979. The parent converted the francs to dollars and invested them to hedge its French franc assets. The franc loan had an interest cost of 11.3 percent and the dollar investment yielded 11.7 percent with matched maturities. This hedge also turned out well because the exchange rate moved from FF4/$ to over FF8/$. The parent's gain on the hedge of approximately $18 million offset the loss in the dollar value of its net operating asset position in francs.

German Mark Applications

A U.S. food company, which recognized a sizable NAP in West Germany after an acquisition there in 1979, provides an interesting German mark application. The parent considered financing the subsidiary by borrowing marks at 8 percent but decided to wait with the financing and use the parent's funds until alternate arrangements could be made. At the same time the parent decided to hedge its German mark exposure.

The amounts required were DM87 million for seven years and DM7 million per year for debt service. A West German bank located counterparties to a series of long-date forward contracts. The pricing for each forward contract was based solely on interest differentials at the time. To illustrate, the seven-year bullet contract was priced at DM1.33/$ when at the time the spot exchange rate was DM1.97/$. This 4.5 percent annual premium was based on the then current interest differential. The pricing on the forward contract for DM7 million that matured in 1982 was at DM1.65/$. The food firm sold this contract in 1982 and realized a capital gain for use to offset the lower dollar value of the 1982 dividend stream from the West German subsidiary whose assets were being hedged. There was also a tax implication on the gain from this asset hedge; the gain on the forward contract was a long-term gain and hence taxed at a lower rate than the dividends from the West German subsidiary.

Other Currencies

Asset hedges are also possible in currencies where the capital markets are less developed than those of the major currencies. A U.S. contracting and oil well development firm used a parallel loan application to cover its exposure in Greek drachmas. This company needed to finance the exploration and development of a mineral that it needed for oil drilling. The mechanism employed was to lend $5 million to a U.S. subsidiary of a Greek company, which in turn provided an equivalent value in drachmas to the exploration subsidiary of the U.S. firm. This long-date parallel loan not only provided exchange rate protection but obtained a lower effective interest cost than the 21.5 percent that would have been otherwise required in Greece at the time.

A final example of an asset hedge illustrates that long-date currency hedges can be implemented even in the less well-known currencies. In this case a U.K. pension fund had a long-term liability denominated in Malaysian ringgits that left it in an exposed condition. The pension fund wanted to match this liability with a ringgit asset. At the same time, an American health care and drug firm needed ringgits to finance an investment in Malaysia. The match was astounding. A U.K. merchant bank skillfully brought the parties together in a currency swap that helped to square the balance sheets regarding currency and maturity for both companies. This combination produced a reduction in the foreign exchange risk and interest rate risk of both parties.

Sale or Purchase of a Large Block of Assets

On occasion the sale or purchase of a very large block of assets denominated in an undesired currency can lead to a significant disruption in a player's otherwise balanced net asset position in the currency. When the asset transaction is nominal, the problem of how to rebalance the NAP or cover the concurrent foreign exchange exposure may be handled in a conventional manner. We saw this earlier in the U.S. food company's use of a stream of German mark forward contracts to cover its DM87 million exposure in connection with its West German acquisition. However, when a significantly large block of assets is involved, the problems of rebalance become more complex as the players attempt to package an overall hedge to mitigate the newly found exposure. Moreover, because of the large amounts exposed and the massive impact of even small changes in exchange rates on the success of the underlying transaction, it is usually urgent that the hedge be assembled and implemented with dispatch. This point is illustrated by a large-scale sale of Canadian assets by a U.S. oil company.

In the autumn of 1980, the Canadian government adopted a National Energy Policy (NEP) whereby it gave notice of its intent to move to a position where majority ownership of Canadian energy enterprises would be held by Canadians. Up to this time there had been a fairly active two-way, long-date currency market in Canadian dollars–U.S. dollars. However, the adoption of the NEP served as a point of demarcation as the impending heavy outflows of capital from Canada reversed much of the flow of forward U.S. dollars into Canada.

Not long after the change in long-date market sentiment on the Canadian dollar, a U.S. multinational oil company sold a portion of its equity holding in its Canadian subsidiary sufficient to reduce its ownership by 25 percent to move toward compliance with NEP. The proceeds of this sale amounted to C$325 million in cash and C$325 in 10-year 14.5 percent fixed-rate notes. The cash was converted into U.S. dollars and was no longer a currency exposure problem. The notes were negotiated at a below-market interest rate in an attempt to consummate the sale. They represented a foreign exchange asset to the parent for both interest and principal and for which a long-date currency hedge was in order. The debt was amortized such that 25 percent was to be retired in the first five years and 75 percent in the last five years.

The hedge selected was a classic balance sheet asset hedge (i.e., selling foreign currency debt to cover the asset exposure). The U.S. multinational oil firm borrowed Canadian dollars and converted them to U.S. dollars with the intention that the cash flows from the Canadian dollar asset note would service its new Canadian dollar debt. At the outset, the net interest cost on the Canadian dollar debt was 16.75 percent, which left a net interest cost of 2.25 percent as a result of the below-market pricing of the original notes. There was no fixed-rate Canadian dollar debt available beyond one year, so it was necessary to obtain the Canadian dollar finance using floating-rate debt. The potential added cost of floating-rate debt was viewed as part of the cost of the sale and was offset in part by an opportunity currency gain. The opportunity gain resulted from the fact that the Canadian dollars were converted at US$0.84/C$ and subsequently moved below US$0.77/C$. Hence, the multinational oil firm was reasonably satisfied with the outcome of its hedge.

Note that as a result of NEP and all that it engendered for discouraging foreign investment in Canada, the U.S. oil company was still looking to sell another 26 percent of its investment in its Canadian subsidiary. Its entire residual investment in Canada also represented a conditional exposure. However, since petroleum products are priced in world markets in U.S. dollars, the currency exposure resulting from its NAP is offset by the flow of U.S. dollars obtained from product sales outside Canada. But, if the parent sold another 26 percent of its ownership, the resulting cash flow from the sale would be in Canadian dollars and would not have the currency advantage to the parent formerly obtained from the sale of product in U.S. dollars. Hence, the foreign exchange exposure associated with a desire to sell more of its ownership represents only a conditional exposure to the parent. Perhaps the sale would produce all cash proceeds, which could be immediately converted. Perhaps the political climate regarding foreign ownership in Canada will change, or perhaps the outlook for the Canadian dollar will improve. Despite the fact that the added sales of 26 percent of its ownership could produce C$800 to C$1000 million, no hedge was planned because of its uncertain impact on the NAP of the parent.

Our discussion of recurrent transactions and net direct investment applications of long-date currency cover is complete. We turn next in Chapter 8 to translation, taxation, and regulation applications of long-date currency cover.

Translation, Taxation, and Regulation Applications

INTRODUCTION

This chapter contains applications of long-date currency cover that result from a variety of causes; some are the result of accounting procedures and regulations. Such applications are novel in that they involve setting up hedge transactions that entail cash flow and tax considerations to offset or hedge the accounting translation of accounts that have no cash flow or tax implications.

Other applications contained in this chapter are driven primarily by market imperfections that result from differential tax rates between countries. Still others exist because of dislocations in the free flow of funds caused by various types of government controls and regulations. In general, these applications continue to exist as long as the external forces that prompt them continue intact. However, when changes in the underlying causes occur, the applications are altered or terminated accordingly.

FOREIGN EXCHANGE TRANSLATION

Foreign exchange translation conventions and procedures are needed to consolidate the financial statements of subsidiaries whose financial statements are denominated in currencies different from the currency of the parent firm. In an attempt to introduce an element of consistency and uniformity into the translation process, various national accounting bodies have developed and promulgated foreign exchange translation procedures to be followed by accounting practitioners in their respective countries.

Alternative translation methods that are typically employed include:

1. **Current:** All assets and liabilities are translated at current exchange rates leaving the equity account to reflect any residual translation effect directly in an equity valuation section on the balance sheet.
2. **Current–noncurrent:** All current accounts are translated at current exchange rates with noncurrent accounts translated at historical rates in effect when the assets or liabilities were acquired.
3. **Monetary–nonmonetary:** All monetary assets and liabilities are translated at current exchange rates with all other assets and liabilities translated at the historical rates in effect when the assets or liabilities were acquired.
4. **Temporal:** Same as current–noncurrent except that inventory valued on a historical cost basis is translated at historical exchange rates in effect at the time the inventory was acquired.

A summary of the predominantly practiced translation methods employed in numerous countries is presented in Table 8–1. The objective at this juncture is not to examine the technical merit or logic for each method but only to show that alternative translation methods exist and that multinational firms in each country more or less employ the translation method prescribed for their particular country.

In some cases the rules are sufficiently flexible to allow discretion in translation exchange rates and permit the firms some latitude. However, because of the impact that various accounting translation methods may have on reported financial statements, many multinational firms have developed very strong positions on the application of inflexible translation requirements. This problem is illustrated by what has transpired in the United States regarding currency translation requirements since 1976.

Financial Accounting Standards

Financial Accounting Standard 8 (FAS 8) first became applicable in the United States in 1976. Prior to that time, official "accounting opinions" required that translation losses flow through the income statement to the balance sheet but that translation gains be held in abeyance except to the

Table 8-1 Translation Methods (predominant practice)*

	Current	Current-Noncurrent	Monetary-Nonmonetary	Temporal
Argentina				X
Australia	X			
Austria				X
Bahamas			X	
Bermuda				X
Bolivia				X
Botswana	X			
Canada	X†			
Columbia	X			
Costa Rica			X	
Denmark	X			
Dominican Republic				X
Ecuador				X
El Salvador		X		
Fiji	X			
France	X			
Germany		X		
Greece	X			
Guatemala			X	
Honduras			X	
Hong Kong	X			
India	X			
Iran		X		
Ireland	X			
Ivory Coast	X			
Jamaica				X
Japan	X			
Kenya	X			
Korea			X	
Malawi		X		
Malaysia	X			
Netherlands	X			
New Zealand		X		
Nicaragua			X	
Norway	X			
Pakistan		X		
Panama				X
Paraguay	X			
Peru				X
Philippines			X	
Senegal	X			
Singapore	X			
South Africa		X		
Sweden			X	
Switzerland	X			

Table 8-1 Continued

	Current	Current-Noncurrent	Monetary-Nonmonetary	Temporal
Taiwan			X	
United Kingdom	X			
United States	X ‡			
Zambia		X		
Zimbabwe	X			

Source: Price-Waterhouse International, International Survey of Accounting Principles and Reporting Practices, Butterworths, 1979.

*Countries surveyed that had no "predominant practice" are excluded from this table.

† Changed from temporal to current with adoption of CICA section 1650 effective July 1, 1983.

‡ Changed from temporal to current with adoption of FASB 52 in December 1981.

extent that they could be used to reverse previously recorded translation losses. FAS 8 reversed this asymmetry and required that *all* translation gains and losses flow through the income statement. FAS 8 was based on the temporal method of valuation in which inventory and fixed assets were translated at exchange rates in effect when the assets were acquired. Monetary assets and liabilities were translated at current exchange rates. As a result of these translation procedures, most firms had a net liability foreign currency translation exposure position. This fact, coupled with a fluctuating exchange rate in which the dollar declined during the late 1970s, produced fluctuating translation effects and frequent reported translation losses during the period.

These events caused much debate centered around the "correct" method to be used in translating foreign accounts. The resolution to this measurement turmoil was a revision to FAS 8 called FAS 52. The proposed revision was first promulgated in 1980 and became effective on December 7, 1981. FAS 52 differed from its predecessor in that it allowed translation gains and losses to short-circuit the income statement and be recorded in an equity account of the balance sheet. FAS 52 also provided that all assets and liabilities be translated at current rates. Similarly, 16 months later, in April 1983, Statement of Accounting Practice No. 20 became effective in the United Kingdom. While more flexible than FAS 52 regarding translation exchange rates, it was consistent with the U.S. standard. A few months later, the Canadian accounting standard for the translation of foreign currencies was also revised. On July 1, 1983, CICA section 1650 became effective. It also changed the currency translation method from temporal to current and accords with current U.S. practice.

With the adoption of FAS 52, companies that were formerly "short" all over the world from a currency translation point of view (i.e., their currency-exposed liabilities exceeded their exposed assets) have now become "long". This has occurred because of the presence of parent company equity or intercompany financing, which is not translated at current exchange rates under FAS 52, and, hence, represents a residual translation exposure to exchange rate changes. Ironically, coincident with this reversed position in translation methodology, the dollar began to strengthen significantly against the currencies of many of the countries in which large U.S. multinational firms had subsidiaries. This combination of events left many of the multinational firms' income statements less sensitive to currency translation effects but had a detrimental impact on some of their balance sheets. In certain cases the balance sheet effect was so significant that balance sheet hedging became appropriate.

Some have called FAS 52 the "son of (FAS) 8." Others have claimed that while FAS 52 changed the problem of foreign currency translation, it did not eliminate it. The major problem is that it is not possible to capture the full impact of economic exposure accurately through any objectively manageable accounting translation method. As a result, firms whose net foreign asset position differs from zero (i.e., whose foreign currency assets are not equally offset by foreign currency liabilities), however calculated, will face some translation exposure. We do not evaluate the issues that underlie "correct" translation methods here, but do note that without the availability of specific translation guidelines, identifying the magnitude of the necessary long-date currency cover required to effectively hedge forthcoming changes in exchange rates would not be possible.

Income Statement Hedges

A good example of a firm that has relied heavily on the use of long-date forward cover to hedge its income statement exposure under FAS 8 is a personal products and drug firm that had established a target rate of growth in earnings per share as one of its operating goals. The management of this firm attached very high priority to this growth objective and did not want to earn too much or too little in a given year. Hence, they have used forward outright contracts in both yen and French francs to hedge much of the translation impact on their reported net income. Because they experienced rapid inventory turnover, they viewed their economic exposure as equivalent to that measured by FAS 8 minus inventory. They adopted FAS 52 for 1982 and have not hedged any translation loss since then because such losses would no longer appear on the income statement.

Another consumer products firm, which viewed its economic exposure in a similar manner due to its short inventory turnover (four to six months), consistently hedged its translation exposure at its perceived economic exposure level (FAS 8 less inventory) up until 1978. At that time they stopped translation cover because, although cover was effective in smoothing earnings, it often resulted in adverse cash flows. With translation cover of the income statement under FAS 8, translation gains, which had no cash flow or tax effect, were being offset by losses on forward contracts that did have an effect on cash outflows and taxes. Here we see a primary reason why firms turned away from translation cover or declined its use from the start.

With the adoption of FAS 52, translation effects on the income statement were avoided and the need for translation cover of the income statement eliminated. This is so because translation charges or credits now go directly to an equity account on the balance sheet. The provision under FAS 52 that translation gains and losses go directly to the balance sheet has some interesting side effects. Under this arrangement, firms can now borrow a low-interest currency (e.g., yen, Swiss francs, or German marks) and record the low nominal interest cost on their income statements. They could then lend the funds downstream to a subsidiary using an intercompany loan, which is treated as a long-term loan in the audit process, and charge the cost of translation cover or the translation loss directly to the parents' balance sheet. Here the asymmetry of FAS 52 enables a multinational firm to manipulate, or at least overstate, reported earnings if it chooses to do so.

A large consumer finance company maintained an interesting attitude regarding FAS 8, in which they were firm believers. FAS 52 made no sense for them because they were not a manufacturing company and had no inventory. This firm attempted to match the currency of its assets and liabilities worldwide to the extent possible and has borrowed sterling, Canadian dollars, yen, and German marks to accomplish this objective. They obtained the necessary translation hedges by hedging their net asset position. That is, they covered exposed assets by financing the assets in the currency in which the assets were denominated. These hedges were among the largest translation-related hedges identified; the hedges exceeded C\$100 million in that currency alone using four separate debt issues with maturities from five to ten years. These hedges were wise indeed because the Canadian dollars were converted to U.S. dollars at US\$0.98/C\$, and the U.S. dollar subsequently strengthened significantly.

FAS 8 had a profound effect on the reported performance of a large cash-rich drug, health care products, and hospital supplies firm. The impact was so great that they changed their philosophy and operating practices regarding international financial management. Prior to 1975 they financed nearly all of their foreign operations with parent equity, using local debt only when the rates were "too good" to turn down. As a result, they had a neutral translation exposure under FAS 8. However, their inventory turnover was high (two to four times per year), causing the inventory valuation at historical rates to hit the income statement quickly so that inventory was effectively exposed. After having lost about 10 percent of their earnings in 1976 due to currency translation effects, the management switched from its philosophy of decentralized international financial management and implemented a central control at the home office. This newly formed department was charged with applying modern financial techniques to manage their translation exposure.

Since the firm was long in every currency due to its large equity position in each foreign subsidiary, it set out to manage the size of its dividend flows and use of local borrowing. In this process it reduced the liquidity of its subsidiaries by more than $180 million. This put it in an exposed liability position (i.e., short) under a pure FAS 8 measure. But since its high turnover inventory was also exposed, it still remained effectively in somewhat of an exposed asset position (i.e., slightly long) under the view that total translation exposure equals FAS 8 translation exposure minus inventory.

In currencies where its exposure was largest or where it could not fully reduce the exposure by borrowing, the firm used long-date forward currency cover to effect the desired liability in the foreign currency. Since it was naturally long, it looked for counterparties such as multinational firms that were capital intensive in the given currency and, hence, naturally short. As an example of this strategy, it was able to sell Belgian francs forward in 1978 for a period of five years through the use of a bank intermediary. This forward deal was priced at the current spot exchange rate on day one (i.e., no forward premium or discount). The other side attempted to obtain a premium of 1.5 percent per annum but this was negotiated away due to the urgency with which the counterparty wanted to deal.

When the health care products firm shifted to FAS 52 in 1981, it had a gain on its long-date forward contracts. Since it no longer needed the cover under FAS 52, it was able to take the gain by assigning the contracts to an appropriate bank. Although there was a cost associated with undoing the forward contracts, it was not large because the firm allowed the bank sufficient time to take the firm out of its former foreign exchange position. In addition, the maturity of the forward position had now shortened progressively, making it easier to find counterparties.

Balance Sheet Hedges

Note that in the previous example the objective of managing translation exposure to the income statement under FAS 8 by using forward currency contracts was removed by FAS 52. Under FAS 52 translation cover is not needed to protect the income statement. Under FAS 52 each company is long in each currency in which it has an equity investment, and this cannot be changed. Firms can hedge to make themselves less long, but they cannot make themselves short without using forward currency cover. This phenomenon may have significant implications for the translation effect on the balance sheet for currencies that may be expected to devalue.

One solution for balance sheet protection is adequate diversification of investment of long positions among strong and weak currencies to obtain offsetting movements in translation. Severe concentration in one or more countries whose currencies are weak and expected to devalue can cause significant deterioration of the balance sheet. If they are large enough and recur from year to year, these translation losses can have seriously adverse effects on debt ratios, credit ratings, and the cost of capital. Conceivably, the credit markets will see through the translation impact on a creditworthy firm's debt ratio, but a deteriorating ratio will not be helpful to a firm that already has a lower rating. The following example illustrates the concern that some firms have regarding the translation impact of FAS 52 on their balance sheets.

A very conservative U.S. industrial and building products multinational firm with low debt has been successful in penetrating foreign markets with new technology. This firm did not hedge translation exposure under FAS 8. Nevertheless, it was eager to adopt FAS 52 for 1981 because of its very positive effect on income over FAS 8. The main reason for the early adoption of FAS 52, despite a great deal of effort in implementing it, was the favorable impact on inventory and depreciation costs, which amounted to approximately $0.23 per share. Under FAS 52 methods, this cost effect flowed through to a $33 million charge in the counterequity (foreign currency translation) account of the balance sheet and a $7 million favorable impact on the income statement.

The impact on this firm's balance sheet was massive and tended to eliminate a significant portion of its reported net worth. Moreover, another large translation hit to the counterequity account was on the horizon for 1982. The reason for these massive translation charges is that the firm's primary overseas subsidiaries were in France, Italy, and Canada—all countries where the currencies had been rapidly devaluing against the dollar during this period. The Canadian dollar did tend to stabilize in 1982, but the French franc and the Italian lira continued to weaken, causing additional concern for the firm's reported equity position. Hence, in mid-1982, just six months after the adoption of FAS 52, the building products firm was seriously considering hedging its balance sheet translation exposure. At that time the firm considered not using the forward market because of the large forward premiums on the strong currencies and borrowing in foreign currency to square up its translation exposure. Of course, high interest rates would be faced in the weaker currencies, which would nearly equate to the forward premium if the foreign currency loans were, in fact, doable.

The firm was also considering another alternative, the use of a low-interest proxy currency where the exchange value may be expected to move with the exposed currencies. For example, the dearth of a long-term debt market in Italy and France has led to the proposition of borrowing German marks at low interest rates and relying on the common market or snake currency alignment to keep the French francs and Italian lira in parity. The snake suffers, as is well known, from periodic realignments in currencies due mainly to differential inflation rates among its members. Hence, such a proxy policy would be bound to failure over any intermediate term period. What remains as a potential solution to the problem of balance sheet exposure is the use of long-date currency cover that would mobilize offshore spot flows of French francs or Italian lira (perhaps from a subsidized export finance project) in exchange for a future liability in these currencies to provide the desired balance sheet translation hedge. The forward premium on strong currencies in this case can hardly be avoided if the insurance of the equity translation exposure is to be obtained.

These examples bring us full circle regarding the impact of translation methodology on the demand for long-date currency cover. Whereas FAS 52 was designed to reduce fluctuations to the income statement, it has introduced potential fluctuations to the balance sheet and has provided a means whereby a multinational firm can alter the true interest costs that hit the income statement and partially smooth reported earnings as a result. The main role of translation of foreign currencies for our present purposes is that it does provide an application for players to engage in long-date currency cover and, hence, represents a demand for long-date cover. We turn next to other accounting and legal forces that prompt long-date currency cover as we consider tax-related applications.

TAXATION APPLICATIONS

Some users of long-date currency cover have argued that tax differentials are seldom the sole driving force behind the adoption of currency cover instruments. They suggest that taxation-related motives must be coupled with other factors to make long-date currency cover a plausible course of action. Nevertheless, the tax aspect is always important and, after examination of the after-tax impact, it often becomes clear that tax factors alone can provide adequate justification to engage in long-date currency cover. In some cases high tax levies act like other more severe forms of currency regulation and are used to block or effectively discourage the removal of assets from a (weak currency) country. Other tax-related applications are rooted in differential taxation procedures between countries. And tax credit limitations for taxes paid abroad prompt financial initiatives that rely on long-date cover. In this section we examine these applications, starting with the role of income taxes to discourage repatriation of funds, moving to differential tax practices between countries as applied to fixed asset depreciation allowances and their impact on lease pricing, and conclude with the movement of foreign source income to prevent the loss of foreign tax credits that would otherwise have exceeded a firm's tax credit limitation.

Income Taxes

Many multinational financial transactions have been conceived to defer or avoid income taxes. In general, the objective is to shift taxable income from a high-tax country to a low-tax country using whatever discretion may be available and allowable in transfer prices on products or services or in interest subsidies on loans. Other strategies involve the mobilization of liquidity from one subsidiary to another without the funds' passing through an intermediate dividend step to the parent and being taxed in the process.

To illustrate one strategy, consider a Panamanian subsidiary of a U.S. electronics firm, which had been cash-rich for some time. The subsidiary had been quite profitable and paid low income tax rates in Panama, but if funds were to be remitted to the parent in the form of dividends, the latter would face a 46 percent tax rate on the payment. Far East subsidiaries of the parent in Singapore and Hong Kong had similar characteristics and could also have been selected as a source of liquidity. Another subsidiary in West Germany had mark revenue because its products were priced primarily in that currency; nevertheless, it incurred dollar expenses for the raw material and parts purchased from the parent and sister subsidiaries. The German subsidiary wished to purchase dollars forward to hedge its own foreign currency flows. This was accomplished by using a bank-intermediated back-to-back (BTB) loan whereby the Panamanian subsidiary lent (deposited) dollars to the Panamanian branch of the bank. The bank in turn provided marks to the Panamanian electronics subsidiary. The Frankfurt branch of the same bank then did an opposite BTB deal with the German electronics subsidiary (i.e., the bank provided forward dollars in return for forward marks). The German subsidiary had been able to pass the exchange risk to the Panamanian subsidiary effectively, which in turn was able to make dollars available to a sister subsidiary without incurring U.S. taxes on dividends.

As in many other instances, a collateral motive was behind this transaction. The German subsidiary was close to bankruptcy, and the parent did not want the foreign exchange risk to force the subsidiary into an intolerable profit or cash flow position. The parent preferred to remove this risk from the German subsidiary and pass it to the profitable, cash-rich Panamanian subsidiary, which could dispose of the DM at a loss if necessary. This was a subtle way of enabling the corporation to manage, within limits, where its profits were taken. The choice, of course, depended upon its perceptions regarding whether the DM would weaken and upon relative tax rates. This use of long-date currency cover enabled the firm to pass risk to a less cost-sensitive subsidiary within a closed system without having to incur U.S. tax on the liquidity used in the process.

Tax Hedging

Another income tax application of forward currency cover is applicable to the use of forward contracts of approximately one year's duration. Obviously, this is not long-date as we have defined it, but the application is so novel that it warrants inclusion as an example of the type of flexibility and choice that operating in multiple currencies, time durations, and tax jurisdictions frequently offers. In this example the actual period of the hedge depends on the tax consequences.

A multinational chemical company had numerous offshore subsidiaries and had regular transaction-related foreign currency flows in multiple currencies. It chose to hedge its expected foreign exchange exposure for one year at a time rather than employ a long-date instrument. In implementing the requisite currency cover, however, the firm used 13-month forward contracts. Then, if at 11.5 months it had experienced a loss on the forward currency contract, it assigned the contract and took a short-term loss, sheltering other income at a 46 percent tax rate. On the other hand, if it had a gain on the contract at 11.5 months, it let the contract run until it passed the one-year mark. Then it assigned the contract at, say 12.5 months, and took a long-term gain taxed at only 28 percent.

Differential Tax Policies

Differential tax policies across countries suggest, where possible, taking profits in the low-tax-rate country. A related strategy is to transfer costs to a high-tax-rate country from a low-tax-rate country. The discretionary uses of transfer pricing and interest subsidies have been mentioned as limited means of accomplishing this. Another notable application of the transfer of cost across borders that relies on long-date currency cover is the transfer of the depreciation cost associated with fixed assets. This transfer has been conveniently implemented by using an international lease.

Long-term international leases have been used in transaction-oriented applications for long-date currency cover, relying on differential tax rates to produce a low-cost means of financing long-term assets like ships, oil drill rigs, and aircraft. Until rather recently lease applications of long-date currency cover have been quite popular because of the liberal depreciation provisions allowed in England since the early 1970s. British law allows first-year expensing of fixed assets. Prior to 1983, when the Inland Revenue disallowed this provision for assets transferred to foreign entities, having an English entity acquire the fixed assets required for offshore applications, which did not allow instant depreciation write-off, was attractive. The strategy then required that the assets be leased to the offshore user. In this way a large fraction of the present value of the tax shield obtained by first-year expensing could be built into the rental payments, and both the lessor and lessee could benefit from this differential tax treatment of depreciation charges.

This strategy produced a foreign exchange problem, namely that the user entity generated cash flows in a currency other than sterling and the lease had to be serviced in sterling. The solution was to employ a stream of long-date currency cover, which created a forward liability in the (undesired) nonsterling currency and a forward asset in sterling to service the lease. Note that one U.K. bank sold so much long-date sterling forward for dollars to implement lease cover that it was prepared to quote the other side (sale of long-date dollars against sterling) from its book for periods out through 15 years in amounts up to $100 million. Although no longer applicable, this example represents anomalies that develop due to differential tax policies. Not surprisingly, we may see others develop from time to time.

Foreign Tax Credits

In many cases income taxes paid to foreign governments can be used as a credit against income taxes levied by the home government. However, the magnitude of such foreign tax credits may be limited. In the case of the United States, the foreign tax credit limitation depends upon foreign source income and is calculated in accordance with the following formula:

$$\text{Overall limitation} = \frac{\text{Taxable income from foreign sources}}{\text{Total taxable income}} \times \text{U.S. tax liability}$$

If the sum of foreign taxes paid on foreign income plus withholding taxes paid on distributions of foreign income to a parent multinational firm exceed the calculated limitation, the firm has exceeded the allowable tax credit and may lose a portion of its advantage. The excess credit may be carried back two years and forward five years and applied against income taxes in those years. Moreover, the limitation is an aggregate worldwide limitation so that foreign source income subject to high taxes can be combined with foreign income exposed to lower taxes in figuring the overall limitation.

The ability to commingle foreign source income and foreign tax credits from different sources presents an opportunity to seek or arrange for low rates of foreign tax credits to be used to offset excess foreign tax credit limitation on income from high-tax-rate countries. As derived from the tax credit limitation calculation, the relevant variables are (1) the U.S. tax rate (i.e., U.S. tax liability/total worldwide taxable income) and (2) the amount of taxable income from foreign sources. Thus, if foreign source income, whose local tax rate is less than the U.S. tax rate, can be arranged, that income will flow to the worldwide income of the multinational firm at a "deficit" foreign tax credit limitation and be available for use to offset other "excess" tax credit limitation from high-tax-rate countries.

Many of the countries in which multinational firms have foreign subsidiaries have combined income and withholding tax rates greater than the 46 percent maximum rate in the United States (e.g., Canada, the United Kingdom, and West Germany). Hence, a potential loss of excess tax credit limitation warrants continued attention by corporate treasurers. The following two examples illustrate how long-date currency cover can be used to implement the balancing of current overall tax credit limitation and to postpone a loss of carry-back opportunity of excess limitation.

In the first illustration, a large highly liquid U.S. health care products company was facing the problem of excess tax credit limitation and a concomitant loss in credit for foreign taxes paid. One way to use the excess limitation was to subsidize an intracompany loan to its U.K. subsidiary. To implement this strategy, the parent gave some of its U.S. liquid assets to a domestic subsidiary that converted them to sterling and on-lent them to the U.K. subsidiary at a slightly subsidized rate. To protect itself from a weakening of sterling, the parent sold the sterling interest and principal flows forward using forward outright contracts across the 10-year maturity of the loan. The parent intended the U.K. subsidiary to service the sterling debt with its natural sterling cash flows. This arrangement provided a stream of foreign source income (interest) to the U.S. subsidiary, which could be transferred to the parent without tax because of the excess foreign tax credit limitation in effect at the time. This strategy produced a higher after-tax return to the parent than possible if it were to have invested the funds in the United States, and the forward contracts provided protection against the currency risk.

This example of long-date currency cover also illustrates the significant role of tax treatment in international financial management. The U.K. subsidiary performed well and began to expand rapidly; consequently, it had substantial additions to fixed assets, which, with the large allowable depreciation available in the United Kingdom, put it in a position where it paid no U.K. income tax. Thus, there was no foreign tax credit associated with the U.K. source income, and then the parent had a deficit overall foreign tax credit limitation. This put the parent in a position where dividends from the U.K. subsidiary became highly taxed in the United States.

One way to offset this problem was to have the U.K. subsidiary partially repay its sterling loan instead of distributing some of its earnings (dividends) to the parent. The difficulty that this course of action introduced, however, was that the sterling loan to the U.K. subsidiary was fully hedged, and to repay the intracompany loan prematurely would place the firm in an unhedged position. The alternatives faced included (1) canceling the forward contracts, (2) assigning them to another party, perhaps the issuing bank, or (3) identifying another need for them within the multinational firm. Because sterling had weakened since the contracts were written, the parent had an attractive gain on them. However, this was offset by exchange losses in the U.K. subsidiary. Hence, canceling the contracts was unwise because the parent could not unwind them at a gain large enough to offset the loss on the books of the U.K. subsidiary. Therefore, it let the forward contracts stand and did not prematurely repay the intracompany loan.

This example clearly illustrates one of the disadvantages of the use of long-date cover (viz, the inflexibility that it can impose on its user). Nevertheless, given a little time, unwinding a hedge is usually possible. In fact, some players use long-date cover to profit from market anomalies in much the same way that bond traders trade bonds to generate trading profits in markets that are out of equilibrium. Thus, with full respect for patience and profit objectives, long-date instruments can have a measurable impact on the future flexibility of a firm.

A second example deals with an excess tax credit limitation that was expiring because of carry-forward time limitations. This situation occurred at a large consumer finance firm. To avoid losing the excess tax credit limitation, the parent arranged in 1980 for its Netherland Antilles subsidiary to borrow 50 million Swiss francs for five years and on-lend them to a U.S. subsidiary at 15 percent interest. To avoid exchange risk, the U.S. party entered into five forward contracts, each to cover one year's interest and the fifth to cover both interest and principal. These forward contracts were written at an 8 percent annual premium on the Swiss francs.

This strategy created a deficit foreign tax credit limitation for the first four years. Two reasons are possible for this additional limitation deficit. First, the Netherlands Antilles subsidiary was heavily capitalized with parent equity so that it could invest the equity financed funds in its local market while facing zero interest cost and, thus, maximize its foreign source income. Second, the 8 percent forward premium was amortized by the subsidiary and, thus, represented income for the purposes of the Netherland Antilles subsidiary. In contrast, the forward premium or discount on forward contracts is not amortized for U.S. tax purposes, but, rather, the premium on the principal is expensed at maturity—at the end of five years in this case. Therefore, this transaction generated increased taxable income from foreign sources based on the profit to the Netherland Antilles, which could then be used to offset the excess foreign tax credits. As a result of the asymmetric timing of the impact of the forward premium on reported income, taxable income to the Netherland Antilles was created in the early years. This accelerated taxable income will be reversed in year five, but meanwhile it allowed an effective deferral of the tax credit carry forward period. This deferral may become a problem if the firm has other tax credits that expire in 1985, but it also provided five years in which to plan on how to resolve similar problems that may occur.

Note that this application of long-date currency cover exists because the U.S. tax law requires that the premium on a forward contract cannot be recognized until the contract closes.

REGULATORY APPLICATIONS

Government regulations of currency flows in various jurisdictions have introduced impediments into free market processes. Regulations or controls that interfere with the free flow or pricing of currencies result in market inefficiencies, which, in turn, frequently give rise to opportunities to reduce all-in capital costs or increase yields.

Regulations of currency flows are designed to preserve foreign exchange balances in those countries that have experienced persistent net currency outflows, frequently due to adverse trade balances. Such countries also typically experience relatively high, in some instances abnormally high, inflation rates and hence face the prospect of devaluation against stronger currencies from time to time. This prospect of devaluation of weak currencies motivates multinational entities to move funds to stronger currencies—a process that often places added stress on the currency and increases the pressures for devaluation. The monetary authority of the country with the weak currency, eager to relieve the pressures for devaluation, may seek to employ currency controls of various sorts to accomplish this end.

Government regulations can range from an extreme of total blockage of the currency, in which case all foreign exchange transactions are unlawful, to the imposition of dual exchange rates for various foreign currency transaction purposes or to the adoption of excessively high withholding taxes on dividends remitted to a parent to discourage repatriation of earnings. Each of the many forms of controls restricts free foreign exchange markets in some way and sets the stage for arbitragelike operations to exploit the market imperfection caused by the controls. The objective here is not to catalog all of the controls employed but rather to provide representative examples of transactions that employ long-date currency cover to extract an advantage from the market anomalies caused by currency regulations. Our discussion is limited to two general categories of government regulations and to those methods that have been popular in using long-date cover to circumvent the effect of the regulations.

Blocked Currencies

Except in the extreme case where all transactions requiring foreign exchange are illegal, currency blockage is a relative term. Total blockage of a currency, such as has occurred in some Communist countries, reduces trade to barter transactions, and currency flows become unimportant. Most cases of relatively blocked currencies occur in hyperinflation countries that have faced recurrent devaluations. A number of Latin American countries have been forced to manage the outflow of hard currency and have effectively blocked the removal of currencies from their shores by devices such as high withholding taxes on repatriated earnings and controls on repayment of intracompany debt.

For fear of an inability to remove funds from a country whose currency is blocked, a multinational parent with liquidity in a strong, freely traded currency seeking to invest in a weak currency country will frequently seek a counterparty with excess liquidity in the blocked currency. The available strong currency resources can then be transferred to the weak currency country without fear of loss by using parallel loans. These instruments allow the blocked currency to be made available to the firm who needs it and, at the same time, make the strong currency accessible to the counterparty whose weak currency was blocked. Although the flows must be reversed at the maturity of the loans, the original holder of the blocked currency may have some prospect of a reduced degree of blockage in the interim. Moreover, it has use of the unblocked currency on which an attractive return may be realized in the strong currency.

An example of the use of a pair of parallel loans to provide for future removal of a currency can be cited using Spanish pesetas. Spain had an effectively blocked currency in that funds were difficult to remove. A multinational soft drink manufacturer wanted to borrow medium-term pesetas, and none were available. To resolve this impasse, the firm made a five-year dollar deposit at a major Paris bank, and the Madrid branch of the bank lent an equivalent amount of pesetas to the Spanish subsidiary of the multinational firm. While it is possible that the French bank took this long-date currency risk on its own book, it undoubtedly found a counterparty with peseta liquidity who was unable to remove its funds from Spain. This party would have provided the five-year pesetas to the Madrid branch in return for a similar term dollar loan. The Spanish party had effectively mobilized blocked pesetas into dollars for use over the next five years.

In another example a U.S. manufacturer of oil field equipment and major construction projects considered its flexibility to remove assets from a currency whenever desired as its primary motive for a hedge. Therefore, its policy was to hedge the dollar value of future currency flows from the outset of any exposure, rather than wait until a deterioration of market forces caused it to become nervous about a currency. This policy is especially appropriate for those hyperinflation currencies that have or are likely to institute severe blockage regulations.

Currency Controls

Many countries place restrictions on the repatriation of dividends and/or repayment of intercompany loans. Such countries would include the high inflation Latin American countries such as Mexico, Brazil, Venezuela, Columbia, and Argentina. South Africa, Spain, Sweden, and Belgium, which limits out-payments to once a year, would also be included. A Swedish example illustrates the type of controls that may be imposed.

Access to the foreign exchange market in Sweden is denied unless the foreign currency is required for a trade-oriented transaction or for the repayment of nonkrona debt. A U.S. construction company, which had accumulated $15 million in retained earnings in Sweden and had difficulty removing it, sought the use of long-date instruments as a means of mobilizing the funds elsewhere in the world. Adjustment to transfer prices of components purchased in the U.S. was considered as a means to transfer the blocked funds progressively, but this technique had limitations on how much could be accomplished, and its implementation was long-term. Hence, long-date foreign exchange instruments became the firm's more appropriate choice. In this example, the firm sought to swap krona for dollars or other strong currency to mobilize the liquidity that was blocked in Sweden.

Note that the market imperfections brought about by currency controls have been among the most effective forces in fostering the early development of long-date currency instruments. In particular, the existence of currency controls in the United Kingdom required that a premium be paid in sterling to obtain foreign exchange to be invested abroad. Prior to the full relaxation of exchange controls by the Bank of England in 1979, a 20 to 30 percent dollar premium market existed for British nationals who wanted to move funds out of England. To convert sterling to U.S. dollars to invest abroad, U.K. unit trusts, pension funds, and others had to pay this premium. This phenomenon provided a major impetus to the development of instruments for long-date currency cover to avoid the premium on dollars. By using long-date currency cover, offshore dollars were made available to U.K. investors in exchange for the use of sterling within the United Kingdom to finance North Sea oil developments and other British subsidiaries of U.S. firms.

These arrangements combined hedged investing of dollars by U.K. institutions with hedged sterling financing of U.K. subsidiaries of U.S. firms. The advantage of avoiding the dollar premium market was the primary driving force behind the development of these parallel loans and currency swaps. With the termination of sterling exchange controls in 1979, activity was slowed somewhat, but, because of the then proven applications of long-date cover, it prospered and developed even more strongly than before.

The exchange controls imposed on sterling by the Bank of England provide an example of how government regulations can cause market inefficiencies to persist. More recently, with the Socialist success in the French election in 1981 and their subsequent imposition of firmer currency controls, another dollar premium market in the French franc arose with premiums exceeding 25 percent. This situation precipitated similar applications for long-date currency cover for those who wished to invest francs outside of France. Although not entirely new in France, where exchange controls have previously existed, the controls were tightened somewhat by the Socialists in 1981.

Sources of Long-Date Flows of Controlled Currencies

Despite the fact that currency controls continue to exist in France, they have not eliminated the availability of long-date franc flows. To understand why term flows would continue to be contracted for in the face of a high inflation rate, Socialist policies, and currency controls, we will examine a typical source of long-date francs as well as who would be a typical buyer of a future stream of a weak currency.

Representative sellers of forward French francs would be multinational firms with subsidiaries in France. Such firms would generate future streams of francs, which their parent might wish to repatriate and hence be willing to sell the francs forward. Other providers of forward francs would be foreign firms that have French construction contracts denominated in francs. These firms might fear the franc's devaluation and would want to lock in a current foreign currency equivalent of the franc. Still other providers would be recipients of franc-denominated subsidized export financing who have non-franc expenses.

On the other side of the transactions, forward buyers of francs would be certain multinational firms that have franc liabilities greater than their franc assets (i.e., those who have borrowed francs in the past to finance assets elsewhere). Those who have decided that the franc was already sufficiently weak to produce substantial transaction gains and were content to lock in the existing gains would be potential buyers of forward francs. More generally, any non-French holder of a net liability position in francs would find forward cover a means of avoiding exchange rate risk and may be content to freeze its exposure if the forward discount on the franc were sufficient. Similar characteristics could be found to influence the supply and demand of other currencies that suffer from governmental controls, making long-date cover a logical means to mobilize blocked liquidity.

Intercompany Financing

In hyperinflation countries the government or monetary authority often has to defend the currency by establishing currency regulations. In these instances various forms of long-date forward cover have been useful not only in hedging exchange risk but also in providing assurance that the funds can be withdrawn when the financing is completed. Recent examples include the MBA (Mexico, Brazil, and Argentina) countries where the central bank has allowed repayment of loans to a financial institution but not to a multinational parent or sister company. The financial authorities view repayment to related firms as a return of capital, whereas repayment of a loan to an unrelated bank is a contractual necessity, which has been permitted. Perhaps this tolerance for the repayment of bank loans is influenced by the fact that many large, money center banks also have financed MBA (and other) governments, and the latter are concerned that any controls imposed on the repayment of bank loans in the private sector may precipitate withdrawal of credits from the public sector. In any event, the ability to repatriate funds that were transferred abroad via bank loans, in contrast with the inability to withdraw intercompany loans, has prompted an on-going application of a pair of two-party back-to-back loans between (1) a multinational parent and a money center bank and (2) a foreign branch of the bank and the foreign subsidiary of the multinational firm.

Both loans could be, but usually are not, in the same currency. Rather, the loan from the parent to the bank takes the form of a term deposit in the parent's currency, say, dollars, and the offshore loan is denominated in local currency. If both loans were not in hard currency, converting the local currency to dollars at the end of the loan for the subsidiary to repay the foreign branch of the bank might not be possible. When the offshore loan is denominated in local currency, the bank incurs an exchange risk that it would attempt to lay off or match. Typical sources of the match would be investors with local currency liquidity wishing to mobilize it for investment in hard currency assets.

In a U.S. example of bank-intermediated parallel loans from a multinational parent to a subsidiary, a medical products manufacturer provided dollars to a U.S. bank, which, in turn, loaned local currency to a foreign subsidiary of the parent at a fixed spread of interest rates for periods up to 12 years.

In another example an electronics firm arranged a pair of back-to-back loans between a cash-rich subsidiary and a bank that extended credit to the firm's Mexican subsidiary to buy land for a future plant.

The same parent also did a single currency deal in Japan whereby it had a Japanese subsidiary take surplus liquidity that it did not want to dividend out to the parent and place in on deposit with a Eurobank. The parent had an understanding with the Eurobank that the bank would on-lend the yen to another Japanese subsidiary. In cases like this the interest difference (spread) between the loans can range from 0.125 percent to 0.25 percent. Since both loans are in the same currency, there was no exchange risk. Such loans enable the private sector to escape some of the constraints imposed by currency regulations and represent applications of long-date currency instruments even where currency exposure is not a consideration. The rationale for this deal was partly motivated by the U.S. tax on repatriated earnings but also by the fact that, when the deal was done in late 1979, a parent could not finance a Japanese subsidiary using intercompany debt. Only equity finance was allowed. Here the use of an intermediary bank between the Japanese subsidiaries provided the solution to the regulatory dilemma because it converted the legal form of finance to a bank loan.

Despite the foregoing mention of a single currency loan, most examples of the use of parallel loans are employed to manage exchange risk and involve multiple currencies. In cases where the opposite side of the deal can be arranged with reasonable dispatch, a bank intermediary is sufficient to facilitate the transaction.

Government Swaps

In hyperinflation countries, funds tend to move primarily one way—from weak to strong currency. Banks cannot intermediate because of the lack of interested counterparties. If the weak-currency country is to attract hard currency for development, it must arrange an alternative way to cover exchange rate risk. In some cases the central bank of the weak-currency country guarantees the future exchange rate in a parallel loanlike arrangement. These deals have been loosely called *government swaps* and have been employed by countries such as Mexico, Brazil, Venezuela, Argentina, Colombia, and Uruguay. Here, the use of a central bank guarantee enables a borrower to obtain a below-market cost of funds in local currency and protect itself against exchange rate risk. These deals are not without other forms of risk, however, and, depending on the prospects for the country involved, the borrower may be merely substituting a broader form of sovereign risk for exchange rate risk. The following cases depict some of the details of representative government swap arrangements.

In an initial example a U.S. medical products firm placed funds on deposit with a Wall Street bank, which in turn loaned $15 million to the Argentine subsidiary of the U.S. firm. The subsidiary then converted the finance to pesos. To protect itself against exchange rate risk, the parent purchased insurance from the Argentine central bank to guarantee the exchange rate on the interest and on the repayment of the loan. This insurance premium depended on the central bank's need for dollars and at the time ranged from 3 to 4 percent per month. This rate was much lower than the local inflation rate or interest rate at the time. The government-controlled interest rate was 6 percent per month; hence, the insurance produced savings of approximately 2 percent per month. Note that this process did not remove sovereign risk, and, unless the investment was a substitute for sovereign risk already committed to by the parent, the government swap may have actually increased the sovereign risk exposure of the parent.

A form of government swap popular in Mexico is its Special Financing Program (SFP). The program was designed to guarantee that the peso–dollar exchange rate on a loan will remain fixed at the initial rate throughout the life of the loan. Nondollar parties would have to borrow or otherwise obtain dollars to participate. The program was first introduced in 1977 and applied to the financing of fixed assets. In early 1982 it was liberalized to include working capital financing as well, but had to be suspended that summer when financial crisis conditions developed.

The financial arrangements employed in the SFP were straightforward,

139

and a few large commercial banks of various nationalities tended to specialize in accommodating multinational firms with Mexican subsidiaries that wished to participate. The process began with the multinational parent's borrowing dollars or using its own liquidity to place a dollar deposit with a commercial bank. The bank, in turn, placed the dollars on deposit with the Mexican central bank. The central bank had set the six-month London Interbank Offer Rate (LIBOR) rate as the interest rate paid to the multinational firm on the dollar deposits. The central bank then guaranteed a floating-rate peso loan from a Mexican commercial bank to the Mexican subsidiary of the multinational parent. The peso loan was priced based on the Mexican bank's cost of funds (approximately 34.5 percent in mid-1982) and revised monthly. In addition there was an 8 percent margin charged by the central bank for three- to five-year loans. This fee was reduced to 6 percent for loans over five years. There was also a 0.25 percent fee for the service of the commercial bank. Thus, the nominal cost of a four-year loan would be 42.75 percent less LIBOR of approximately 15 percent at the time or 27.75 percent. This cost represents a kind of insurance premium to obtain a guarantee from the central bank that the dollar exchange value on the principal will be protected. The guarantee was not extended to the interest on the dollar loan.

A relevant cost comparison would be a contrast between the cost of the peso loan of 42.75 percent and the cost of direct peso borrowing. Such financing was very difficult to obtain at the time because of the extremely tight liquidity in the country. But, if it were available, direct peso borrowing would have cost about 70 percent per annum. Thus, even after allowing, say, 4 percent for the difference between the cost of dollar financing of the deposit at the central bank and the after-withholding tax proceeds on the LIBOR interest payments, SFP swaps still represented a saving of more than 23 percent over direct peso financing if it were available. In addition, the SFP provided a central bank guarantee of the exchange rate on the principal.

The question of sovereign risk that the central bank will honor its guarantee of the exchange rate on the principal of the loan still remains. In confronting this risk, one solution for a U.S. manufacturer of capital equipment that was evaluating an SFP facility was to attempt to convince the bank provider of dollars to accept the sovereign risk. However, the dollar provider, a large Japanese commercial bank, was unwilling to accept the political risk associated with unwinding the dollar loan at the Mexican central bank. As a result, the U.S. manufacturing firm finally agreed to assume the sovereign risk based on its assessment that the guaranteed loan really was a substitute for its extant country risk position. It reasoned that it had the sovereign risk anyway, and the real question was whether or not to exit its economic activity in Mexico. If it chose to remain in Mexico, it already had the country exposure.

The U.S. manufacturing firm's decision was to accept the parallel loan guaranteed by the Mexican central bank. The financing was a six-year facility with a three-year grace period on repayment of principal. It was put on in the early part of 1982, so amortization of principal had not occurred by 1984, and the possibility of dishonor has not yet been tested. Because of the serious financial problems in Mexico, interest payments coming out of the country had been delayed, but no defaults had been recorded. At the time this loan was put on, the peso–dollar exchange rate was 47:1. By mid-1984 this rate had moved to over 200:1. The original peso loan was for $11 million. This loan principal had subsequently devalued to a dollar liability of only $3 million on the books of the U.S. manufacturing firm. This has resulted in $8 million of exchange gains on the firm's balance sheet.

Some argue that the question of sovereign risk has been overstated. They contend that no knowledge or indication of the prospect of dishonor in Mexico exists. Since financial conditions have improved in that country, perhaps this risk will be avoided. More recent attempts to reschedule private sector debt at fixed exchange rates may also provide some solution to the problem. Such attempts have not been successful because they require a peso deposit at the outset, which represents a very high financing cost to insure the fixed exchange rate.

Experience in other countries offering government swaps has been mixed. Uruguay has honored every swap offered in 1981. Argentina issued a few million dollars in short-term swaps in 1981 that matured in 1983. Because of local conditions, including the Falkland Islands war, the Argentine peso devalued many times; and the government did not have the dollars to repay. The upshot was that the original one year loans were rolled over for three years in the form of a dollar bond issued by the Argentine government with interest at LIBOR plus 1.5 percent. These bonds are said to have sold down to approximately a 50 percent discount in subsequent trading.

This result would suggest that sovereign risk on government swaps may be real in some cases and that reliance on government swaps may not end a firm's exposure to the ravages of exchange rate changes in hyperinflationary or unstable countries. Stated more succinctly, currency swaps cannot fully substitute for sovereign risk. Assumption of sovereign risk is a long-run strategy, however, and is difficult to reverse quickly when problems arise. Hence, many firms tend to take a long-run view of their particular assortment of country risk exposures and evaluate government swap opportunities within a long-run context. In doing so many firms are willing to participate in government swaps even in high-risk countries if the cost or rate is sufficiently attractive.

Our discussion of translation, taxation, and regulation applications for long-date currency cover is complete. In the next two chapters we turn to the use of long-date currency contracts and swaps to exploit numerous differences and imperfections found across world capital markets. In Chapter 9 we consider capital market applications that deal with the financing of operations in alternative currencies to obtain a lower cost of capital in the process. Chapter 10 then treats those portfolio investment applications that seek to improve the overall yield obtainable from separating the currency of the investment from the currency of the investor by the use of long-date currency cover instruments.

Chapter 9

Hedged Financing

INTRODUCTION

In the development of long-date cover of currency risk, the classic balance sheet hedge of an exposed net asset position provides many of the earliest applications. These applications were followed by other applications associated with currency controls and blockages. Transaction-, translation-, and taxation-oriented applications added to the volume. This growing demand for long-date currency cover led to the development and refinement of instruments and to the identification of counterparties to use the advantages of long-date currency cover more fully. At the same time, innovations in finance began to focus on new or modified applications for currency cover that would use the arrival of refinements in instruments.

The liability or capital market hedge was the most popular application resulting from this evolution. A liability hedge typically employs a long-date currency agreement to take advantage of a prevailing market anomaly to obtain a lower all-in cost of financing in another currency than what may have been possible in one's local capital market.

Liability hedge techniques were also applied to hedged investing in what became known as portfolio hedges. Portfolio or investment hedges were employed to improve investors' all-in rate of return over what was otherwise available in their own national capital market. Because of the importance of these two techniques, hedged financing is treated separately in this chapter, and hedged investing is covered in the next.

LIABILITY HEDGES

Whereas translation, transaction, and direct investment hedge applications of long-date currency cover result from a mismatch of currency positions that arise from ongoing operations, hedged financing applications are associated with the *planned* creation of a long-date mismatch in the currency denomination of a firm's assets and liabilities. In general hedged financing applications became attractive due to inefficiencies across world capital markets. They involve financing in currencies other than the currency of intended use. The primary motive is to reduce the all-in cost of capital to the firm; however, sometimes hedged financing occurs because national capital markets are temporarily unavailable or saturated and long queues prevail.

To make the all-in cost explicit when financing assets denominated in one currency with debt denominated in another currency, the asset (home) currency must be sold forward to acquire the necessary currency with which to service the (foreign) debt. The purchase of forward foreign exchange is a natural role for long-date currency cover in that it requires the creation of a term liability in the home currency and a term asset in the foreign currency. Because inefficiencies in world capital markets abound, this application has grown substantially in recent years. It promises to continue to develop as improved knowledge and understanding of available instruments and increased market depth make arbitrage of world capital markets more commonplace.

It is, of course, not possible to record all of the prevailing inefficiencies in world capital markets. Moreover, as they become apparent and are arbitraged, many former inefficiencies disappear or are even reversed, providing alternate arbitrage opportunities. As we have seen, inefficiencies may be caused by government regulations, which range from fully blocked markets to limited control or taxation on the movement of funds. Other anomalies are caused by dislocations in supply or demand for funds in a given currency. Such saturated or "stuffed" markets result in excessive interest rates to those who choose to use them. Financing in alternative, nonsaturated markets and covering with long-date currency instruments often produces a lower cost of world capital.

The major types of market inefficiencies that give rise to liability hedges were presented in Chapter 4. Examples of each major type of application are presented in the following sections.

Market Segmentation

Market segmentation occurs when a preponderance of the flows are in one direction. One-way flows can be caused by regulatory or legal pressures or by economic forces. The former types of applications were covered in Chapter 8 under regulatory applications. We treat economically-induced market segmentation in this section.

When examples of one-way flows occur, it is often a difficult and lengthy process to find the other side of the transaction, and a cost incentive is often necessary to attract interest. Consider as an illustration the eight weeks that a U.S. optical products firm took to sell South African rand forward, despite the fact that the maturity was only six months and a Wall Street bank was acting as agent. The point is that, at the time (1981), the forward market in the rand was very one-sided with little interest in buying forward rand.

Just as the seller of forward currency in a segmented market with little demand may have to make a cost concession, a forward buyer may expect a significant cost advantage. The Italian lira provided a good example of this in 1982. At that time a large U.S. commercial finance conglomerate could get better terms than would have been theoretically obtainable based on interest differentials. This was possible because, in 1982, most players were sellers of forward lira and had little interest in buying. The finance firm was able to take advantage of this anomaly and obtain a larger forward discount than theory would suggest in satisfying its need for forward lira.

A similar situation occurred in the Mexican peso and to a lesser extent in the Canadian dollar in 1982. At that time, nearly all spot flows were away from the United States and forward counterflows to service the spot conversions were toward the United States. This situation caused forward prices to swing away from the theoretical formula to the advantage of forward providers of U.S. dollars against either currency. Although a two-sided market had previously existed in Canadian dollars out to five years, the market subsequently became very thin. The demand for forward U.S. dollars by Canadian fixed-rate borrowers in the U.S. capital market remained, but the supply of forward U.S. dollars by the natural resource firms had diminished significantly by mid-1982. As a result bid–ask spreads widened markedly. For example, quotations on the five year Canadian dollar discount from spot reflected a spread of 250 basis points, and have reached spreads up to 300 basis points. Normal spreads for this maturity would be 100 to 150 basis points. Traders refused to quote some clients. With very few players and very little money in the market, a single trade could move the market significantly. At that time these forward contracts appeared not to be priced to trade but only to speculate.

The cost opportunities afforded by even modest degrees of market segmentation associated with one-way flows can lead to a tendency to speculate on the part of certain players. In one example a large Canadian bank borrowed US$30 million for three years to fund its mortgage loan department. Of course, it wanted to hedge the resulting foreign exchange exposure. In searching for a forward seller of U.S. dollars, a Toronto merchant banker located a subsidiary of a large U.S. bank, which took a 5 percent premium on the forward sale of U.S. dollars. Essentially, the provider of forward U.S. dollars was betting that the Canadian dollar would *not* fall by 5 percent per year against the U.S. unit.

In late 1982 and 1983 the French franc provided another example of oversupply of forward positions. The existence of currency controls and the lack of a free flow of currency encouraged many players to sell forward. Pricing of five-year forward contracts depended on the interaction of supply and demand, but, with a dearth of demand, the forward prices departed measurably from a level consistent with external interest differentials.

A final example of a long-date market that exhibited one-way flows in most of 1983 is Japan. Because of the strength of the dollar against the yen during this period, most players wanted to buy yen forward at a fixed exchange rate. Their rationale was that the yen would appreciate as western real interest rates fell. Hence, players with long-date supplies of yen were able to find attractive deals. Japanese multinational firms would have done well to borrow western currencies, convert to spot yen to finance their domestic operations, and sell the yen forward to cover their currency exposure, while reducing their cost of capital against domestic alternatives.

Market Saturation

Market saturation occurs when a relatively large borrower insists on tapping a relatively small capital market to the point that the market is no longer willing to absorb the issuer's paper. In such instances, questions of adequate diversification of investors' portfolios take on major importance. AT&T, a massive borrower, has not had to face this problem in the U.S. capital market because of the vast size of the dollar market. Sovereign governments are also often massive borrowers but can tap their domestic markets because of the loyalty and financial respect of their national capital markets for the sovereign. Market saturation has become an impediment to market efficiency when nonindigenous institutions attempt to continue to penetrate a relatively small capital market to take advantage of its relatively low interest rates.

Classic examples of market saturation are seen where a supranational organization persists in borrowing in the low-nominal-interest currency of a country that has a well-developed but relatively small capital market. Borrowers that could fall into this category include the World Bank and the Inter-American Development Bank. National agencies of the Austrian, French, and Italian governments have placed similar burdens on a term debt market in a low nominal interest currency.

The capital market that has experienced the most saturation by such borrowers is that of the Swiss franc, although some degree of saturation has also been observed in the market for German marks. When a market approaches saturation with a borrower's paper and the borrower insists on having its debt denominated in that market's currency, an anomaly is introduced. This anomaly may then be used by borrowers that are welcome in the saturated market to obtain ultimate finance in another desired currency at a below-market all-in cost of funds. The following examples illustrate some of these transactions and provide an insight into representative arrangements. The first example repeats the case study presented in Chapter 4. It is summarized to develop the concept of market saturation more fully.

In mid-1981 a BBB-rated U.S. rubber company was seeking fixed-rate term dollar financing. At that time it faced a 17.625 percent effective cost of funds in New York. Meanwhile, the World Bank with an AAA rating could obtain term dollar debt for a 16.5 percent effective cost. Since the BBB-rated rubber company was well-known in Switzerland, it was able to borrow francs in Zurich at just slightly below the 8 percent rate cost objective available to first-class credits such as the World Bank. The strategy that was followed was for the U.S. rubber firm to borrow francs; the World Bank borrowed an equivalent amount of dollars at the prevailing exchange rate; they exchanged the initial currency flows and agreed to service each other's debt.

The terms of this arrangement imposed the World Bank's dollar interest cost on the U.S. firm, a rate with which it was pleased because the rate was lower than it could otherwise access in New York. Moreover, the rubber firm's natural cash flows were in dollars, so servicing the debt introduced no currency exposure. The World Bank, extremely sensitive to nominal interest cost, was able to obtain a lower cost of funds denominated in Swiss francs. Since the World Bank had the ability to make a unilateral decision to lend in the currency of its choice, it did not view liabilities denominated in Swiss francs as imposing an exchange risk.[1] The upshot was a lower nominal cost of finance to the World Bank (viz, approximately 7.75 percent in Swiss francs versus 16.5 percent in dollars) and a lower dollar interest cost for the U.S. rubber company of 16.5 percent versus 17.625 percent. Some of this cost advantage was lost to the costs of the spot and swap transactions and to the credit intermediation fee necessary to implement the currency cover. The remaining benefit was negotiated between the parties so that both obtained

147

what each viewed as a cost advantage obtained from the application of long-date currency cover to a currency market that was saturated with the obligations of a major issuer.

Note that the World Bank did in excess of $2.5 billion of swapped currency deals through the second quarter of 1983.[2] Of this amount, most was in Swiss francs with approximately $200 million in German marks. The World Bank was aware that it had virtually saturated these currency markets and viewed these swap transactions as a means of increasing, not substituting for, its direct access to Swiss francs and German marks. It planned to continue to borrow directly in the capital markets of Switzerland and the Federal Republic of Germany when propitious to do so.[3]

The World Bank has had to get the consent of appropriate government agencies in the currency of the swap for every currency swap transaction that it has done. The Swiss have been liberal in this regard, and the West Germans, while more cautious, have also granted approval. Concerns that may result in denial of access include the impact of the foreign bond issue on balance of payment outflows or the effect of excessive borrowing in a given capital market on the level of interest rates. Normal West German concerns over capital export were not applicable in this particular case because the German mark debt, which was swapped, was seasoned debt rather than newly issued debt.

Among the other U.S. multinational firms participating in World Bank swaps was a BBB-rated conglomerate firm with heavy interests in the metals industry. This firm did Swiss franc financing in April 1982, borrowing SF30 million for six years at 7.75 percent. This liability was swapped for a U.S. dollar liability with the World Bank at an all-in savings to the U.S. firm of 150 basis points over what it would have had to pay in New York. The credit risk on the BBB-rated firm was taken by a U.S. bank, leaving the World Bank with a low nominal cost of funds without concern for credit or currency exposure.

In another application a BBB-rated U.S. forest products firm saved 75 basis points in April 1982 by borrowing SF100 million and swapping it for dollars with the Austrian Control Bank (OKB). Even though the BBB-rated firm was a lesser credit than OKB, it was able to borrow Swiss francs more cheaply than OKB because the latter had saturated the Swiss capital market. On the other side of the Atlantic, given its sovereign status, OKB could borrow more cheaply than the BBB-rated firm. This deal was orchestrated by a U.S. investment bank, and a Canadian bank took the credit risk for OKB. The all-in cost to the BBB-rated issuer was 15.3 percent, a 75 basis point saving over market rates in New York.

In many of the examples of long-date cover of currency exposure, each side may have a different rationale or driving force for dealing. This point is illustrated in an example discussed more fully in a subsequent section on locking in foreign exchange gains. In that example a U.S. multinational firm used the World Bank's appetite for Swiss francs and German marks to serve as the counterparty and enable it to realize significant foreign exchange gains.

Spread Compression

Another anomaly that occurs between certain capital markets allows certain lower credit-rated U.S. firms to obtain lower cost financing than in their home capital market. In the United States, a BBB-rated firm may pay up to 2 percent over AAA-rated firms for term financing. In contrast, continental capital markets, such as Switzerland, have required the poorer credits to pay only 50 basis points over the best credits for term money. This intermarket anomaly has been called *spread compression* and represents an interesting application for hedge financing. A typical transaction would call for a weaker-credit U.S. borrower of Swiss francs at a lower risk premium than obtainable in the United States. The U.S. borrower would convert to spot dollars for investment in the United States and simultaneously contract to sell forward dollars to acquire the Swiss francs needed to service the franc loan. This application works best for lower credit-rated firms that have a broad international presence and names that help facilitate foreign market acceptance of their debt. Examples of spread-compression-driven hedged financing have also occurred in marks, sterling, and guilders.

Implementation of the concept of spread compression has already been seen in the ability of BBB-rated credits to obtain interest rates that approximate those available to supranational and sovereign borrowers in the foregoing illustrations describing saturated markets. In fact, the existence of spread compression builds a sufficient incentive into the deals to enable the massive borrowers to entice proxy borrowers to secure the low-nominal-interest-rate loans desired. Examples of spread compression also exist in currencies with higher nominal interest rates (viz, an A-rated U.S. consumer and commercial finance company borrowed sterling at a lower risk premium than they faced in New York, converted to dollars, and hedged its sterling exposure to obtain a lower all-in cost than if they financed directly in dollars).

The Swiss franc appears to offer the greatest opportunity for compression of spreads. The degree of compression can be illustrated by the following example. In mid-1981 the rate faced by AAA- and BBB-rated industrial borrowers in New York was 16 and 17.5 percent, respectively, with an even larger spread for utilities. At the same time the rates in Zurich were 7.25 percent for an AAA-rated firm and 7.5 percent for a well-known BBB-rated firm. One reason for this is that Swiss investors do not have to conform to requirements imposed on U.S. pension funds and other investors by governmental entities such as ERISA.[4] This freedom makes it possible for modestly creditworthy bonds to be placed in the portfolios of individual investors in Switzerland indefinitely. Hence, if the name is appealing and the issuer meets investment grade credit standards, Swiss investors have been willing to absorb the issue without a large risk premium. This compression in risk premium spread can then be used to serve as an incentive to conduct the arbitrage operation, provide for transactions and credit intermediation costs, and still leave a cost advantage to both parties.

Name Arbitrage

In our discussion of spread compression, we relied on the use of a borrower's name to help it access funds in one national capital market to obtain an advantage over another national capital market. In this section we advance that idea. Essentially, the concept that underlies name arbitrage is this: If you have an advantage in one market over another, use it to obtain a lower cost of funds.

A number of large, well-known U.S. firms in industries such as auto, soft drink, and health care products have used their names and credit ratings to borrow dollars and then transfer the funds using intercompany loans to finance subsidiaries in countries where repatriation is not a problem. This example shows the parent straddling capital markets, using its name in a well-developed market to obtain a cost advantage for its subsidiaries. Note, however, that this strategy does produce a foreign exchange exposure that, unless managed, may mitigate the cost advantage obtained.

A striking illustration of name arbitrage took place within a short period of time in the first quarter of 1982. In a given week during this period, an AAA-rated credit, the Republic of Austria, and a well-known A-rated Canadian consumer products company each floated similar debt issues in the U.S. dollar market. As we would expect, the AAA-rated credit received a 50 basis point rate advantage over the A-rated credit. During the same week both issuers also floated Swiss franc debt, and the A-rated Canadian firm obtained a 25 basis point advantage over the AAA-rated credit based on a strong preference of Swiss investors for its name. As we have seen, there have been numerous examples where "name" A-rated companies can borrow in Switzerland at rates below other AAA-rated issuers whose paper has saturated the Swiss capital market.

A final example of name arbitrage applies to certain well-known U.S. firms about to be closed out of the commercial paper market because they have reached their limit of borrowing short-term, floating-rate funds in this market. Such firms would typically have their bonds classified **BBB** by U.S. rating agencies, but, because of their names, they can go to the Swiss franc market and sell five- to ten-year bonds at reasonable coupons. The fixed-rate foreign exchange could then be swapped for dollar floating-rate notes to obtain for the issuers the type of finance they desire. At the same time it would provide fixed-rate term funds to other borrowers who prefer to have their interest costs specified for a long period of time. This process may also require a second swap of fixed-rate Swiss francs for fixed-rate dollars to implement the needs of all of the players fully. These concepts will be developed more completely in Chapter 14 where we examine complex applications of long-date currency and coupon cover.

Differential Financial Norms

As we focus on the various applications of long-date currency cover, specific market anomalies that give rise to each type of application tend to blend into one another. Thus, the concept of differential financial norms from one capital market to another rests in the background of the concept of name arbitrage. It surfaces more forcefully, however, in applications where cultural or behavioral patterns cause significantly different financial standards to be evident. A notable example of this difference lies in the differential standards that prevail for corporate debt ratios between Japan and the United States.

As indicated in Chapter 5, creditworthy Japanese borrowers would be prudent to borrow yen in Japan and convert to dollars for investment in their U.S. subsidiaries rather than face the high risk premiums required in dollar borrowings associated with their abnormally high (by western standards) debt ratios. Because the subsidiary's dollar cash flows would be at risk in servicing the yen debt, a long-date forward contract to sell dollars against yen would be indicated.

In an example of this application, a Japanese leasing company borrowed term yen in 1983 at the Japanese equivalent of the long-term AAA rate of 8.4 percent. The parent leasing firm on-lent the yen to its Hong Kong subsidiary who then executed a currency swap for U.S. dollars. This strategy effectively converted the yen borrowing to a covered dollar borrowing at 12.5 percent interest cost. This rate was 50 basis points cheaper than the leasing company could have obtained directly with dollar term investors. The advantage obtained by applying acceptable financial norms is further improved by the low cost of credit intermediation available to Japanese firms by Japanese banks. Since the banking-industrial complex is so intertwined, Japanese banks do not view "related" borrowers to be as risky as, say, U.S. banks may

151

view equivalent unrelated U.S. borrowers. The upshot was a lower price for the credit guarantee of about 0.25 percent per annum.

Credit Arbitrage

A credit arbitrage application relies on the fact that, within limits, more risky issuers usually encounter a rising risk premium in the debt markets but not in the spot or forward foreign exchange markets. This difference in pricing is due to the differing operating conventions in the respective markets. Whereas increased risk is reflected in a risk premium component of the interest rate charged to a borrower in conventional debt markets, it is handled differently in foreign exchange markets. In the latter, risk is incorporated in the overall assessment of a foreign exchange client and incorporated in the trading volume limit allowed for spot and forward foreign exchange transactions. Foreign exchange dealing rooms then trade with all approved clients at the foreign exchange spot and forward quotations in effect at the time of trading.

The concept of credit arbitrage is often difficult to grasp because it derives its arbitrage advantage from these differential intricacies involved in pricing in the credit and foreign exchange markets. We will study it more thoroughly by building on the illustration used in Chapter 4 and specifying the characteristics of typical players. Recall that in this illustration the interbank German mark deposit ask rate was 7 percent and the dollar deposit ask rate was 10 percent. The AAA- and BBB-rated German mark loan rates were 7.5 and 8 percent, respectively.

The first player could be a BBB-rated West German borrower, which required five-year German marks and could borrow them at 8 percent. The second player might be a dollar investor who was planning to place a five-year dollar deposit. The third player may be an intermediary who was willing to convert the dollars to German marks on day one to on-lend them to the BBB-rated West German borrower for five years for a stream of German mark interest and principal at 8 percent. To consummate the deal the intermediary would need to locate a fourth player to serve as a counterparty. The role of this player would be to swap the German mark interest and principal cash flows at a 7 percent interbank deposit rate in exchange for the necessary dollar cash flows to service the dollar deposit (investment) at 10 percent.

The dollar investor (depositor) could possibly fill the role of the counterparty if the dollar provider happened to have a need for a future stream of German marks to service a lease, debt, on-going trade, royalty, or license fee transaction. If chance does not supply such a dollar provider, a financial intermediary is required to identify appropriate players who have natural or planned cash flows that suit the needs of the swap. The 1 percent per annum profit potential that resulted from the differential pricing conventions applied to risk in the respective markets is the incentive to formulate and participate in credit arbitrage transactions. This example deals with a rather small risk premium rate differential for reasons of conservatism. At times risk premium differentials in the bond market turn out to be considerably larger, providing a much greater incentive to assemble and execute the credit arbitrage. To understand the credit arbitrage concept and to clarify the cash flows associated with this example, a flowchart is presented in Figure 9-1.

Figure 9-1   Cash Flows Associated with Credit Arbitrage

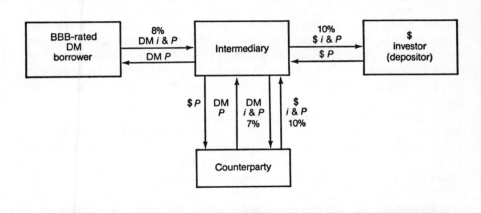

Confidentiality

There are many reasons why a firm may want to keep its borrowing behavior in a particular capital market confidential. Although the amount borrowed is revealed in the firm's consolidated financial statements at year's end, the terms, conditions, and maturities need not be disclosed prior to the borrowing except in the case of public offerings. We have already seen the reaction of the Swiss capital market to an oversupply of an issuer's paper. The reaction of the World Bank and Austrian, French, and Italian governmental agencies was to find proxy borrowers of Swiss francs and avoid excess direct confrontation with Swiss investors. In essence these institutional borrowers have attempted to avoid having their names appear too frequently in the Swiss capital market (i.e., achieve a degree of confidentiality by their [indirect] borrowing of Swiss francs).

Borrowers may have other objectives in keeping their names out of a particular market. These objectives may be accomplished by using proxy borrowers in that market and long-date currency cover to achieve ultimately liabilities in a desired currency. In one example a syndicated floating-rate seven-year dollar term loan was swapped by a U.S. industrial firm for fixed-rate Swiss francs. The counterparty was a bank that wanted floating-rate dollar financing to match the interest sensitivity of its floating-rate assets. The bank was easily able to sell a fixed-rate Swiss franc issue to be used to swap for floating-rate dollars. The pricing to the bank would be only slightly below what it would have had to pay directly for floating-rate dollars, but the swap provided incremental funds to the bank without its having to go to a dollar lender. This strategy kept the bank's name out of the dollar market for this financing, an objective important in a market that is intensively name sensitive, has limits on amounts available to each name, and severely discriminates against excessive usage. More generally, the long-date currency swap enabled the bank to widen its borrowing power to nondollar capital markets, while maintaining the denomination of liabilities in its desired currency.

In another interesting example of the sale of long-date currency cover to maintain confidentiality, an A-rated U.S. pulp and paper firm was concerned about having its credit rating downgraded in the United States to BBB as a result of the review process associated with floating a new dollar public offering. To avoid the need for a rating review, it decided to borrow SF75 million for five years in Zurich. This borrowing occurred in March 1982 and was hedged into dollars using a series of forward contracts for interest and principal. The funds were provided by a major Swiss bank at an all-in cost to the borrower below 16 percent. Although the primary objective was to avoid the credit rating review and not to minimize the cost of funds, the borrower also realized a saving of 50 basis points under current dollar rates for its term paper.

The desire for confidentiality can also render alternative strategies more appropriate. In another example a U.S. health products company had been financing its Japanese subsidiary by borrowing dollars and on-lending them to that subsidiary. In June 1979 it sold 3 billion yen forward for three years to cover its yen exposure. When it came time to renew this hedge, the parent declined. The reason for foregoing the continuation of the hedge in June 1982 was not because of a change in view regarding the yen, but because renewal would have required approval by the Japanese Ministry of Trade and Industry (MITI). The parent feared that, as a result of the review process, MITI would have required an additional infusion of equity capital, which the parent preferred not to make. To avoid the review and maintain its confidentiality, the parent instructed the subsidiary to borrow the needed funds directly in yen.

A final example of an attempt to maintain secrecy in financing contains an interesting combination of players. A U.K. industrial firm sought to swap sterling for Euro sterling prior to 1979 when U.K. exchange controls were abolished. The counterparty to the swap was a U.S. multinational oil firm. Both primary players were AAA-rated credits. To obtain secrecy in this deal, they brought in a U.K. merchant bank subsidiary of a U.S. commercial bank to intermediate the loan and assume credit risk. The irony of this arrangement is that the bank intermediating the credit risk between two AAA-rated parties carried a lower credit rating than either of the primary parties. The cost for intermediating the credit risk was 0.25 percent per annum to each party. However, despite their attempt to maintain it, the secrecy of the deal was lost; its existence became well-known in financial circles.

Avoidance of Queues

Just as instruments for long-date cover of currency risk are useful to obtain confidentiality and avoid review by rating agencies or governmental bodies, they can also be used to avoid other undesirable features of the international finance process. Long-date currency swaps or forward contracts have also been used occasionally to avoid waiting in a financial queue to obtain finance in a desired currency.

To control the flow of investment funds to the private sector, financial authorities in many countries establish a quota of financing that is available to the private sector in each financing period. Borrowers apply for permission to borrow and, if approved, are placed in a queue until their turn to borrow arrives. Such a practice has long been the custom in Germany and France and also operates in Japan. At times the queue can become quite long, far exceeding one year.

As an example of queue avoidance, a U.S. electronics firm with a subsidiary in Japan was in the queue for Samurai issues. Samurai bonds are yen-denominated issues sold in Japan by foreigners. Its position in the queue substantially delayed the U.S. firm's obtaining the necessary yen finance for its very rapidly growing business. The investment opportunities and returns that it faced were too attractive to tolerate waiting so long for the needed yen capital.

The parent considered a number of alternatives available to accelerate the funding of the planned growth of its Japanese subsidiary. After thorough analysis and with the aid of a financial intermediary, it succeeded in effectively swapping its position in the queue with another borrower who was at the head of the queue. The counterparty to the swap was indifferent to the currency of its finance. The counterparty borrowed yen and swapped them for dollars with the U.S. electronics firm, which the latter had obtained in the Euromarket.

Locked-In Gains and Losses

Unless fully hedged, long-term cross-currency transactions may result in accumulated foreign exchange gains or losses after their inception. Rather than run the risk that a book gain will be dissipated, or a book loss worsened, by subsequent changes in exchange rates, players may employ long-date cover to freeze the size of the gain or loss at its current level. To illustrate, a Japanese entity borrowed Swiss francs on an uncovered basis when the exchange rate was 150Y/SF. The rate subsequently moved to 110Y/SF in mid-1981 representing a profit of 40Y/SF. The Japanese party could guarantee that this book profit would not be subsequently lost by employing a long-date currency swap. Then, regardless of what developed in the Swiss franc-yen exchange rate, the borrower would be assured of this foreign exchange gain at the maturity of the loan.

Similarly, many U.S. firms borrowed Swiss francs in the early 1970s to finance their overseas investments in the face of controls on dollar foreign direct investment. Much of this borrowing was not hedged, and, to the borrower's displeasure, the Swiss franc subsequently appreciated significantly against the dollar. Somewhere along the way, the U.S. firms should have stopped their exchange losses from further increasing by engaging in long-date cover to hedge their Swiss franc obligations. As it turned out, a number of firms prepaid their franc liabilities to terminate their exposure and took realized losses in the process. Many of these firms remain unwilling to sustain similar losses in the future and tend to be prime participants in the current use of long-date cover instruments.

In our discussion of market saturation, we deferred discussion on a notable case study where the other side was motivated by an opportunity to lock-in sizable currency gains. We turn now to this example. In March 1980 a large U.S. computer manufacturer borrowed DM300 million for six years at 10 percent interest. In April 1980, the same firm borrowed SF200 million for six years at 6.375 percent interest and borrowed another DM200 million for eight years at 10.18 percent interest in the following month. None of these foreign currency debt issues was covered against the risk of changes in exchange rates.

By August 1981 the dollar had strengthened significantly, and the U.S. multinational firm decided to lock-in its sizable exchange gains on its Swiss franc and German mark liabilities. This decision occurred at the same time that the World Bank was seeking proxy borrowers of currencies with low nominal interest rates. Hence, the World Bank was a natural counterparty for the U.S. computer manufacturer. All of its foreign currency loans that were placed in 1980 were swapped with the World Bank, which had borrowed dollars for this purpose. Since the exchange rate at the time of the swap reflected a much stronger dollar than at the time of the foreign currency loans, the U.S. firm assumed a much smaller dollar debt than the dollar value of the foreign currency received at the time the loans were initially placed. This difference represented the gain that the firm wished to protect by swapping the debt. In addition to these transactions, the same U.S. multinational firm later swapped SF300 million that it had borrowed in March 1981 with the Inter-American Development Bank. This counterparty, another supranational organization, had motives similar to the World Bank's, and, of course, the U.S. firm was again protecting gains from adverse exchange rate movements.

Two additional points bear noting regarding these transactions. First, unlike hedged financing, the placement of the original debt and the initiation of the swap were not simultaneous deals. Therefore, there was some foreign exchange exposure for a period of time, unless it was offset by cash flows or asset positions in the currency in which the liabilities were denominated. Second, the form of the swap was not a cancellation of the original debt issue, but rather an exchange of obligations whereby a new party serviced the old foreign currency debt in return for the original party's servicing the other debt in a more desired currency—in this case, dollars. This point illustrates an important concept underlying the use of liability and portfolio hedges (viz, the original debt issue remained intact on the books of the original issuer and investors). This concept is also fundamental to another financial device for protecting gains or limiting losses that arise from changes in exchange rates or interest rates. This financial instrument is called a *defeasance*, a subject to which we next turn.

Defeasance

The term *defeasance* means a making null or void; an annulment. In finance it describes a strategy that is used to undo or extinguish an existing liability by replacing it with another obligation. Its primary applications are (1) to freeze or lock-in a current exchange rate or interest rate or (2) to shift a firm's capital structure quickly by replacing old debt with new equity. Our chief interest is in the first application. When a new debt instrument is used to replace an outstanding issue in the same currency, a defeasance is conceptually similar to a fixed rate for fixed-rate interest rate or coupon swap. Where two currencies are involved, a defeasance accomplishes many of the same objectives as a currency swap. In this section we are primarily interested in the latter application. Two examples will illustrate the relevant features of a defeasance.

In 1973 a domestic U.S. oil company with international involvement sold a DM100 million, 15-year bond issue with a coupon of 7.5 percent. When the issue was placed, the dollar-German mark exchange rate was DM2.30/$, and the issue produced approximately $45 million of finance. The German mark subsequently strengthened to DM1.70/$, and, along the way, the company did a six-month forward hedge at DM2.10/$. This hedge did not provide the total long-date protection that the firm really needed, so it considered a liability assumption with the World Bank. Evaluation of the liability assumption and available alternatives led to the concept of a defeasance, which it subsequently undertook in 1982.

The defeasance is a course of action that allows a debtor to extinguish a given debt for accounting and tax purposes by placing an impeccable credit between the borrower and the original investors. The oil company accomplished this by buying long-term West German government bonds with sufficient cash flows to service interest and principal of the original liability. When the defeasance was done, the new bonds were yielding 11 percent whereas the original debt had a 7.5 percent coupon. Thus, only about DM65 million new bonds were needed to service the remaining DM75 million outstanding debt.

A saving in the principal amount required to extinguish an outstanding debt issue arose due to increases in interest rates since the issue was originally placed. This saving represents the primary motive for a domestic defeasance. However, in this case, the oil firm also had a sizable German mark exposure that resulted from its uncovered borrowing of a low-interest currency in 1973. By undertaking the defeasance it locked-in an interest rate gain and an exchange rate loss. The 20 pfenning per dollar foreign exchange loss was more than offset by the interest rate gain, making the transaction profitable in dollar terms while reducing the firm's currency exposure.

The mechanism used in the defeasance was the placement of the new asset and the original liability in an offshore trust; this was done to keep them off the balance sheet of the defeasing firm. To protect the original mark creditors, the trust must have sufficient mark cash flows that are properly timed to service the mark debt. The trust should never be short marks; thus, it is conservative to provide for slightly more mark cash flows than are expected to be required. Any residual amount reverts to the defeasing company when the trust terminates.

The use of a trust has other advantages as well. With the trust, the firm retains control over the sinking fund that is set up to retire the original bonds. Any income effect that accrues to the sinking fund due to further increases in interest rates ultimately can be taken into income. Moreover, any gain on the subsequent purchase of outstanding bonds at a discount can augment income in the future. In addition, the trust is a tax-paying entity, and any gain that it generates from buying discounted bonds would be taxed as a capital gain. In contrast, if the firm itself held the bonds and managed the sinking fund, any gain might be deferred but taxed at higher rates as regular income.

While similar to a long-date forward currency contract or currency swap in obtaining long-date currency cover, a defeasance had a few additional advantages in this case. For one thing, the foreign exchange loss that was locked-in could not be amortized in a long-date forward contract and could only be taken as a tax shield at the end of the contract. In contrast all the cost was effectively amortized in the defeasance, and the timing of the tax benefit accelerated.

Interestingly enough, the computer firm that locked-in a foreign exchange gain discussed in the previous section could have obtained an improved outcome with a defeasance over that with a currency swap. This is true for a number of reasons. First, the timing of the tax benefit associated with any currency loss could have been accelerated. Second, because of the inverted yield curves in mid-1981 (short-term rates higher than long-term rates), the cost of the series of the German mark and Swiss franc government bonds needed to provide the cash flows to service the mark and franc debt would have been lower than if it were all done with term paper as in a swap. Third, with the use of a currency swap, the U.S. firm lost its ability to manage its sinking fund and garner any potential advantage from further increases in interest rates. Instead, this advantage accrued to the party that assumed the obligation for the foreign currency debt. The sinking fund arrangement on the dollar debt, which may have added restraints in its operation, replaced this advantage. On the other hand, the relative attractiveness of a defeasance over a currency swap depends on where the appropriate government debt instruments are trading relative to corporate bonds. If, say, West German goverment bonds are trading at higher yields than German mark corporate bonds, to defease using government bonds would be more propitious than to swap using corporate bonds. Opposite arguments also apply.

Another defeasance application to terminate a liability position involved an A-rated U.S. commercial credit conglomerate. This firm borrowed SF80 million for 10 years at a 7 percent coupon. The financing was done unhedged in February 1981. Borrowing Swiss francs uncovered was a daring move in light of the losses on franc loans in the early 1970s. However, the difficulties encountered during that time were viewed to be due to the fact that the dollar was artificially controlled at too low a rate. In 1981, because the Swiss interest rates were very low compared to dollar rates, the Swiss franc would have had to rise from $0.53/SF to $1.10/SF over the life of the loan to offset the interest advantage. The U.S. firm did not expect such an increase in the franc, so it borrowed francs naked.

By spring 1982 the firm felt that U.S. interest rates would soon fall. Thus, in June 1982 they cleared out their Swiss franc debt by defeasance. Their liability was assumed by an AAA-rated credit in exchange for spot francs, the present value of which was then sufficient to service the debt. In this case the original debt was defeased by spot foreign exchange rather than by using other financial assets to generate the cash flows needed to service the original debt. As a result, the U.S. firm ended up borrowing SF80 million for 16 months at 7 percent compared with the 16.5 percent interest on comparable dollar instruments. This interest difference on the equivalent of $42 million amounted to an overall saving of $6 million in financing cost. Although defeasance deals were temporarily halted in mid-1982, this application was completed two months before the moratorium. It provides an example of defeasance applications that have again become possible.

Domestic Defeasance

Defeasance deals are also useful for domestic balance sheet purposes. They have been used to swap a new high coupon debt for deep discount debt and significantly reduce the book value of the outstanding debt. Domestic defeasance arrangements have also been funded by selling equity to retire debt. These deals were brought to a halt in the United States in mid-1982 while the Financial Accounting Standards Board (FASB) studied alternative means of accounting for defeasance transactions. The temporary suspension of defeasance deals was the result of the FASB's concern that the placement of assets in a trust did not qualify as extinguishment of the old debt and that the balance sheet should be grossed-up to show both old and new debt.

These restraints took much of the appeal away from defeasance, and few were done while the review took place. Then, in June 1983, FASB voted in favor of defeasance to qualify for extinguishment of debt for accounting purposes. A new exposure draft was released, and a revised accounting standard was released in late 1983. Following the new exposure draft, defeasance arrangements regained some popularity, and a few were done in anticipation of the revised accounting standards.

Liability Diversification

Just as diversifying assets among various industries, locations, and currencies with the objective of spreading the risk of an asset portfolio is wise, diversifying liabilities among currencies may also have merit regarding the balancing of currency and interest rate risk. A representative example of the potential advantages of liability diversification draws on expectations for the future value of the French franc after its weakening in 1981–83.

Because it expected the French franc to continue to devalue, a Swedish firm was looking to include French francs in its liabilities. In mid-1983 it swapped a $25 million dollar five-year fixed-rate liability for an equivalent French franc liability. In this way, the Swedish firm also diversified out of primarily dollar-denominated debt and into franc-denominated debt to reduce currency exposure and to take advantage of its view on the future value of the franc. The counterparty or forward buyer of francs and seller of dollars was a multinational firm that, in its own view, already had too much franc debt and wanted to balance into dollar-denominated liabilities. Here we see liability diversification as the motive for both parties to the swap to obtain the desired liability portfolio balance.

Generalized Liability Hedges

Despite our attempt to classify examples of liability hedges into related groupings, a few hedges, which warrant inclusion as helpful examples of liability hedges, remain. Hence, the following examples are presented on their own merit as generalized liability hedges.

The first example considers a Canadian subsidiary of a U.S. multinational firm that, in mid-1980, wanted to borrow Canadian dollars but found Canadian dollar interest rates too high. The Canadian subsidiary sold U.S. dollar-denominated debt in New York and converted to Canadian dollars. It easily obtained long-date currency cover to service the debt because U.S. dollars were, at the time, flowing freely to Canadian firms that did business in the United States. By financing in U.S. dollars, converting to Canadian dollars, and selling Canadian dollars forward, the subsidiary was able to lock-in an all-in cost 40 basis points below what it would have had to pay for fixed-rate dollars in the Canadian capital market.

In another example a year later, a U.S. finance company wanted to raise U.S. dollars but could not obtain the desired dollar finance because the U.S. markets were effectively closed. No financing window existed due to the fact that U.S. investors expected rates to rise. Consequently, the U.S. finance company went to London and obtained a ten-year sterling loan, converted it to dollars, and entered into an agreement to sell dollars forward to buy the sterling needed for the interest payment each year and the principal in the tenth year. This was done at an all-in cost (including transactions costs and placement fees) of 25 basis points below what would have been possible in the U.S. market based on secondary market quotes at the time. While more difficult to arrange, note that long-date cover in the form of a stream of foreign exchange to service sequential payments has been possible to obtain in major currencies when needed. Hence, the more easily found bullet or single payment cover normally need not be resorted to when a stream of currency flows is really required.

Another interesting example occurred in early 1981 when a U.S. auto manufacturer needed to obtain seven-year dollar financing. Interest rates at the time were 13.25 percent in New York. At the same time a West German bank was interested in making the dollar loan but could not easily fund the dollars. As an alternative the German bank funded the loan in marks and converted into dollars to on-lend to the U.S. borrower. At this point the bank had a currency mismatch to manage. A counterparty was found in a U.S. food company that had been pressured by banks to raise seven-year German marks in the private placement market. The food company could raise dollars easily from the Middle East, which it did, and then swapped the dollars into marks with the German bank. This arrangement lowered the cost of German mark funds to the food company by 100 basis points, the auto firm obtained lower cost dollar financing in Frankfurt than was available in New York, the German bank earned a swap fee and two placement fees, and all wound up with liabilities in the currency desired and avoided currency exposure.

Another cluster of examples is derived from a problem faced by many large Canadian borrowers, based on the fact that in mid-1982 the Euro-Canadian dollar market was not large enough to source a C$50 to C$75 million financing. Hence, the borrowers looked to the U.S. dollar Euromarket for size. Despite the more recent shortage of forward flows to the north, borrowers still have been able to obtain funds in this way at approximately 10 to 15 basis points more cheaply than with direct Canadian dollar financing. This result can be illustrated by comparing quoted rates in July 1982. At that time the direct quote for five-year Canadian dollar funds was 17.5 percent. The quote for five-year U.S. dollar funds was 15.5 percent. The Canadian dollar forward premium in the five-year long-date market was 1.85 percent. Hence, by financing in U.S. dollars and covering, a firm wanting Canadian dollars could obtain a 15 basis point advantage over borrowing Canadian dollars directly *and* obtain its funds in larger size as well.

In another straightforward application designed to reduce its cost of capital, a U.S. finance company borrowed eight-year Eurosterling through its Netherland Autilles subsidiary. The sterling was on-lent to a U.S. international bank, which, in turn, provided U.S. dollars to the Netherland Autilles subsidiary at the prevailing spot rate. The underlying currency swap contract required that the U.S. company effectively borrow dollars from the bank and repay dollar interest and principal. Thus, the bank will service the sterling debt (or swap it with someone else), and the finance company will service the dollar debt and repay the principal. In this arrangement the currency swap provided that the forward exchange rate would be the same as the initial rate. The sterling loan had a 14.25 percent coupon, and the dollar bank financing to the Netherland Autilles subsidiary was at 12.5 percent, 65 basis points below the prevailing dollar rate for the U.S. company.

In a final example, Finance for Industry (FFI), a U.K. agency owned by banks and formed to lend funds to industry, had access to the Eurodollar market but needed sterling to make its loans. At the same time in 1982, a U.S. multinational conglomerate had access to Eurosterling but wanted dollars. The obvious solution was for FFI to raise Eurodollars and for the U.S. firm to raise Eurosterling and for them to exchange their obligations using a currency swap. This deal was arranged by a U.K. merchant bank with a U.S. bank intermediating the credit risk. The result was that the U.S. firm raised dollars at a cost of 25 basis points less than borrowing directly, and FFI had a similar saving and was able to access sterling without appearing in the sterling market, an added incentive.

Since liability hedges have been the most popular applications of long-date currency cover, many more cases could be cited. We have provided examples of the various generic applications, showing, whenever possible, how they tend to blend into one another and how counterparties can employ vastly differing objectives and still accommodate each other's needs. Having seen how liability hedges can effectively separate the currency of the liability from the preferred currency of the borrower, we turn the table, as it were, and in Chapter 10 examine applications where investors separate the currency of an asset from their currency of choice in what are called *portfolio investment hedges*.

Footnotes

[1] Actually, the interest rate that the World Bank charged was the same regardless of the currency denomination of its loans. Since July 1982 the rate charged has floated based on the average cost of funds to the bank. This policy provided the motive for obtaining the lowest nominal cost of funds.

[2] C.I. Wallich, "The World Bank's Currency Swaps," *Finance and Development* (June 1984), vol. 21, no. 2, pp. 15–19.

[3] The World Bank Annual Report. (Washington, D.C.: The World Bank, 1982), p.53.

[4] ERISA is the Employee Retirement Income Security Act. This legislation was enacted in 1974 to provide for pension reform and places certain restrictions on pension fund investment practices.

Chapter 10

Hedged Investing

INTRODUCTION

Hedged investing operates in a similar but reverse manner to hedged financing. It draws on market imperfections to increase the all-in rate of return on investment, and employs instruments denominated in alternative currencies using much the same logic as hedged financing, but opposite linkage. In capital markets where the supply of funds exceeds local demand, returns tend to be bid down. With efficient world communication and funds transfer, transferring funds to another currency where risk-adjusted returns are higher is a relatively simple matter. Such a strategy not only can produce superior risk adjusted returns, but it can also improve the allocation efficiency of *the* world capital market. Avoidance of the concomitant exchange risk requires long-date currency cover. Despite the need for cover, investors have been able to increase their all-in rate of return by shifting some of their investments to fully hedged instruments in alternative currencies.

INVESTOR CONSIDERATIONS

Professional investors might have a very positive view on a country and its investment performance but might not want to take a currency exposure in that country; they might prefer one country's securities over another's for political, geographical, or economic reasons. Hedged investment began when U.K. and Dutch life insurance companies and unit trusts developed an interest in U.S., Canadian, and Australian dollar instruments. The Dutch were also interested in sterling securities. In other applications Japanese investors wanted to diversify out of Japan with dollars available from U.S. trade deficits because of their fear of the potentially devastating effect of earthquakes on investments in Japan. Although much of the flow has been to dollar instruments because of their political stability, U.S. institutional investors also often prefer a foreign stock market because of its prospects for capital gain. Frequently these investors do not want to assume the concomitant currency risk. The long-date currency cover of swaps and forward contracts permit investors to unbundle the choice of issuer from the currency of the investment.

A deterrent to the process of covered investing is the perceived or actual need for liquidity (i.e., the ability to exit the swap or sell out the forward contract). This does not tend to be a problem for most private placement-type investors, which generally hold their assets to maturity, but, at times, it may be a serious consideration for other types of investors. Nevertheless, liquidity can usually be managed by alternative means of liability management such as gap management, lines of credit with lenders, and maintenance of alternative sources of purchased funds. Moreover, as we discuss in this chapter and Chapter 11, exit from long-date currency agreements in major currencies can be readily accomplished. In addition, documentation ease has reached the point that, if the other side is known, forward contracts can be handled on foreign exchange tickets.

Ease of exit is also illustrated by the fact that, in portfolio investment hedges and hedges of a firm's exposed net asset position, the player may reverse the hedge and take the gain if the hedge runs well and a sizable unrealized gain is evident. This practice represents a speculative action based on the view that the direction of the exchange rate move will reverse and the hedge can be reinstituted when exchange rates have moved back down. Note that policies of this type are similar to those applied in the portfolio trading activities of banks and other financial institutions. These policies have contributed to the increase in volume of long-date foreign exchange activity. They illustrate clearly that entry and exit to long-date foreign exchange deals are no longer a formidable obstacle to hedged investing.

MARKET ANOMALIES

An intriguing application of hedged investing to exploit market inefficiencies lies in two alternative currency liabilities of a captive finance company of a major U.S. multinational. In this example a U.S. investor in mid-1981 converted to Canadian dollars and bought the five-year Canadian dollar obligations of the finance company on a fully hedged basis to yield an all-in rate of return of 17 percent. At the same time the U.S. dollar five-year obligations of the same finance company were yielding only 15 percent. In this case, we have the same issuer, maturity, and terms but a 200 basis point higher yield. Such opportunities resulted from the natural supply at the time of forward U.S. dollars by Canadian firms operating in the United States.

Despite their attractiveness, opportunities such as this often went unexploited. A major reason why they were *not* done is because investors generally felt more comfortable in their own currency. They feel, for example, that they could not dispose of the Canadian dollar bonds as readily as the U.S. dollar units. When a hedge is used, players tend to feel considerable inertia of being locked into that currency until maturity. This attitude is unfortunate because unwinding a hedge is virtually as easy as creating one. To unwind a hedge, another party must take the opposite position. Developments in long-date currency markets discussed in Chapter 11 will clarify how this now appears to be a much less onerous problem. A major hinderance to unwinding a hedge used to be the timing factor; market developments have now reduced this period significantly in the major currencies. The transaction cost of unwinding still remains a consideration as well.

An application of hedged investing, which has been popular over the last few years, is illustrated by Japanese life insurance companies, which sell spot yen for dollars and invest the dollars with a full hedge to improve their yield by more than 20 basis points. This strategy created a forward seller of dollars and a forward buyer of yen, a natural offset to the U.S. multinational firm that would hedge a net asset position in Japan and be both a forward seller of yen and forward buyer of dollars.

Another application of an investment hedge involved the reverse of a foreign currency debt financing operation described in Chapter 8. Prior to the authorization and establishment of International Banking Facilities (IBF) in the United States in December 1981, a large corporation wanted to place a Swiss franc deposit in the United States. This firm preferred U.S. country risk but not U.S. currency risk. At this time (pre-IBF) U.S. banks could not accept foreign currency deposits. Instead, a large U.S. bank offered the firm a guaranteed Swiss franc yield on a dollar certificate of deposit (CD). This offer was implemented by converting the spot Swiss francs to dollars and purchasing a five-year dollar CD. The periodic dollar cash flows on the CD were reinvested to produce a compound dollar cash flow (interest and principal) at the end of the period. The dollar proceeds of the CD were sold forward for Swiss francs to produce a franc yield that was satisfactory for the investor.

Another illustration of a typical investment hedge is a U.K. Investment Trust that in mid-1981 wanted to invest £20 million in U.S. equities. The

U.K. trust liked the investment prospects of the year-old bull market in dollar equities. However, it wanted to separate the currency risk from the equity risk because it believed that the dollar would weaken against sterling. It accomplished these objectives by swapping the £20 million for dollars for five years. The other side was a U.S. multinational firm who was employing an asset hedge to cover its investment in plant and equipment in the United Kingdom.

Simulated Investment Alternatives

Since the advent of markets in financial futures, astute institutional money managers have used futures transactions in conjunction with cash market trades to produce investment alternatives that are more attractive than other strategies currently available. Such simulated investment alternatives tend to be self-extinguishing and may be self-funding. These domestic transactions, often called *cash and carry,* involve buying a term asset and funding it in the repurchase (repo) market with short-term funds when possible, while simultaneously selling an appropriate number of futures contracts to hedge the price risk on the term asset. The futures position should normally be in instruments that have approximately the same maturity as the term asset. The maturity of the simulated investment would then equal the maturity of the futures position.

In the context of cash-and-carry investment strategies, the role of financial futures contracts is an integral part of the overall investment process. They are used to simulate investment alternatives in domestic markets that exploit anomalies between the cash and futures markets by converting long-term instruments to short-term investments at above-market returns. In a similar manner long-date forward currency contracts can be used to simulate investment alternatives across international capital markets that produce above-market yields without increased currency risk. In this sense the use of long-date currency cover widens the availability of investment opportunities to an international scale and facilitates the extraction of improved returns from market anomalies almost anywhere in the developed world.

Simulated investment alternatives are typically put together by financial traders to improve yields. When done for customers, it would be expected that the simulated investments would be held to maturity. But when done for the financial trader's firm, the investment is more likely to be taken off the books at a propitious time. Such unwinding often makes possible the set-up of another opportunity to exploit another anomaly in the near future.

Simulated investment deals using long-date forward contracts are not widely done. Only a relatively few traders have been involved, but the resulting transactions illustrate how long-date currency cover can be used to improve yields.

The way in which forward currency agreements are priced facilitates an improvement in yields using long-date currency cover. As we indicated previously, most banks price their forward contracts off the interbank term deposit market. Because of the low volume of interbank term deposit transactions, these quoted rates are frequently artifically distorted, thereby prompting an opportunity for profitable arbitrage. To exploit such an opportunity, a trader may seek a compound investment strategy, which would require building a position in the long-date currency market (i.e., a strategy in which a long-date currency contract is one leg of a multifaceted transaction). Two examples illustrate this concept.

In the first example consider a yen investor that in the spring of 1983 sought to improve its return on 2.5 year money over the 6.9 percent available on Japanese government bonds. To implement an improved yield it converted the yen to spot dollars, invested in 2.5 year U.S. government notes, and sold the dollar interest cash flows forward for yen at each coupon date and the principal for yen at maturity. The result was an all-in yield of 8.2 percent, a return equivalent to Japanese prime industrial rates but in an investment with U.S. government credit quality.

In the second illustration a U.S. investor sold spot dollars for sterling and invested in a three-year gilt (U.K. treasury obligation) at 1/8 point over the offer rate. At the same time it sold the sterling interest cash flows forward for dollars at each coupon date and the principal cash flow at maturity. The result was an investment with U.K. government credit quality at yields that approximate the three-year interbank rate. Note that when these deals are assembled, traders can usually operate within the quoted bid–ask spreads and thereby further improve their investment outcome.

COMPREHENSIVE CASE STUDY

Financial innovation and creativity are essential ingredients in the original development and refinement of most applications of long-date currency cover. After having developed the instruments and mechanisms for long-date cover, master investment and merchant bankers can deploy these tools to solve various classes of problems that involve separating the currency of a transaction from the currency of preference. Intermediaries simply need to identify the source or need for future currency flows and then set out to locate counterparties. In this process a supply and demand for future currency flows which is no more than a notional or imaginary flow can be created (i.e., a flow that does not really take place but is necessary conceptually to facilitate the real currency flows required to satisfy the needs of the parties). These concepts are illustrated in the following rather comprehensive case study.

A West German firm held a term yen asset with a 6.5-year maturity on which it had a sizable book gain and wanted to recognize the gain for accounting purposes. This player, whom we will call the hedger, went to a merchant banker for assistance. What was needed was a long-date source of marks against yen for the hedger to lock-in the mark price of its asset and thus recognize its future value in marks for accounting purposes. The obvious solution to this problem was to take a German mark security to a Japanese life insurance company (JIC) and offer a better all-in yield in yen than was available in the Toyko market (i.e., sell a mark security with a hedge to convert the marks to yen at maturity). Naturally, the JIC was interested in an above-market yen yield, which, if implemented, would create a source of forward marks and a demand for forward yen—just what the hedger needed to recognize an accounting gain.

At this point a problem, which caused the merchant banker to exercise a high degree of creativity, arose. The issuance of German mark securities is regulated by the German Capital Market Subcommittee, and, at the time, the Subcommittee had a moratorium on all foreign issues of mark securities. Hence, West German domestic issues could not be purchased by the JIC. The merchant banker devised a remedy to this problem requiring a highly creditworthy borrower of marks (i.e., an issuer of Schuldschein domestic promissory notes) to issue a sterling bond instead of a German mark bond and swap the sterling into marks. This course of action produced a forward provider of German marks without legal constraints and, of course, a forward buyer of sterling to be used to service the sterling debt.

While this strategy produced a forward provider of marks, it did not resolve the need for a forward demand for yen. This need was filled by arranging for the U.K. buyer of the sterling bonds that were issued by the top-quality German borrower to swap the future sterling cash flows for future yen flows. This could be accomplished by selling the sterling bond to a representative of the JIC, which would simultaneously sell all of the future sterling flows for yen. In this way the merchant banker created a forward buyer of yen against which the forward yen flows of the hedger could be offset. Note that the sterling flows were notional and represented a complete wash. In actuality no sterling flows took place. Instead, the hedger provided the forward yen in return for the forward German mark, which was provided by the JIC. A proxy for JIC bought the sterling bonds and simply passed them along to JIC. When the mark provider covered its forward positions in marks, the marks flowed through the JIC to the hedger, which was the actual provider of forward yen.

The forward flows of this multiphase, sophisticated transaction are illustrated in Figure 10–1. In putting it together, the borrower received the going interest rate on German mark instruments for its risk class, the JIC investor received an all-in return after fees of 30 basis points above equivalent yen yields in Tokyo, and the hedger received a better forward rate after fees than was quoted in the long-date forward market plus the locked-in profit of DM12 million for accounting purposes.

Figure 10–1 Forward currency flows associated with mark–sterling–yen forward transactions

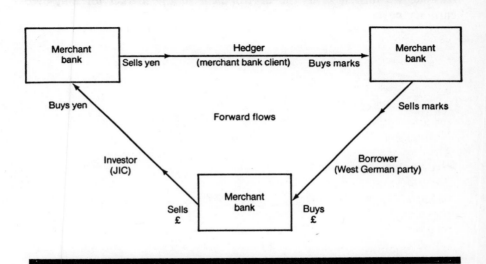

The spot and forward flows associated with this transaction can be summarized as follows: the investor (JIC) was a spot yen provider against sterling and a forward sterling provider against yen. The borrower (the West German party) was a spot taker of marks and a forward provider of marks. The hedger seeking to lock-in a gain on its yen asset was a forward provider of yen and the forward taker of marks. A merchant bank intermediary served as proxy for the JIC by investing in the sterling bond. This merchant bank intermediary was the spot provider of sterling against marks and the forward taker of sterling against marks. As we already indicated, the sterling flows were notional, and sterling–yen and sterling–mark transaction flows were self-canceling. Instead, the investor provided spot yen, which could be converted in the spot market to fill the borrower's need for spot marks. The West German borrower provided forward marks to the hedger, who, in turn, provided the forward yen to the investor. The investor used the forward sterling receivable from the intermediary bank to satisfy the obligation for the forward yen obtained.

While this transaction appears to be rather complex, its currency flows are quite straightforward. What often does prove to be difficult is the arrangement of equal transferred amounts in each period and the negotiation of the forward exchange rates on the stream of interest and principal flows. There is no doubt that other, more involved transactions have been attempted. To see why such comprehensive strategies are becoming more and more feasible, we turn next to the development of the market for long-date currency cover.

Chapter 11

Development of the Market for Currency Cover

INTRODUCTION

Since the advent of floating exchange rates in 1973, changes in economic fundamentals among countries have been promptly reflected in currency values. More recently, the increased volatility of interest rates and inflation differentials has led to wide swings in exchange rates and has enlarged the exchange rate risk faced by international traders and investors. As we have seen, foreign exchange exposure results not only from commercial and financial transactions but also from accounting translation methods employed in various countries and from planned financial or operational strategies, which occasion long forward foreign exchange exposure. Moreover, most sources agree that volatility in interest rates, inflation, and, hence, exchange rates, will continue to prevail.

SHORT-DATE FORWARD CURRENCY MARKETS

The high volume and relatively short duration of many commercial and financial transactions has led to the development of efficient instruments and markets in short-term forward exchange through which traders can avoid exchange risk. However, the volume of transactions decreases significantly for maturities beyond one year, and mechanisms are not as readily available to hedge long-date currency exposures that arise from financial, operational, or translation positions that span several years.

In forward markets with maturities up to one year, spreads widen and transaction costs increase with the period to maturity.[1] The widening of spreads occurs due to a decreased volume of transactions, increased prospect of adverse price movements, and increased difficulty in finding counterparties as maturity lengthens. Although a relatively active market exists for forward cover through 90 days, the volume of transactions for longer maturities diminishes markedly due to both reduced demand for longer forward cover for transactions purposes and reduced supply on the part of market makers. The latter occurs because of the increased risk that the market maker may not be able to find the offset to a longer forward position and, thus, wind up the day with an unbalanced position.

LONG-DATE CURRENCY TRANSACTIONS

As we move to forward maturities beyond one year, spreads widen even more[2] and some of the marketlike characteristics of actual transactions disappear. The criteria for a true market require that a market maker exist who is willing to execute transactions at quotations whose bid–ask spreads are not so large as to preclude transactions at these quotations. Many prospective long-date transactions in foreign exchange have not met these criteria, and the concept of vibrant markets must be rejected in the strictest sense. At present the finding of counterparties to take opposite currency positions is usually still too unstructured an event to characterize all of the transactions in long-date currency cover as "market" transactions.

Nevertheless, if the gains from trade in particular types of transactions are great enough, institutions will arise to accommodate these transactions. The nature of the transactions might be such that a brokerage function would be appropriate. In such a case the brokers would match parties to the transaction without becoming principals. On the other hand the facilitating agents may play the role of principal by assuming the price risk associated with holding the asset. If the agents inject themselves as principals into many transactions simply to facilitate (and profit from) the transactions of others, they become dealers. If they are willing to make quotations at which they will deal to accommodate transactions, then they perform the role of market makers.

Presently, some intermediaries display a marked tendency to perform the role of market makers in long-date currency contracts in the major currencies. One of the issues that dealers must address in making long-date markets is the equivalence between a series of short-date currency contracts and a long-date currency contract and, hence, the ability to substitute short-date transactions in long-term applications. This question was examined in Chapter 5. We now examine in more detail the forces involved in market making and the tendency toward a more resonant market in long-date currency cover.

AVAILABILITY OF LONG-DATE FOREIGN EXCHANGE POSITIONS

Demand for long-date currency cover is indicated whenever investors and borrowers take positions in long-term instruments that are denominated in foreign currencies. This latent demand for currency cover by primary parties suggests that some semblance of a long-date forward currency market should exist. Although some activity in long-date currency cover has existed since the return of convertible currencies following World War II, larger volumes of actual demand for long-date currency cover did not become apparent until the transition to floating exchange rates was completed in 1973. Hence, any substantive activity in long-date currency cover is scarcely more than 10 years old, and the availability of positions and related market mechanics are still developing. In Chapters 2 and 7 through 10, we saw how long-date instruments and applications have evolved in the last decade; we now examine the market for long-date currency cover with emphasis on its development, resilience, and durability.

TRADING VOLUME OF FORWARD TRANSACTIONS

We begin by recognizing the vast growth in spot and forward foreign exchange trading activity and then attempt to estimate the relationship between trading volume and the future delivery date of forward contracts. In a survey conducted in April 1983, the Federal Reserve Bank of New York reported that gross foreign currency transactions by 119 banking institutions in the U.S. foreign exchange market averaged $33.5 billion each business day that month.[3] This was $10 billion more than the turnover reported in an earlier survey conducted in March 1980. After correcting for double-counting resulting from interbank transactions, the average daily gross turnover was an estimated $26 billion, an increase of about 44 percent over the March 1980 adjusted figure of $18 billion. A still earlier survey conducted in April 1977 revealed an average daily turnover of only about $5 billion in 1977.

175

This represents a compound growth rate of 32 percent in the volume of foreign exchange dollar transactions in the six-year period and reflects the significant growth in all types of international transactions.

The data released by the Federal Reserve Bank of New York also indicate that 63 percent of all foreign exchange trading in April 1983 was in spot contracts, generally for delivery in two business days. Of the balance, 33 percent was in swap contracts consisting of both a spot transfer and a reversing forward transfer at the maturity of the swap. The remaining 4 percent was in forward outright contracts in which currencies were traded for future delivery. No other firm data are known to be available regarding the proportion of foreign exchange trades made for lengthening future delivery dates.

Other estimates of trading volume versus maturity date were obtained from foreign exchange traders, bankers, and market participants. Using these estimates, a tentative plot was constructed of the relative volume of foreign exchange transactions versus their forward delivery dates. This plot is shown in Figure 11–1. Approximately 63 percent of all foreign exchange transactions are spot transactions in accordance with the data from the Federal Reserve Bank of New York, about two-thirds of the balance (24 percent) mature within 3 months. Another 8 percent have delivery dates from 3 to 6 months, and 5.9 percent mature from 6 to 12 months, with only 0.1 percent of the foreign exchange transactions estimated to have a maturity beyond one year.

Those who participate in foreign exchange transactions know that, in most currencies, the market for deposits becomes quite thin as the maturity lengthens. This condition is also prevalent in forward contracts and is reflected in Figure 11–1. As maturities approach long-date levels of, say, five years, market characteristics take on a different tone. Some of these differences are evident in the behavior of bid–ask spreads and in the role of quotations in the market-making process.

BEHAVIOR OF BID-ASK SPREADS

As reported elsewhere, bid–ask spreads of forward foreign exchange quotations tend to widen as the period of maturity lengthens.[4] As with quotations for most other financial instruments, the size of the bid–ask spread depends upon both trading volume and risk of adverse price movements to the market maker. Since volume tends to decrease and forward premiums/discounts increase as maturity lengthens, these forces operate to cause a widening of bid–ask spreads.

In the case of long-date currency transactions, other factors prompt increasing bid–ask spreads as maturity increases. Important among these is

Figure 11-1 Estimated Foreign Exchange Trading Volume Versus Forward Delivery Date

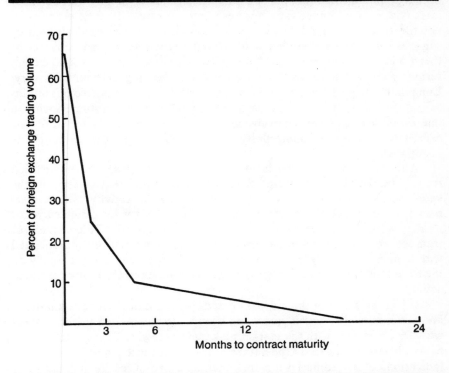

the fact that banks maintain credit limits for each of their customers, and long-date currency contracts tie up portions of customer credit limits. Since the banks realize higher revenue on loans than on currency contracts, they perceive the use of limited credit lines for long-date currency contracts as an opportunity cost that must be compensated for by higher spreads on long-date currency contracts. And to the extent that a bank offsets a long-date currency contract by borrowing and investing the currency sold forward, it (reluctantly) enlarges its own balance sheet. The bank is naturally inclined to widen its bid–ask spread to prevent its return on average assets from excessive erosion due to the expanded asset position.

Because bid–ask spreads on long-date currency quotations are so wide, they are frequently not perceived as dealable quotations. Evidently a similar perception is held by both long-date foreign exchange dealers and long-date foreign exchange players. Based on ongoing observation of long-date currency quotations, the quotations are apparently updated infrequently. This occurs despite the fact that the two major determinants of long-date currency rates (viz, spot exchange rates and term interest rate differentials) are more volatile than the long-date exchange quotations themselves. This finding suggests that dealers are either well covered by the wide bid–ask spreads, or they do not really intend to deal at quoted rates and hence do not take them seriously enough to prompt revision when underlying determinants vary. Long-date foreign exchange users, on the other hand, view posted quotations as mere advertising by dealers, used to bring on potential customers with an interest in dealing. Others perceive long-date quotations as a kind of fishing exercise in search of a counterparty with whom final rates can ultimately be negotiated.

Although a wide spread in bid–ask quotations appears to be justified from a market maker's perspective, the transaction costs implicit in the widening spread undoubtedly tend to retard market activity. Many intermediaries have argued that considerably more use of the long-date currency market would be made were it not for the wide spreads. This element of transaction cost can at times consume all of the potential profit associated with a market anomaly leaving nothing to the parties who would actually do the transaction, thereby stifling the profit advantages of the long-date transaction.

Given the width of the bid–ask spreads in long-date currency quotations and the inertia that resists imparting changes to the quoted prices, players who are unfamiliar with the market maker strike few deals at quoted prices. Most players are aware of the nature of the quoted prices and view them as indications of a trading level rather than as a firm price. As a result most informed players try to get inside the quoted values and can usually do so unless the bank's appetite for their name (i.e., the player's credit limit) is approached. Thus, we have seen that many of the elements for a market in long-date foreign exchange are generally present in a more-or-less rudimentary form. Perhaps a genuine market is developing and will continue to evolve as players become more aware of the role and advantage of long-date currency cover and as the concomitant volume increases.

AVAILABILITY OF LONG-DATE CURRENCY POSITIONS

Although a "market" for long-date currency cover may not yet exist in the conceptual sense that many market makers stand ready to sell or buy long-date foreign exchange at quoted bid and ask prices, a form of shadow market exists, given that a sizable volume of long-date foreign currency transactions take place each year. In many instances these transactions are arranged by a financial intermediary such as an investment banker, merchant banker, or commercial banker with wide international contacts and reputation. The necessary arrangement in most cases still requires finding a counterparty with opposite currency needs and matched timing, size, and risk. Although an occasional fast fit can be found, the arrangement process normally takes considerable time and involves intensive search, and, often, extensive financial creativity on the part of the intermediary. An added element of difficulty in consummating a deal is the need for simultaneous execution of the contract by the often geographically disparate parties. Clearly, one party would not want to be bound until the other has signed. This impasse can usually be resolved by joint Telex confirmation to the intermediary or by both sides dealing with the intermediary as principal.

The scale of activity that exists in the shadow of a full-fledged market is the result of a cadre of up to 30 intermediaries who are active in most of the important financial centers throughout the developed countries of the capitalist world. Although still operating somewhat in the shadow of other financial markets, some of the intermediaries have recently been taking on more of the functions of a fully developed market maker. For instance, subject to the limitations discussed earlier, 5-year quotations have been readily available on dollar–sterling, dollar–German mark, dollar–Swiss franc, dollar–yen, and dollar–Canadian dollar since 1981. Moreover, in some cases, transactions can be quickly accommodated up to $50 million. More recently, 10-year quotations have been offered to regular customers by a few banks in dollar–sterling and dollar–German mark positions.

In the case of all bank quotations, long-date foreign exchange services have been offered only to the commercial customers that the bank knows well. The size of the foreign currency quotation depends on the credibility of the customer, not the exposure of the bank. Expected stability of foreign exchange rates is also considered in the extension of quotations.

In a few instances banks have been willing to keep an open transactions book in long-date dollar–sterling positions (i.e., to assume the risk of unmatched trading positions). They carefully monitor maturity mismatch for each day throughout the first three-month maturity period and for each month thereafter up through 15 years. Despite a number of overbought and oversold maturities, an aggregate mismatch in the entire book of open transactions positions would not be expected to exceed $10 million.

Whenever a given maturity's mismatch exceeds a nominal limit, the bank will attempt to offset its position through a more-or-less restricted market that exists between banks. This availability to offset forward foreign exchange positions among large international banks is based on reciprocal access to each other's forward foreign exchange mismatched positions. Availability of this service is restricted from any bank that does not maintain an ongoing interbank relationship, and only a relatively few players participate. These arrangements enable exposed market makers to square up their open transactions book and contribute to moving the long-date foreign exchange market out of the shadows.

Foreign exchange brokers are also active in arranging foreign currency transactions between banks. Although long-date brokered transactions have increased in the last few years, their volume remains small, with very few deals beyond $5 million or one-year maturity.

CHARACTERISTICS OF MARKET PARTICIPANTS

In our discussion of the availability of long-date positions, we focused on the nature and behavior of market makers and intermediaries. In this section we study the characteristics of representative participants or users of the long-date currency market. We also look at some of the more recent thinking of market participants that may contribute to a deeper market in long-date currency contracts in the future. Finally, we illustrate the role of various types of interested players by examining the nature of typical participants in the long-date market of a particular currency.

Size Threshold

Any firm of any nationality with a net long-date foreign currency exposure of nominal size could be a candidate for long-date currency cover. As we have seen, the foreign exchange exposure may result from transaction, translation, tax, regulation, financing, or investment applications. In an attempt to identify threshold parameters for potential users of long-date currency cover, we focus on the characteristics of players choosing to employ long-date cover in its most popular application (viz, a liability hedge).

The minimum size of users who seek long-date currency cover from the foreign exchange dealing rooms of banks should be sufficiently large to warrant lines of credit adequate for both their borrowing and currency cover needs. This might place potential users in a category exceeding $100 million of sales per year. In these cases their covered financing needs in a single transaction may be on the order of $3 million to $5 million.

Despite their potential need for long-date currency cover and the potential availability of cover in the major currencies, the financial management of many of these small-sized firms may not have the sophistication needed to pursue long-date cover. Undoubtedly, many smaller firms employ long-date currency cover, but a more appropriate threshold for users of cover are those larger firms engaged in covered financing. Recognizing the minimum transaction fees and other fixed costs of long-date cover, minimum threshold parameters would seem to be sales of at least $1 billion per year with concomitant financing requirements of a minimum of $25 million per trip to the capital market. Larger firms can also be easily accommodated by packaging a number of traunches of long-date cover to fit the needs of the larger players.

Data Banks

In their search for counterparties, financial intermediaries have been quite aggressive in soliciting firms that may have potential applications for long-date currency cover. Astute merchant bankers continue to search for reasons why parties may want to do a long-date currency deal. One of the major intermediaries maintains a data bank of customers' needs and availabilities for cover of currency exposure. This data bank is reported to contain in excess of 3,000 entries and represents an efficient means to initiate a search for counterparties.

The rationale behind the use of a data bank of interested parties is supported by the announced policies of many present users of long-date currency cover. Having experienced protection against the ravages of a deteriorating foreign exchange rate on a net asset exposure or a sizable saving in financing costs, many players have become confirmed users of long-date currency cover. With certain limitations, they are eager to make their continued interest known to financial intermediaries seeking counterparties. For instance, one electronics systems manufacturer has made known to its financial intermediaries that it has had good experience with currency swaps and is quite willing to fit its needs into another party's long-date currency picture to reduce its own world cost of capital. This firm stands ready to be a counterparty in currencies in which it conducts business if the price is right. Despite the fact that it has rejected deals that were brought to it because the price was too high, it remains willing to be a counterparty to a long-date currency deal where it can lengthen the maturity or reduce the cost of its debt.

In another example of the willingness to engage in long-date deals, a multinational oil firm has maintained a strategy of informing its financial intermediaries of its appetite for long-date currency cover. It openly seeks applications to cover its nondollar investment exposure, provided the price is right. Similarly, a multinational consumer finance company informed its

181

investment bankers when it had a need for foreign currency financing and was pleased to react to what was brought back to it in terms of opportunities.

Minimum Cost Savings

Other situations reflect user initiative in establishing criteria for a hedging strategy. A large U.S. multinational food company in assessing its financing needs in mid-1982 informed its investment bankers that if the yen appreciated to Y220/$, it would consider a five-year Samurai bond. The firm assumed that the five-year premium would place the repayment exchange rate at Y140/$, resulting in a saving of 150 basis points over what would have been available to the firm at the time in straight dollar finance. In addition, this strategy would have provided the firm with an in-house hedge because it could have serviced the yen loan with the cash flows from its Japanese subsidiary, thereby facilitating an asset hedge.

Criteria for hedging strategies used by participants are not always as unique as the foregoing yen example. Frequently, firms will notify their financial intermediaries of the minimum all-in rate savings necessary to induce them to engage in a liability hedge. For example, a U.S. building products firm announced that it would not be willing to borrow a foreign currency for a rate saving of less than 50 basis points. In contrast, a large U.S. finance and conglomerate firm that does extensive borrowing has indicated that it would be interested in deals that reduce its all-in cost of capital by as much as 25 basis points. Still other players will only deal in currencies where they have a business interest and hence a close watch on the expectations for the currency.

Cost Monitoring

Just as intermediaries attempt to keep informed regarding the needs and applications of potential users, many players maintain systems to keep an up-to-date knowledge of effective costs. A major U.S. chemical firm monitors the cost of covered financing in four currencies on a monthly basis to evaluate which is the most cost effective. The results of this effort have suggested direct dollar financing in 90 percent of the cases. However, occasionally a window opens up for covered financing because of opportunities to negotiate the forward cover with someone who, for whatever reasons, is willing to offer a below-market forward rate. Another chemical and office systems firm has a minicomputer programmed to compare market quotations for forward foreign exchange with "do-it-yourself" hedge pricing to quickly identify market anomalies that become reflected in forward foreign exchange price quotations. Finally, a major U.K. merchant bank maintains computer listings of the cost of funds in each currency plus (minus) the swap cost to identify any apparent savings obtainable from deploying long-date liability hedges to reduce a client's capital cost. These real-time computer applications provide immediately available, accurate computations to be used to make long-date foreign exchange deals accessible to interested clients.

Proxy Currencies

Another strategy that has furnished some flexibility to user applications is use of one currency closely tied to another to serve as proxy for the second in the choice of long-date currency cover. For example, the lack of long-date availability in the Austrian shilling caused one auto firm to use a strip of short-date forward contracts to hedge its long-date net asset position. Obviously, it took the risk of changing interest differentials discussed earlier in Chapter 5. An alternative course of action could have been to hedge its shilling exposure by selling Swiss francs or German marks forward, since the shilling has strong economic ties with each of these currencies. The use of one currency to serve as proxy for another related unit whose capital markets may not be accessible is not without risk, but it may serve well to reduce the risk of either short-date cover or complete lack of cover.

Borrowing proxy currencies has also been used within the European group of Common Market currencies, commonly called the *snake*. The paucity of long-term debt markets in France and Italy have led some players to borrow term German marks and rely on the snake agreement to maintain currency parity. While this strategy employs the proxy currency concept, it can be quite risky unless covered because the frequent realignment of the snake currencies tends to thwart the security of their initial parity.

Representative Players

Having examined the characteristics of users of long-date currency cover and many of the practices that they employ to deploy long-date cover effectively, we turn next to a roster of the representative major players in a national long-date currency market. The particular national market selected in Japan, but most of the typical players could also appear in many of the other national markets where long-date currency cover is available.

As the Japanese financial markets continue to open up to foreigners, natural buyers of forward yen are attracted to the low yen interest rate. Such borrowers might include supranational and national borrowers that are primarily influenced by low nominal interest rates and that, consequently, would need forward yen to service the yen debt. Other typical buyers of forward yen at prices fixed on day one would be those that fear or expect an appreciation of the yen. Here we see what may appear to be a contrast in views because a forward purchase of yen against say, dollars, is the economic equivalent of borrowing dollars and investing yen. That is, when a player borrows dollars on day one, it will have a dollar outflow in the future when the debt must be repaid. And when it lends or invests yen, it will have a yen inflow in the future when the yen is repaid. These future flows are the same as those associated with a forward purchase of yen against dollars. The contrast in views that is reflected here is that typical buyers of forward yen are (1) those who seek a low nominal interest rate (i.e., borrowers) and (2) those who fear or expect an appreciation of the yen and wish to engage in the economic equivalent of investing in yen securities by purchasing yen forward.

This apparently divergent logic associated with the same strategy of buying forward yen is consistent, however, when viewed in terms of the underlying economic forces at work. Japan has had a low rate of inflation that along with its very high saving rate, high degree of economic prosperity, and credit controls has resulted in an artificially low interest structure. This low nominal interest cost would be attractive to borrowers that seek primarily low nominal capital cost. On the other hand if the yen is currently undervalued and should be expected to appreciate by more than the rate implicit in the forward premium, players with a speculative bent or others with yen liabilities would be well advised to purchase forward yen to alleviate their expectations or fears.

A more complete list of the natural buyers of forward yen would include:

• Japanese investors that seek a higher all-in return in nonyen, say, dollar, assets; sale of dollar proceeds at maturity for yen.
• Japanese multinational firms with recurrent nonyen cash flows from profits, royalties, fees, and depreciation that prefer to hedge the yen value of these cash flows.
• Non-Japanese players with yen-denominated liabilities or leases that need forward cover.
• Receivers of yen-denominated subsidized export credits.
• Purchasers of assets on long-term contracts from Japanese trading companies or construction firms where payments must be made in yen over future periods.

Natural sellers of forward yen would include:

• Non-Japanese players with yen-denominated assets that require forward cover.

- Non-Japanese multinational firms with recurrent yen cash flows from profits, royalties, fees, and depreciation that prefer to hedge the foreign exchange value of these cash flows.
- Japanese borrowers of nonyen currencies; sale of forward yen to obtain the necessary foreign exchange for debt service.
- Non-Japanese investors in yen assets to exploit the rate advantage of market anomalies that occur.
- Japanese purchasers of recurrent imports or capital assets requiring future payment in foreign exchange.

A salient characteristic of the Japanese capital market in recent years has been its extensive liquidity. This liquidity is the product of the savings rate in Japan (the highest in the world), its protracted period of prosperity, and the artificially low structure of interest rates. Its future is not without concern, however, because of the major national deficits that the country has been running which impose a large public sector borrowing requirement on the capital markets.

The low nominal interest rates currently available in Japan (and in Switzerland and West Germany) have been tempting to some borrowers. Moreover, we have recently gone through a period when uncovered borrowing in low-interest currencies has turned out to be profitable (i.e., exchange rates of low-interest currencies have not increased in lock-step with inflation and interest differentials). When this recent phenomenon is contrasted with what occurred in the early 1970s when large losses accrued to those borrowing uncovered in low-interest countries, some are tempted to argue that the risk inherent in uncovered positions has abated. We examine this and other issues regarding the risk of long-date positions in the next section.

RISK OF LONG-DATE POSITIONS

Despite the fact that implementation of long-date currency cover is designed to manage or reduce the foreign exchange exposure of the user, other collateral risk considerations, which should be evaluated, crop up. We have previously examined the uncertainty associated with the size and timing of the future cash flows that long-date cover assumes will occur and on which it is predicated. This risk, while significant in some instances, can be resolved by trading only that portion of the future flow that is believed to be reliable. A policy of selling some fraction of expected foreign currency flows or using a declining formula related to the distance into the future when the flows are expected has proved helpful. Actually, except in extreme devaluations, some mismatch of size or timing is bearable. The uncovered balance due to uncertainty in flows, like the deductible on a liability insurance contract, can usually be absorbed without severe adverse impact on a player.

Many firms have adopted this policy of covering most of their uncertain exposure with available long-date cover size and date without the concern and delay associated with fine tuning. Moreover, in those numerous instances where future currency flows are contractual, they can be swapped without worry as to size or date.

In addition to the uncertainty regarding the size and date, users of long-date currency cover face some degree of credit risk, currency or exchange rate risk, and, perhaps, sovereign risk.

Credit Risk

The credit risk encountered in long-date currency arrangements consists of two types. The first, usually called *settlement risk,* deals with the risk of insolvency of one of the parties during that short (two-day maximum) period in which settlement must be made at the start and at the maturity of a long-date swap or equivalent. The settlement risk on day one of a swap should be readily accessible using conventional credit analysis or could be managed by requiring simultaneous transfers of guaranteed funds through a bank or other third party. This latter provision should allay fears of settlement risk at maturity as well.

The second type of credit risk depends directly upon currency or exchange rate risk. Ironically, an instrument designed to hedge long-date currency exposure also faces a credit risk that depends on changes in exchange rates. Nevertheless, if one counterparty fails during the period of the contract, the other party faces a credit exposure equal to the size of the contract times the change in exchange rate from the outset until the date of failure. Put differently, the exposure is equal to the cost to replace the long-date currency contract in the market at the prevailing forward rate at the time of default. Theoretically, this exposure could produce a gain as well as a loss. If a failing party had a gain on a long-date contract, the contract would probably be assigned before default; hence, only contracts with loss positions are likely to be defaulted.

In the early days of long-date currency cover before the right of offset became well established, each party conceivably faced a credit exposure for the entire amount of the contract. With the advent of the right of offset of claims against each counterparty, this exposure was reduced to the impact of a change in exchange rates on the value of the contracts. Recall that this degree of credit exposure is what precipitated the need for a topping-up clause in back-to-back and parallel loans. Bank intermediation and assumption of credit risk for a fee was a well-used alternative to the awkward topping-up clause. Moreover, bank intermediation of credit risk is still used in long-date currency swaps where less than impeccable credits are involved. However, the intermediation fees are considerably smaller in magnitude than normal letter-of-credit fees charged by banks because the size of the exposure is limited to the potential change in exchange rates times the principal of the contract rather than the full amount of the currency contract. And even then the exposure is limited to the party whose currency devalues and not to both parties to the contract.

This limitation on credit exposure is also reflected in the rearrangement of a bank's lending limit to a customer when applied to forward foreign exchange contracts. For instance, a customer with a $10 million lending limit may be granted a forward limit of $100 million up to one year, $50 million for one- to three-year forward contract maturity and $33 million for forward contracts beyond three years. These enlarged (but declining) limits on forward contracts over outright lending limits would be based on the general assumption that a major currency would not devalue by more than 10 percent in one year, 20 percent in three years, or 30 percent in the life of a term-forward contract.

Exchange Rate Risk

We have seen that exchange rate risk directly influences the credit risk exposure of users of long-date currency cover. Exchange rate risk has also had an indirect effect on the willingness of players to engage in covered financing arrangements. Many firms remember vividly the adverse effects of exchange rate risk that they incurred following their uncovered Swiss franc borrowings in the early 1970s. Prompted to secure foreign direct investment financing offshore by the Foreign Direct Investment Controls in effect at that time and attracted by the low Swiss franc nominal interest rates, many U.S. firms borrowed francs uncovered. Unfortunately, the value of the dollar was controlled at that time at an artificially low rate. Subsequent devaluation of the dollar after the onset of floating exchange rates caused huge foreign exchange losses on uncovered franc liabilities.

Most managements have not been able to forget these injurious events, and many are still reluctant to borrow foreign currencies even though long-date cover would prevent a recurrence of the Swiss franc experience. Such managements would rather commit financial acts of omission of potential savings in cost of capital and use the higher cost of domestic finance than incur alternative acts of commission and the high balance sheet visibility associated with foreign borrowing and long-date currency cover. They believe that use of higher-cost domestic finance without visibility would cause them to have fewer problems than borrowing foreign currencies. They argue that

187

the latter strategy places them in the awkward position of having to explain why foreign borrowing would be wise now with long-date cover despite the fact that severe losses occurred in the 1970s. Hence, earlier adverse experience with exchange risk continues to influence the management process in rejecting favorable financing initiatives using long-date currency cover.

Sovereign Risk

A final element of risk in certain long-date currency contracts is that of sovereign risk. *Sovereign risk* is the risk that the government of a country may take actions to devalue, block, or otherwise interfere with the recovery of assets denominated in its currency. This risk is faced by every player who holds unmatched assets and liabilities in a foreign currency. However, because the implications of severe government interference with normal trade and currency movements can be so adverse to the conduct of trade and investment and detrimental to a country, relatively few incidents have occurred where full value has been permanently lost.

The deployment of long-date currency cover to reduce the currency mismatch of a net asset or liability exposure is itself a step to reduce a player's exposure to sovereign risk. However, in cases where a government agency is a party to a long-date currency contract, the risk of performance by the government or sovereign takes the place of credit risk in private contracts. Applications involving government swaps discussed in Chapter 8 provide working examples. Just as a private party may fail to perform on its obligation in a long-date currency instrument, a government agency could conceivably dishonor its obligation. The following comments provide some insight into this possibility.

Despite the difficulties that the Mexican government has had in obtaining foreign exchange since 1982, no outright defaults have occurred on their swaps with multinational firms. In most cases the three-year grace period before principal was to be amortized had not expired, so a true test has not yet occurred. There have been some delays in paying dollar interest, and rescheduling of principal has been a possibility. More recently, conditions appear to be improving in Mexico, and perhaps the severe foreign exchange squeeze will be relieved before the bulk of the principal payments become due. In Argentina, where inflation was much higher and hard currency very scarce, the government unilaterally rolled over dollar swaps due in 1982 for three more years. This extension of maturity, while interest bearing, effectively blocked the removal of the swapped principal until the new maturity date.

These examples illustrate the fact that the question of credit risk as related to governments in countries with high inflation can be more serious than that related to private players in more stable inflationary environments. In the case of sovereign risk of governments and their agencies, nearly the entire principal and interest may be at risk because of the potential for large-scale devaluations. On the other hand, in the case of private players in countries with lower inflation, the exposure is limited to the effect of a more modest change in exchange rate on the principal and interest payments.

MARKET SIZE AND GROWTH

The volume of long-date currency transactions has continued to expand since its inception in the late 1960s. This volume is a function of the demand for long-date currency cover, which in turn depends upon the awareness of potential users of its availability and usefulness. Some curtailment of volume came in 1979 with the abolition of U.K. exchange controls. However, the pause in market volume was very short. A rapid expansion followed as market intermediaries developed innovative roles and configurations for long-date foreign exchange applications and as a greater number of potential users became aware of the advantages of long-date cover. It has been estimated that market volume was the equivalent of approximately $2.5 billion in 1980 and grew to the equivalent of $5 billion in 1981. User aversion and reluctance has become further reduced due to improved understanding of the potential of long-date currency cover to reduce risk or increase profitability. And application innovation has continued to progress. Thus, market size is expected to continue to develop vigorously throughout the 1980s.

No firm data exist on market size. Sources have estimated that 75 percent of all long-date currency swaps are never publicized and the far forwards are almost never reported. Despite a potential lack of precision, a crude attempt has been made to estimate the size of the long-date currency market by currency and by major application.

Based on a preliminary survey of market intermediaries and market participants, the various types of long-date foreign exchange transactions clearly have been transacted in most of the actively traded currencies (e.g., sterling, marks, guilders, yen, Swiss and French francs, Swedish kroner, and U.S., Canadian, and Australian dollars). The deals range in size form $5 million to $100 million with an average size of about $25 million. About 30 active financial intermediaries operate worldwide. The range of estimated volumes for 1983 that have been done by each intermediary may vary from $100 million to $1,500 million with an average volume per intermediary estimated at about the equivalent of $250 million. When both sides of the transaction are considered, this results in approximately $500 million per intermediary. Multiplying this average firm volume by 30 intermediaries places a crude estimate of world market size for 1983 at the equivalent of approximately $15 billion. No official data are available on the size of the market with which to test this estimate; however, it is believed to be conservatively based. The only challenge that it has received by intermediaries is that it might be on the low side.

It is equally difficult to divide the market by application and by currency. Nevertheless, to provide some idea of its composition, estimates have been made based on multiple inputs from active intermediaries. These estimates are presented in Tables 11-1 and 11-2.

Because of its importance in world trade and finance, U.S. dollar applications make up the largest share. This is followed by Swiss franc-

Table 11-1 Estimate of composition of long-date currency transactions in 1983 by application

Application	US$ Million
Transaction	
Balance sheet hedge	$ 3,000
Long-term, recurrent contracts, and leases	3,000
Export financing	2,000
Translation	300
Blocked currency, taxes, and other	700
Hedged financing	5,000
Hedged investing	1,000
Total	$15,000

Table 11-2 Estimate of composition of long-date currency transactions in 1983 by currency

Currency	US$ Million
U.S. dollar	$ 6,000
Swiss franc	2,000
Yen	2,000
Canadian dollar	1,500
German mark	1,500
Sterling	1,000
Other	500
Total	$15,000

denominated deals since Switzerland is at the forefront as a world financial center and supranational agencies prefer its low nominal interest rates. Canadian dollar deals peaked at a higher volume than that shown but have fallen somewhat due to the recession and the national energy policy adopted in Canada; however, recovery is expected in the near term. Yen-denominated transactions have shown striking growth due to Japan's very strong trade position and the relaxation of controls on the issuance of Samurai bonds and the ability of Japanese companies to issue foreign and Eurobonds. The sterling and German mark volumes have exhibited normal size and growth for these currencies because they are important in international trade and investment.

PROSPECTS FOR THE FUTURE

The data presented above reflect the recent rapid growth in adoption of long-date currency cover for an expanding list of applications. This growth in long-date currency cover has exceeded 80 percent per year. It has been attainable because of the huge volume of latent demand for long-date currency cover, as evidenced in the data presented in Chapter 6, and the initiative of financial intermediaries in locating interested counterparties. Given the size of U.S. foreign direct investment alone of $221 billion in 1982, growing at 9.2 percent per annum, and foreign direct investment in the United States of $102 billion and growing at 22.5 percent per annum, the potential application for cover of exposed net asset positions remains extremely large. When international portfolio investment and non-U.S. direct investment in other countries are added, the potential application for long-date currency cover increases manifold. To this must be added the trade-driven applications and the important function of long-date cover in exploiting market inefficiencies. The potential for growth in the long-date market can be likened to the record historical growth in the foreign exchange spot and forward markets and in the Eurocurrency markets as international trade and capital market development have operated to facilitate their growth. The latent demand for long-date currency cover is immense and awaits continued development by market intermediaries.

Productization of Instruments

As more potential users of long-date currency cover become aware of its advantages, rates of growth should be sustained. To aid in realizing this high growth, intermediaries have begun reacting to the widespread requirements for cover by standardizing terms and otherwise productizing their offerings. These actions facilitate increased access to counterparties and reduce the time necessary to implement or unwind a long-date swap or forward contract. Intermediaries are also finding that syndicated long-date contracts are helpful in packaging together a number of counterparties to offset a single large desired long-date forward position. While still in its infancy in long-date currency cover, syndication will be able to provide the same benefits that it has provided for years in term loans.

The flexibility and ease with which contracts can be written has added to the attractiveness of long-date currency cover. Documentation has become so simplified that implementing a long-date forward currency contract on a foreign exchange ticket is now possible if the parties know each other well. Long-date currency swap contracts are now only a matter of a few pages—a marked contrast to the formerly voluminous parallel loan documentation. The ease and flexibility with which contracts can now be written, coupled with the increased volume, has made it increasingly easy to unwind a long-date position when necessary. This feature has made the use of long-date currency cover more flexible and materially reduced the apprehension of boards of directors, thereby relieving some of the impediments to the approval process necessary for the adoption of long-date currency cover.

Channels of Distribution

There are two distinct channels through which intermediary activity is focused on marketing long-date currency cover to clients. In many cases both channels exist within the same intermediary or bank, and in other cases a given firm offers only one channel. The two channels are the corporation finance department of an investment or merchant banking organization and the dealing room of a bank that makes a market in foreign exchange. The corporate finance department typically encounters more-or-less unique long-date currency applications that require tailor-made size and maturities for a stream or single payment forward transaction. These deals require much effort and client contact to find an appropriate counterparty. In contrast bank dealing rooms deal off their foreign exchange trading book and offer rather standardized positions in only the major currencies. In recent years some of these dealing rooms have extended size and maturity of forward contracts up to $25 million to $50 million and up to 5 to 10 years to acceptable clients in the major currencies.

In addition, both channels of the long-date foreign exchange market have access to foreign exchange brokers. Brokers exist in major financial centers and arrange enormous volumes of spot foreign exchange transactions for dealers. While some forward currency transactions are arranged by brokers, they tend to be small (under $5 million), with a short maturity (one year or less) and only in the major currencies (U.S. dollar, Canadian dollar, sterling, Swiss franc, and German mark). Actually, the dealing rooms of a few of the large international banks serve as more of a back-up source of long-date currency cover to the corporate finance departments and to the dealing rooms of smaller banks than do the foreign exchange brokers. This points out an interesting interrelationship between the role of the dealing room of the large international banks and the corporate finance groups: The latter often rely on the former to assist in filling the need for counterpositions, and the former are essential to the increased ease and flexibility now available in long-date currency cover. But the dealing rooms themselves are not adapted to the need for tailored positions, nor are they likely to be able to handle the diversity in size and maturities of many swaps and forward contracts. Hence, both channels will continue to be needed to accommodate the routine and special demand for long-date currency cover.

Market Practices

The financial intermediaries operating in the market have found that an inquiry to potential clients often creates an awareness of potential applications of long-date currency cover in the client's asset or liability portfolio. Because of the legal, accounting, and financial complexities of many applications and instruments and the worldwide network of contacts required for success, not all intermediaries have developed the expertise necessary to operate in this market. Long-date currency transactions require extensive international relationships and are generally linked to other business normally conducted by investment or commercial bankers. Those intermediaries that have participated in long-date foreign exchange arrangements have generally prospered and have found that long-date currency applications have led to other types of merchant banking business with their clients.

Since most all the available long-date foreign exchange instruments are similar regarding the foreign currency exposure of each party, an intermediary could negotiate one side as, say, a currency swap and the other as a back-to-back loan. Most other combinations are also possible. Moreover, an international bank could package alternate positions regarding size and timing together with its own foreign currency asset and liability position and take a short-term exposure on a long-date instrument until it was able to lay it off in another long-date transaction. The bank could protect itself against foreign exchange risk by offsetting its exposure in the short-term forward market. The remaining exposure to interest rate risk, one quite normal for banks, can be managed by movements in its own asset or liability portfolio or in the urgency with which it is willing to negotiate concessions in pending offsetting long-date deals with clients or other financial intermediaries.

A final note on the development of the long-date foreign exchange market seems warranted in terms of the ambitious forecasts made earlier. As the flexibility of the market improves due to its increased size and assumption of principal positions by intermediaries, the need for a full-fledged market maker should become apparent soon and be implemented. Some say that this function is now fulfilled in a limited way by the dealing rooms of a few large international banks. When the demand by intermediaries for more rapid access to long-date foreign exchange positions in a larger number of currencies becomes sufficiently regular, a long-date foreign exchange market maker will appear to breach the gap in a matter of time and with a little initiative. At that point long-date currency quotations will become more than just indications of price, and the former barterlike market in the long-date currency will have been transformed into a more fully operable and complete financial market as we know them in other applications. Much progress has been made in recent years in achieving such a market. The continued growth that is expected in long-date currency cover will unquestionably provide the needed impetus for full market status in all major currencies by the late 1980s.

Footnotes

[1] J.L. Hilley, C.R. Beidleman, and J.A. Greenleaf, "Why There is No 'Long' Forward Market in Foreign Exchange," *Euromoney* (January 1981), vol. 22, no. 1, Table 4.

[2] Ibid., Table 4.

[3] Federal Reserve Bank of New York, "Summary of Results of U.S. Foreign Exchange Market Turnover Survey Conducted in April 1983," and Press Release No. 1550 dated September 7, 1983.

[4] J.L. Hilley et al., op. cit.

Chapter 12

The Conceptual Basis
for Coupon Swaps

INTRODUCTION

Recall that a currency swap represents an exchange of two currencies on day one with the agreement to re-exchange them at the maturity of the swap at a predetermined exchange rate. Similarly, a coupon or interest rate swap is the exchange of a coupon payment or periodic interest obligation on a bond with a given configuration, say, a floating interest payment that is tied to the London Interbank Offer Rate (LIBOR) as its basis, for a coupon obligation with a different configuration, say, fixed, or fluctuating on a different variable-rate basis. In coupon swaps the principal is not exchanged; only the interest obligations are swapped.

This development of the swapping of coupon or interest rate obligations has enabled financial managers to apply well-known portfolio management techniques to the liability side of the balance sheet as well as to their asset positions. It provides the flexibility to the management of interest rate risk that currency swaps provided to the management of foreign exchange risk. Through the use of coupon swaps many of the concepts of modern liability management that have recently become available to financial managers of financial institutions can now also be extended to nonfinancial corporations.

Just as the choices available among alternative types of short-term purchased funds currently used to finance banks and financial institutions have increased their flexibility, coupon swaps provide means of arranging and rearranging the long-date funding of financial and nonfinancial companies to better match their financial requirements.

As we explore these intriguing possibilities in this chapter, we examine the nature of coupon risk, the financial characteristics of a coupon swap, and the configuration of cash flows of potential users.

COUPON RISK

The concept of coupon risk is closely related to a broader phenomenon known as interest rate risk. In its truest sense *interest rate risk* is the risk or uncertainty associated with the course of interest rates. Although periods of exceptional stability have not existed for decades, U.S. interest rates in recent years have become far more volatile. This has been primarily due to a major policy change announced by the Federal Reserve Board in October 1979. At that time the Fed announced that it planned to target its money management operations on the monetary aggregates rather than on the level of interest rates. As a result of that change in policy, movements in rates have become much more volatile than they were previously.

This change in Fed policy, coupled with the high inflation rates in the earlier portion of the period since 1979, have resulted in heightened volatility in interest rates and, hence, in exceedingly high levels of interest rate risk. In terms of its impact on financial management and its effect on a firm's profits and residual cash flows, this change ranks closely with the adoption of floating exchange rates over fixed exchange rates in 1973. The difficulties that each of these watershed events has imposed on financial managers regarding the increased uncertainty associated with changes in exchange rates and interest rates have been addressed by various means, including currency cover and coupon cover, respectively.

Whereas interest rate risk deals with the uncertainty in the course of interest rates, coupon risk is used to focus on the impact of changes in interest rates on the cash flows and market values of borrowers and lenders that employ contractually determined or fixed income securities. These effects are also more commonly referred to as *reinvestment rate risk* and *price risk*. Additional dimensions of coupon risk are concerned with which side of an investment instrument a player is on (e.g., borrower or lender). This consideration is necessary because what would be a favorable outcome to one party due to a given change in rates could be an unfavorable result for the other.

The Borrower's View

Accepting the prospect that interest rates will continue to fluctuate, we direct our attention first to the impact of changes in interest rates on fixed-income securities of various maturities. Basically, the longer the maturity of a fixed-income security, the longer the period until the principal or some part of it must be repaid, and the longer the period over which the level of interest payments are held rigid and fixed. Thus from the standpoint of a borrower, a long-date bond would lock-in an interest cost over a long period and would delay repayment or defer amortization of principal. Borrowers who have stable, long-term cash flow or profit expectations, such as might be expected from investment of the borrowed funds in manufacturing or distribution facilities, may demonstrate a strong preference for such long-term, fixed-cost capital. A necessary proviso, of course, is that the aftertax expected return on the investment projects exceed the overall aftertax cost of capital. Thus, by locking in a positive spread of their expected return in excess of their expected cost of funds across a long investment horizon, these players have properly matched both the maturity and the yield versus the cost of their assets and liabilities. For such firms a substantial fraction of their assets are long-lived, and they can tolerate the rigidity of fixed interest cost over the expected lives of their underlying fixed assets.

Others that borrow funds to finance shorter term assets or assets with yields subject to change may choose to avoid having their interest cost fixed over long periods of time. They prefer the flexibility of refinancing in the short-term at the current rate of interest. Borrowers who view interest rates as being cyclically high and anticipate a subsequent decline in rates would also fall into this category. Such borrowers could obtain the flexibility they desire by financing with short-term debt and rolling the debt over each three or six months at the market rates that prevail at the time of refunding. Alternatively, if such a borrower wished to avoid the uncertainty and nuisance of this requirement to refinance its short-term debt continually, it could establish a line of credit at a bank and pay the appropriate administered market rate of interest (i.e., prime or LIBOR plus some risk premium). Or it might source its funds using floating-rate term notes where the interest rate is reset each three or six months based upon some predetermined formula related to short-term market rates. In any of these cases, the borrower has obtained the flexibility of paying a floating-rate for its finance based upon current market rates and has avoided the funding rigidity associated with long-term fixed rates of interest.

The market valuation of a fixed income security like a bond or note also fluctuates in response to changes in market rates of interest. The direction of the change in value is inverse to the direction of the change in interest rates.

199

Thus, an increase in the market rate of interest would cause the market value of a debt instrument to fall, and vice versa. The magnitude of the change in market value of a fixed-income security for a given change in market rate is directly, but not linearly, related to the maturity of the security. Thus, market values of long-date debt instruments tend to fluctuate a great deal more than market values of short-date instruments for a given change in the level of interest rates.

The financial mechanics require that, if interest rates go up from the time of issue, the market value of the debt falls, and vice versa. However, if borrowers elect to continue to service the debt until maturity, their principal may not be affected. The major economic effect to the borrowers will occur if the debt issue has a sinking fund. Under these conditions, if interest rates have risen since the time of issue, the borrowers may be able to profit from a periodic retirement of debt at market prices below the debt's par value or principal. Furthermore, if the issuers have sufficient liquidity to retire the issues or choose to execute an equity for debt swap or other type of defeasance of the debt, they may be able to augment income by effectively retiring the debt at its below par, market value. On the other hand, if rates go down, the borrowers may, within the limitations set forth in their debt agreement, consider refinancing at the lower current market rates. Certain duplicative costs are associated with refinancing debt issues that preclude their application in cases where interest rate changes have not been significant or when the current period to maturity becomes rather short.

In summary the impact of coupon risk regarding financing costs can be managed effectively by borrowers by properly matching the maturity of their liabilities to the maturity of their assets. The impact of price risk on borrowers is not terribly significant and often operates in their favor. We turn now to the impact of coupon risk on investors and focus on the uncertainty of interest flows and market values for various periods to maturity.

The Investor's View

From the point of view of an investor, the dual dimensions of coupon risk can, unless properly managed, have extremely serious implications as interest rates change. For one, the market value of a fixed income security moves in the opposite direction to the change in interest rate, and the magnitude of the change increases with the maturity of the security. This is the risk of principal or price risk faced by investors. This price risk on long-term debt instruments is much more significant to investors than to borrowers. We see this significance surface in the potential adverse impact on long-term securities if investors are forced to dispose of them following an increase in rates or if they are forced to finance their investment with higher-cost floating-rate funds.

As before, effective asset and liability management involves carefully matching the maturities of assets and liabilities. Thus, life insurance companies and many pension funds with distant liabilities can, in a cavalier fashion, invest in fixed-rate, long-term bonds with little concern for interest rate-induced changes in market values. This carefree attitude is possible because these investors fully intend to hold their assets to maturity to match the maturity of their liabilities or claims.

On the other hand, investors with short-dated liabilities would view long-dated investments with great apprehension because of the potential loss in asset value if interest rates subsequently rose. The potential gain in portfolio value associated with a possible decline in rates receives little attention by prudent investors when the same investment strategies also present serious loss possibilities. As a result investors with short-dated liabilities prefer short-term or repriceable instruments for their portfolios. Contrariwise, investors with long-dated claims prefer higher-yielding, long-term instruments through which they can lock-in known interest returns over a long period and set up principal receipts that approximate the maturity of their claims.

The second dimension of coupon risk to an investor deals with the risk involved with the reinvestment rate that may be earned on the repaid principal. Here the impact of the risk runs counter to the risk of principal. A long-dated bond provides a known fixed rate of interest over the life of the bond, whereas the owner of a short-dated instrument faces the risk of reinvestment at more frequent intervals. Given that interest rates are expected to continue to fluctuate, investors in short-dated instruments cannot be assured of what their interest returns will be beyond the maturity of each of their holdings. To the extent that investors depend on their investment income for their support or otherwise rely on investment income to support some enterprise, this risk can be quite serious. For instance, if a college endowment fund is totally invested in short-term instruments and rates fall, the reduced level of income may be insufficient to provide such necessities as basic maintenance, faculty salaries, and student aid, all of which were expected. Management of reinvestment rate coupon risk for such investors may be accomplished by holding a strip or sequence of medium-term instruments so that only a few mature in each year, thereby reducing the impact of reinvestment at a different current rate on the total income provided by the portfolio.

While some investors are averse to the risk of changing reinvestment rates, others prefer it. Those in the latter category would be investors that have liabilities that are also being continually repriced. Notable examples of this type of investor are commercial banks that face variable rate funding costs where some of the rates may change on a daily basis as market rates change. Investors of this type would prefer to hold matched variable rate assets whose returns also fluctuate with market rates but at a sufficient spread above funding costs to provide the necessary net interest margin to the bank.

The Function of Coupon Swaps

As market participants seek to match the maturity of the asset and liability cash flows that redound from both interest and principal payments or receipts on fixed-income securities, players tend to favor either long-date or short-date instruments. As these characteristics of market participants become sorted out, players tend to seek the maturity of financing or investing that suits their needs. However, because of certain market anomalies, attaching funds with undesired maturities is often easier than obtaining funding with preferred maturity characteristics. Moreover, some anomalies have been large enough to provide a significant cost advantage to those who move to breach the market imperfection to obtain a more preferable form of finance. The instrument available for this manoeuvre is called the *coupon swap*. We turn next to the driving financial characteristics of a coupon swap and then focus on the nature of the cash flows of typical users.

FINANCIAL CHARACTERISTICS OF COUPON SWAPS

A coupon or interest-rate swap is a simple extension of the concept of a currency swap. In a currency swap the parties exchanged a given (and fixed) amount of national currencies on day one and re-exchanged the currencies at the maturity of the swap. In a currency swap each party bore the obligation to re-exchange the currencies at the contractual exchange rate regardless of the future spot rate. Similarly, in a coupon swap the parties agree to bear the obligation to service the interest cost on a common principal amount with the same maturity but a different basis for interest determination. Coupon swaps generally exchange a fixed-interest obligation for a floating-rate or variable-rate interest obligation. Floating versus floating-rate coupon swaps have also become popular in certain applications and are discussed in Chapter 14.

Note that in a straight coupon swap, the principal is in the same currency and is not swapped. Only the debt service or coupon is swapped.

Hence, the principal can be new or existing debt and in some sense is only notional to the transaction. As a result principal is not at risk, and the need for credit intermediation is significantly lessened. Moreover, in straight coupon swaps, only one currency is involved, removing the uncertainty associated with changes in exchange rates.

The risk that is incurred or removed in a coupon swap is the risk associated with changes in interest rates (i.e., coupon risk). Floating-rate payers and receivers encounter a relatively short maturity until they face a possible revision of contract interest rates and incur the coupon risk associated with short-term instruments. On the other hand, fixed-rate payers and receivers are locked into a fixed coupon rate over the term of the swap and incur the coupon risk earlier identified with term instruments. Therefore, depending upon the characteristics of players' underlying operating cash flows, they may be natural floating-rate payers or natural fixed-rate payers, if borrowers, or natural floating-rate receivers or natural fixed-rate receivers, if investors.

CHARACTERISTICS OF COUPON SWAP PARTICIPANTS

Whether a potential participant to a coupon swap is a natural floating-rate or fixed-rate payer or receiver depends upon its underlying operating cash flows. In classifying players in the coupon swap market, we look first at natural fixed-rate payers followed by natural floating-rate payers. We then direct our attention to fixed-rate and floating-rate receivers.

Natural Fixed-Rate Payers

Natural fixed-rate payers are entities whose minimum cash flows are reasonably predictable regardless of the level of interest rates. A reliable minimum level of revenue and net income sufficient to provide a margin of safety necessary to service fixed-rate debt is essential to the successful placement of fixed-rate debt.

A large class of natural fixed-rate payers (borrowers) are manufacturing and distribution firms in the developed countries. The cash inflows to these firms arise from their manufacturing and/or distribution activities. Although the cash flows may be cyclical, they can be forecast with some degree of assurance. Moreover, if the borrowing firms had not previously engaged in excessive debt or financial leverage, they would normally be expected to generate sufficient cash inflows to service their fixed-rate debt annually.

203

In addition to their assumed ability to service a moderate volume of fixed-rate debt, many managements of production and distribution firms prefer fixed-rate debt because of the assurance that it provides to their cost of capital and to the capital investment decision process. For instance if a capital investment in production or distribution facilities is expected to produce an aftertax return of 14 percent, a firm may be quite willing to undertake the project if its overall cost of capital is 12 percent after taxes. Such an aftertax cost of capital may have been based on a fixed-rate debt component that has a pretax cost of, say, 14 percent and approximately 7 percent after taxes and an aftertax cost of equity of, say, 17 percent. This favorable deployment of financial leverage would be beneficial to the stockholders provided the capital cost was fixed. On the other hand if the pretax debt cost floated up to, say, 22 percent, driving the overall cost of capital above the 14 percent earned by the fixed-asset investment, the elevated interest bill would erode earnings, and both management and shareholders would be disappointed. Thus, fixed-rate debt with predictable cost is desirable for many borrowers.

This preference for fixed-rate debt comes through with even stronger force for one group of borrowers that have done extensive financing in past years. The gas and electric utilities have a special interest in the predictable cost features of fixed-rate debt because of the impact of regulators on a utility's performance. When a utility submits a request to a regulatory agency for a rate increase, the regulators need to know the utility's costs, a difficult procedure regarding interest costs unless rates are fixed.

Another major class of natural fixed-rate payers are financial institutions with large portfolios of fixed-rate assets. During the period of rapid escalation of interest rates after the change in Federal Reserve Board policy in 1979, many thrifts and savings-and-loan associations (S&L) suffered serious earnings erosion. This phenomenon, frequently referred to as the *S&L syndrome,* was the result of extensive maturity mismatch of assets and liabilities. At the outset the asset portfolios of thrifts and S&Ls were largely filled with fixed-rate mortgages. When market interest rates rose and deregulation eliminated many of the preferential ceilings on rates paid to depositors, thrifts faced a grave profit squeeze, which caused erosion of reserves, near failures, and numerous financial restructurings.

There are two potential solutions to this problem of maturity mismatch. One is to shift the current portfolio of fixed-rate assets (mortgages) to variable-rate instruments. The other is to swap the extant stock of variable-rate or floating-rate liabilities for fixed-rate debt with a low enough coupon to allow a reasonable net interest margin. Of course, some combination of the two would also be appropriate. Although much effort has been underway to write variable-rate mortgages and other floating-rate assets have been sought out, this strategy does not change the payment features of outstanding fixed-rate instruments. Hence, the process of shifting to variable-rate assets may be slow and somewhat unpredictable. On the other hand with the reduction in market interest rates since 1982, the swapping of a floating-rate interest obligation for a fixed-rate commitment represents a rapid means of shifting the maturity of liabilities to match the maturity of assets more properly. Moreover, the existence of a major market anomaly can help reduce the cost of fixed-rate money below that obtainable by a thrift directly in the fixed-rate market.

Many of the smaller U.S. banks have also suffered from the S&L syndrome and should be included in the group of natural fixed-rate payers. Because the size of their maturity mismatch is modest relative to many of the larger players, the coupon swap requirements of individual small banks and thrifts may have to be packaged together in some way to accommodate a larger coupon swap counterparty. Such assembling or syndication of coupon swap interest has been performed by market intermediaries as the coupon swap market has become more standardized or productized.

Another set of international natural fixed-rate payers is the national agencies of certain developed countries that have difficulty accessing fixed-rate funds because of local capital market or regulatory constraints. Examples here would include various national agencies of the Italian or Spanish governments. These agencies prefer fixed-rate debt with predictable debt service for planning purposes, but they cannot readily access fixed-rate money in their currencies. The relatively protracted high inflation rates experienced in these countries have made term loans something of an endangered species in their currencies. These agencies, with sovereign guarantees, have been able to access floating-rate Eurocurrency debt, which, because of their preference for fixed-rate debt, they have been inclined to swap with natural floating-rate payers.

The foregoing major types of players have been instrumental in launching the concept of coupon swaps. Undoubtedly other classes of natural fixed-rate payers will come to the fore as the coupon swap market becomes more institutionalized. Next, we examine their natural counterparties, those that have underlying operating cash flows that make them natural payers of floating or short-term market rates of interest.

Natural Floating-Rate Payers

Whereas natural fixed-rate payers are primarily concerned with locking in a cost of funds across some borrowing horizon and have relatively reliable cash inflows with which to service the fixed-rate debt, natural floating-rate payers tend to be more sensitive to changes in short-term market rates of interest. This sensitivity is found mainly in large money center, international banks that have large portfolios of floating-rate assets. The interest rates on the assets held in their loan portfolios may be indexed to U.S. prime rates, LIBOR, or other short-term market rates. An income stream tied to short-term market rates, which should be matched with liabilities whose interest cost is similarly indexed, results. Hence, we find a preference of large, international, money center banks for floating-rate liabilities.

The demand for floating-rate liabilities by money center banks had surfaced initially on the part of non-U.S. Eurobanks. The large European banks have participated actively in extending Eurodollar credits to borrowers where the interest rates are based on LIBOR. Because of deposit structures abroad, sourcing sufficient variable-rate deposits to fund the Eurobank's assets tied to a LIBOR or other market index has become difficult. Hence, the large, European, money market banks sought variable-rate funds in large amounts and became the natural floating-rate payers to serve as counterparties to natural fixed-rate payers in a coupon swap.

When coupon swaps were first introduced in spring 1982, the floating-rate payers were primarily European, money market banks. Soon afterward the large Japanese international banks entered the picture and have since become a major factor in the supply of fixed-rate funds to the coupon swap market. In fact, of the coupon swap volume undertaken in 1983, Japanese banks have been estimated to exceed the European banks in participation. The rationale in each case was the same (viz, to procure floating-rate liabilities to be used to fund the bank's floating-rate assets).

Large U.S. money center banks have been slower to participate directly in coupon swaps for their own account primarily because of the large availability of floating-rate deposit liabilities that accompanied deregulation of financial institutions since coupon swaps were launched. More recently, however, some large U.S. money market banks have participated in coupon swaps as floating-rate payers to augment their domestic sources of floating-rate funds. U.S. bank participants are also driven by the cost savings inherent in the coupon swap transaction that enables them to create cheaper floating-rate debt than is otherwise available. In a contrary vein, as we shall later expound, U.S. international money center banks also find use of the coupon swap market appropriate to procure fixed-rate funds at a cost below equivalent term U.S. government bonds (treasuries) without putting demand pressure on fixed-rate markets.

The role of international money center banks as natural floating-rate payers has been paramount in the organization and early development of the coupon swap market. In fact, for quite some time a bank had represented at least one side of nearly every coupon swap. This nearly universal posture has changed, however, and now coupon swaps are being done without a bank as one of the players. Moreover, because the international money center banks have placed so much demand on the private placement, fixed-rate market in Eurocurrencies, rates have increased relative to fixed-rates paid by potential counterparties, reducing the advantage of the market anomaly that initially made coupon swaps so attractive.

Despite the fact that the presence of large international banks as parties to coupon swap transactions has somewhat diminished, the market has continued to prosper. Other natural fixed-rate payers have become attracted to the cost advantages of a coupon swap and have caused this to occur in part. High-quality corporations' swapping new or existing fixed-rate debt service for floating-rate payments indexed to LIBOR has not been uncommon. The AAA- or AA-rated borrower can exploit a market anomaly by funding its side of a transaction at prime credit (A_1/P_1) commercial paper rates, which are typically 75 to 100 basis points lower than the LIBOR-based rate that it receives. This results in a reduction in fixed-rate funding costs of, say, 75 basis points and provides fixed-rate funds below equivalent term treasuries.

A final component of natural floating-rate payers is that group of borrowers who have fixed-rate debt outstanding and prefer to convert it to floating-rate debt. This group would include those who have low coupon fixed-rate debt and, by swapping, could obtain a very low floating-rate cost of funds. That is, if a 5 percent fixed-rate coupon were swapped when equivalent risk fixed-rate rates were, say, 13 percent, this issuer could expect to pay a floating-rate of nearly 8 percent under LIBOR. If LIBOR were to drop below 8 percent, a negative interest rate to the floating-rate payer could be produced.

Unfixing of fixed-rate debt could be desirable for other reasons as well. The operational nature of a player's cash flows might have changed such that they feel more comfortable with floating-rate debt. Or a player's asset or liability structure may have been reassessed suggesting a shift in the nature of its liabilities. The newly found application of liability management concepts on the right-hand side of the balance sheet may suggest the unwinding of a given long-date obligation. This flexibility is now available to finance managers and introduces a presently indeterminate volume of supply of floating-rate payers.

Credit Risk on Coupon Swaps

For the most part coupon swaps have been arranged between natural fixed-rate payers and natural floating-rate payers. In some cases a credit intermediary might be necessary because of the unknown credit risk of the parties. However, in most cases where a U.S. bank was one of the parties to the coupon swap, the need for a credit intermediary was removed. The reasons for this are that (1) most banks are sufficiently creditworthy to satisfy most nonbank players and (2) banks have adequate credit-rating capabilities to assess and assume the credit risk of their counterparties. Those foreign banks that are not prepared to evaluate the credit risk of a corporate U.S. or other counterparty are exceptions.. In these cases a domestic bank may be engaged to take the credit risk for the foreign bank.

From a credit viewpoint, note that in no case is principal at risk. Each party maintains the obligation to repay the principal and interest on its own debt when due. Hence, the credit risk reduces mainly to the willingness and ability of each counterparty to honor its chosen variety of debt service. And even here the risk is not the total risk of full debt service but only the risk of the *difference* between the periodic floating-rate payment and the fixed-rate payment. A related risk in the event of default is the risk of refinancing or reinvesting the fixed-rate principal at the, then, current rates. This component of risk is evaluated more fully in case examples provided in Chapter 13.

Natural Fixed-Rate Receivers

In most cases coupon swaps have been put in place with natural fixed-rate payers servicing fixed-rate debt that is owed by borrowers who prefer floating-rate obligations but have been able more handily to access fixed-rate funds. On the other side, natural floating-rate payers serviced new or existing floating-rate borrowers that prefer the certainty of fixed-rate debt service but are unable to place fixed-rate debt at reasonable rates. In addition, one more class of market participants is natural fixed-rate receivers.

The natural fixed-rate receivers are well-known in the capital markets and are the primary sources of fixed-rate funds. Institutions such as life insurance companies, pension funds, wealthy investors, and managed trust accounts are notable examples of natural fixed-rate receivers. Although most such funds find their way into original fixed-rate issues, natural fixed-rate receivers can become quite interested in taking down floating-rate instruments at market rates to be subsequently swapped for above market fixed-rate coupons at no incremental risk to principal. This application of coupon swaps entails an asset hedge, which is discussed in detail in Chapter 13.

Natural Floating-Rate Receivers

Investors sometimes park funds in short-term instruments because they think interest rates will subsequently rise, at which time they will move the money to higher-interest fixed-rate instruments. Because many floating-rate instruments are of intermediate-term maturity, say four to ten years, there is some credit risk if used for this purpose, and other reasons must be sought for their demand. The primary preference for floating-rate income is from investors who fund their assets with variable-cost funds (i.e., funds whose costs are indexed to some base rate such as LIBOR, prime, treasury bills, certificates of deposit, or commercial paper). If such investors can lock-in a reasonable net interest margin or spread between their return on floating-rate instruments and their floating cost of funds, they can enjoy a positive return at the end of the day. Such investors are typically the funds managers of financial institutions, especially smaller commercial banks and thrifts.

This strong preference for floating-rate income represents an alternative that smaller banks and thrifts have to obtaining fixed-rate finance in their attempt to match the maturity structures of their assets and liabilities. Since the supply of floating-rate assets has been more institutionalized and accessible than the supply of fixed-rate liabilities, most astute banks and thrifts have sought out floating-rate assets in their attempt to manage the interest sensitivity of their institutions.

The other large component of floating-rate receivers is the large international money center banks. These banks source their funds in the interbank market at short-term market rates and want to place floating-rate assets on their books, usually indexed to LIBOR. These banks represent the primary source of funds to the floating-rate borrowers that enter into coupon swaps to obtain fixed-rate finance.

Our discussion of the characteristics of coupon swap participants and the conceptual basis for coupon swaps is complete. We turn next to an examination of the instruments, pricing, and applications of coupon swap agreements. As we can see, coupon swaps can be used to improve the match between the parties to a debt contract based upon their underlying preferences.

Chapter 13

Coupon Swap Instruments, Pricing and Applications

INTRODUCTION

In this chapter we continue our discussion of coupon swaps turning our attention first to the nature of the instruments used and the financial relationships between the parties to a swap. Because a single credit market anomaly is so dominant as the driving force behind most coupon swaps, it is examined in detail, and a typical application is presented. Next follow some observations regarding the rapid institutionalization of the coupon swap market and the way in which contracts are priced. The chaper concludes with additional examples of general applications of coupon cover.

INSTRUMENTS FOR COUPON COVER

The instruments used to obtain coupon cover are similar to those that have been developed for currency cover. Since the instrument development process had already occurred for currency cover applications, reinventing a set of parallel instruments for coupon cover was unnecessary. As a result only the most refined and adaptable instrument that was developed for a stream of cash flows has been transferred to coupon cover applications. This instrument is the coupon swap, which provides for the mutual assumption of each counterparty's coupon or interest obligation. Although a notional principal amount is necessary to effect the coupon swap, the principal amount is identical for each party and in the same currency. Hence, nothing would be accomplished to also swap the principal sum. This feature considerably reduces the risk exposure of the counterparties because no principal is at risk. Only the differential in interest streams is exposed.

The mechanics of a typical coupon swap call for an international money center Eurobank to go to the fixed-rate debt market and issue term dollar Eurobonds, and a lesser quality, say BBB-rated, U.S. industrial firm to go to the floating-rate debt market and borrow floating-rate funds for the same term. Simultaneously with both placements, the bank and the company agree to exchange each other's interest obligations. This transaction is illustrated in Figure 13–1.

In this example, the company pays the bank's fixed-rate interest payments to the bank, and the bank makes floating-rate interest payments to the

Figure 13–1 Coupon swap between a bank and a manufacturing or distribution company

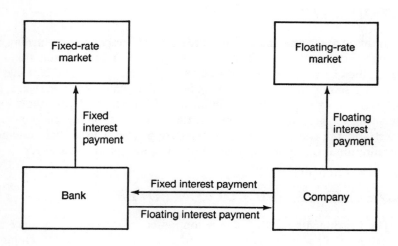

company which are used to offset the company's payments on its floating-rate loan. In the event the parties require intermediation of each other's credit risk, an intermediary bank is brought in to assume credit risk for payments to and from both parties. This additional participant is shown in Figure 13–2.

Figure 13–2 Coupon swap between a bank and a manufacturing or distribution company with credit intermediation

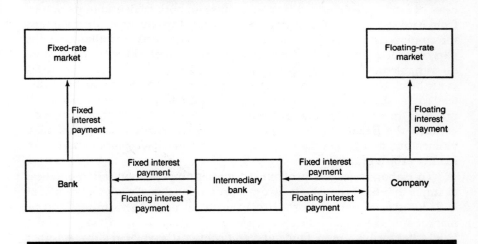

The documentation for a coupon swap is similar to that of a currency swap and can be contained in as few as five or six pages. The concepts employed have been so standardized that coupon swaps now trade as standard products of investment, and some commercial bankers see coupon swaps as similar to other standardized financial commodities. Moreover, their prices will undoubtedly be found on routine quotation devices like the Reuters quotation screen soon.

We will shortly discuss the way in which coupon swaps are priced to lend themselves to such standardized treatment. That discussion depends upon an understanding of a dominant market anomaly that underlies the huge volume of coupon swap transactions that have taken place. Hence, we turn next to this foremost anomaly responsible for coupon swaps and then to a discussion of the ways in which they are priced.

213

THE CREDIT MARKET ANOMALY AND
A TYPICAL TRANSACTION

The single driving force behind virtually all coupon swaps in the early stages of their application was the differential risk premium attached to credit risk in the floating- and fixed-rate debt markets, respectively. This market anomaly is the result of the fact that term bond investors such as insurance companies, pension funds, and other institutional investors demand an increasing risk premium for increasingly large credit risk. In some sense this premium is related to their protracted commitment of funds at fixed rates of interest. In contrast weaker credits can borrow floating-rate money from banks at only a modest risk premium over top-quality credits. Perhaps the continuous repricing of interest payments and closer surveillance on the part of lenders accounts for their willingness to accept a lower-risk premium on variable-rate loans, or, perhaps lenders' desire for floating-rate assets contributes to a greater tolerance for credit risk than found in fixed-rate lenders. A characteristic upward sloping yield curve may also explain this practice. In any event this differential pricing of incremental credit risk between the fixed- and floating-rate term debt markets has produced a momentous market anomaly, which the deployment of coupon swaps can readily arbitrage.

To elaborate on this pronounced market imperfection, a hypothetical example that has been adapted from a promotional package by a prominent U.S. investment banking firm is convenient to use.[1] The arbitrage of this market anomaly enables many companies to execute coupon swaps to raise fixed-rate, medium-term funds at significant cost savings relative to other fixed-rate financing alternatives and money center banks to raise floating-rate funds at below market rates. A coupon swap opportunity is created by the fact that the floating-rate market generally requires a smaller premium for credit risk than does the fixed-rate market.

Two parties are needed to complete the transaction: a borrower (the company), which is a natural fixed-rate payer, and a stronger credit (typically a large bank), which is a natural floating-rate payer. Relative to the company, the bank could borrow at an incremental advantage in the fixed-rate market versus the floating-rate market. An example of the relative advantage is provided in Figure 13–3. In this example, the bank's borrowing cost is 150 basis points lower than the company's borrowing cost in the fixed-rate market but only 50 basis points lower than the company's in the floating-rate market. This 100 basis point difference in incremental borrowing costs between the two markets creates a credit arbitrage opportunity that can be shared to help both sides reduce their respective borrowing costs.

Under the terms of such a hypothetical coupon swap, the bank would

Figure 13–3　An interest rate swap takes advantage of a credit arbitrage opportunity

	Actual Fixed-Rate Cost of Funds*	Actual Floating-Rate Cost of Funds
Company	12.5%	LIBOR + 0.5%
Bank	11.0	LIBOR
Premium	1.5%	0.5%

1.0%
Credit arbitrage opportunity

*Not including issuance expenses.

Source: Goldman, Sachs & Co.

access the fixed-rate market at 11 percent and pass this rate on to the company. The company would access the floating-rate market at London Interbank Order Rate (LIBOR) plus 0.5 percent and pass an improved rate of LIBOR less 0.25 percent on to the bank. From the company's perspective, 150 basis points would be saved by effectively borrowing at the bank's fixed rate, but 75 basis points would be given back by receiving 75 basis points below the actual cost for the floating-rate funds. The net result is a 75 basis point saving in fixed-rate borrowing cost to the company. Conversely, the bank saves 25 basis points versus its alternative floating-rate funding cost. Both parties share in the 100 basis point credit arbitrage opportunity to reduce their respective funding costs via the swap. In addition to the cost savings, other advantages of a coupon swap to the company include the absence of a requirement for filing with regulatory agencies or rating agencies, straightforward documentation, and the availability of an alternate source of fixed-rate capital when combined with floating-rate borrowing.

Other details of the investment banker's representative presentation are provided in Figures 13–4 and 13–5. Figure 13–4 describes the transactions by each party before the coupon swap. It also describes the coupon payments actually made by each party as a result of the swap. This delineation of

215

Figure 13–4 Interest rate swap Illustration of a $100 million seven-year transaction

---

Before

- Bank issues $100 million 7-year Eurobond with 11% annual coupon and issuance expenses of 2%

- Company obtains $100 million floating-rate funds at six-month LIBOR + 0.5%

After

- Bank pays six-month LIBOR less 0.25% to company on $100 million swap amount

- Company pays 11.00% coupon on bank's $100 million Eurobond plus issuance expenses and swap fees*

---

*Includes 0.5% swap fee and 0.15% intermediary bank fee if required.

Source: Goldman, Sachs & Co.

before-and-after payments clearly illustrates the impact of the swap on the ultimate cost of fixed- and floating-rate funds to each respective borrower. It also indicates the typical levels of frictional transaction costs (i.e., fixed-rate issuance expenses of 2 percent on a $100 million seven-year Eurobond placement, 0.5 percent swap fee to the arranging banker, and 0.15 percent annual fee for assumption of credit risk if required).

Figure 13–5 presents calculations of the all-in cost of funds to the fixed-rate payer. As shown, the fixed-rate payer is required to pay all the placement and arrangement fees plus the fee for credit intermediation. This hypothetical cost of 12.125 percent per annum on a semiannual basis should be compared with its alternative cost of fixed-rate money. In the present illustration this alternative cost is 12.5 percent plus placement fees or approximately 12.56 percent on a semiannual basis. This represents an all-in saving to the fixed-rate payer of approximately 0.43 percent, to be compared with the 0.25 percent saving to the floating-rate payer. As is evident in these calculations, approximately 0.32 percent of the 1.0 percent interest differential available from the original market anomaly was lost to the intermediation and credit assumption process. This friction would be reduced, of course, by 0.15 percent if the credit intermediation function were not required.

Figure13-5 All-In cost of funds for a $100 million seven-year transaction

All-In Cost of Funds	=	All-In Cost of Fixed-Rate Debt	+	Floating Interest Differential	+	Intermediary Bank Fee
						11.00% annual payment

All-in cost of fixed-rate debt

Bank's Eurobond coupon	1.875%
Front-end Eurobond spread	0.125%
Front-end Eurobond expense	0.50%
Swap fee	
Total front-end costs	2.500%
All-in cost of fixed-rate debt	11.540% annual basis
	11.225% semiannual basis

Floating Interest Differential

Floating interest payment paid by borrower	6-month LIBOR+ 0.5 %
Floating interest payment received by borrower	6-month LIBOR– 0.25%
Floating interest differential	0.75% semiannual basis

Intermediary Bank Fee

Provision for intermediary bank fee	0.15%

All-In Cost of Funds   12.125% semiannual basis

Source: Goldman, Sachs & Co.

A flowchart of the periodic interest payments is presented in Figure 13-6. This flowchart follows the same format as Figures 13-1 and 13-2 and illustrates a representative percentage interest costs of the payments made by each of the parties in this hypothetical example. The savings reflected on Figure 13-6 relate to alternative interest flows faced by the parties. However, since the company faces all of the transactions costs of the deal, refer to Figure 13-5 for the determination of its all-in savings that result from the swap.

Figure 13-6   Interest rate swap Illustration

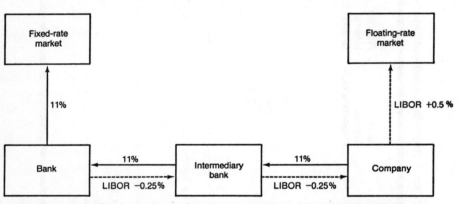

- The company's fixed-rate borrowing costs are reduced by 75 basis points.
- The bank's floating-rate borrowing costs are reduced by 25 basis points.

Source: Goldman, Sachs & Co.

PRICING OF COUPON SWAPS

The example just presented provides a representative set of pricing parameters for coupon swaps. The credit market anomaly is exploited by the strong credit that borrowed fixed-rate funds and the weaker credit that procured floating-rate finance at a lower-risk premium than would have been faced in the fixed-rate market. Coupon payments are then swapped so that each player obtains a below-market rate for the type of funds it prefers. As coupon swaps have moved from a special arrangement to a more productized financial commodity that depends on a structure of interest rates that is in a constant state of flux, pricing coupon swaps relative to some clearly understood dynamic price basis has become convenient. Actually two price bases or thresholds are used in pricing each swap, a fixed-rate basis and a floating-rate basis.

The fixed-rate basis used is typically some spread over term treasury bonds of the same maturity as the instruments being swapped. At the time of this writing, the fixed-rate pricing of a five-year coupon swap was approximately 55 basis points over the current rate on five-year treasury bonds. This basis spread over term treasuries takes into consideration the level and term structure of interest rates at the time of the quotation. The spread also reflects the size of the interest differential between normal risk profiles typically faced by the fixed- and floating-rate credit markets, along with many other factors.

As in the case of any market inefficiency, arbitrage of that inefficiency tends to eliminate its own advantage. Even though the underlying credit market anomaly was initially very deep in this case, Eurobanks have partially sated the fixed-rate Eurobond market from time to time since coupon swaps originally became attractive to them. Moreover, recovery from the recession of 1982 has reduced the fixed-rate credit risk differential faced by BB-rated firms, causing the fixed-rate basis spread over term treasuries to fluctuate and narrow as the coupon swap market has developed. Subsequently, the spread widened and fluctuated as would be expected in a dynamic market.

Pricing on the floating-rate side can be done off a number of indices or bases. From the outset floating-rate pricing has primarily used LIBOR as its basis. However, banks are also sensitive to returns on short-term treasury bills, and this has also been an acceptable basis for pricing. More than an estimated 80 percent of all coupon swaps index their floating-rates to either LIBOR or treasuries. Other floating-rate bases that have been used are prime, certificates of deposit, and commercial paper. More is said about alternate floating-rate indexing when floating versus floating-rate coupon swaps are covered in Chapter 14.

As we have seen in the foregoing coupon swap example, the floating-rate paid by the bank was 0.25 percent under LIBOR. Typical rates indexed to LIBOR have varied from more than 1 percent below to 0.5 percent above LIBOR. The rate consistent with the above quote of 55 basis points over term treasuries on the fixed-rate side was a zero spread over LIBOR on the floating-rate side.

To understand the full implications of the concept of spread pricing of coupon swaps, yet another arbitrage opportunity available to most strong-credit, natural floating-rate receivers must be studied. This additional arbitrage is based on the fact that commercial paper interest rates available to first quality (A_1/P_1) credits are typically 75 to 100 basis points below LIBOR. Hence, if the natural floating-rate receiver chooses to fund its side of the borrowing in the commercial paper market, it can get a further reduction of, say, 75 basis points below the market rate on fixed-rate coupon swaps. That is, the 55 basis point over term treasuries available to fixed-rate payers could be reduced to a real cost of approximately 20 basis points under term treasuries. This represents cheap fixed-rate financing for AA-rated credits. Whereas some credits with favored names have been able to finance through (below) treasuries in the Eurobond market, similar rates have seldom been directly available to most creditworthy borrowers.

APPLICATIONS OF COUPON COVER

The most popular application of coupon swaps has already been presented. Similar swaps between a strong credit desiring floating-rate finance such as a Eurobank and a weaker-credit industrial borrower desiring fixed-rate funding have accounted for coupon swaps of more than $10 billion annually since their inception in spring 1982. We will not dwell on this type of application other than to stress its prominence. Moreover, a review of the characteristics of coupon swap participants presented in Chapter 12 provides an array of potential applications for using the magic of swaps to tailor the asset or the liability side of the balance sheet to that preferred by a firm's financial management. In this section we provide a modest tally of some of the other applications of fixed- versus floating-rate coupon swaps as applied to both the liability and asset sides of a balance sheet, leaving some more interesting and complex examples of floating- versus floating-rate coupon swaps and combined currency coupon swaps to Chapter 14.

Liability Coupon Swaps

One interesting extension of the typical application of a coupon swap to a natural fixed-rate payer is found in the financing of certain poorly capitalized subsidiaries of a major U.S. financial services company. Because the subsidiaries were poorly capitalized and relatively small, they were unable to borrow long-term fixed-rate funds directly. They could, however, borrow short-term funds from banks. This was done, and the floating-rate coupons were simultaneously swapped for fixed-rate money. In this process the subsidiaries obtained a fixed-rate coupon that approached AAA-quality-credit interest rates. Their counterparties were continental European banks that wanted floating-rate dollar finance in exchange for fixed-rate money, which they obtained in the Eurobond market.

Coupon swaps also find application in many instances where temporary, short-term financing is initially employed to effect some form of permanent arrangement. Examples include leveraged lease transactions, leveraged buy-outs, sale and leaseback transactions, unsecured short-term loans, project financing, and specialized single projects. In many cases these types of activity are initially financed with short-term floating-rate money with the intention to sell fixed-rate debt to convert the funding to a more permanent status. With the advent of fixed- for floating-rate coupon swaps, this conversion can now be accomplished without having to appear directly in the fixed-rate market. And, depending upon the circumstances, the conversion can often be obtained at a lower fixed-rate cost than available in direct term debt.

As the range of coupon swap unit sizes become more continuous and swaps of various sizes become more readily available, banks and other lenders can make use of them to fund fixed-rate loans with variable-rate liabilities. As indicated earlier many players prefer fixed-rate finance to protect themselves and their operating profits from the vagaries of changes in interest rates. On the other hand, banks prefer to put on variable-rate loans to match the interest configuration of their deposit and other floating-rate liabilities.

With the arrival of fixed- for floating-rate coupon swaps, both preferences can be satisfied. That is, coupon swaps of the correct size can serve a bank in much the same way as financial futures have been used to convert floating-rate funds to fixed-rate funds effectively. This could be accomplished by going into the certificate of deposit (CD) market, selling a floating-rate note and then swapping the interest obligation for a fixed-rate contract. Other forms of purchased funds such as short-term repo, short-term CDs, or commercial paper could also be used. What is required is that the swap pricing produce a fixed-rate cost of funds sufficiently below the yield on the fixed-rate loan to provide an adequate net interest margin on the deal. Moreover, more aggressive banks could lock-in their cost on a block of fixed-rate funds obtained by swapping floating-rate money and then proceed to market fixed-rate loans to their commercial and industrial borrowers as a special service to them.

Many other examples of coupon swap applications in a financial or nonfinancial firm's liability management could be adduced. In most cases they would follow a similar theme of more perfectly matching or adapting the characteristics of their liabilities to their underlying cash flows. Instead of extending the list, we turn now to another interesting application of coupon swaps. Although initially developed to assist in liability management, coupon swaps also find application in managing debt instruments held in investors' asset portfolios to better suit the investors' underlying needs to match their expected cash flows. The next section provides two disparate asset management applications and reveals additional elements of the comprehensive aspects of coupon swaps.

Asset Coupon Swaps

A representative portfolio coupon swap can be used to highlight the limited risk features of a coupon swap. In this case a U.S. life insurance company purchased five-year floating-rate CDs in mid-1983 at six-month LIBOR plus 0.25 percent. The life insurance firm preferred term fixed-rate assets where cash flows more nearly coincided with its expected disbursements and where fixed-rate returns could be relied upon to produce assumed returns for policyholders. Thus, the life insurance firm swapped the floating-rate CD interest income with a weak corporate credit. Although it could consider weaker credits without undue fear of loss, the life insurance firm swapped its floating-rate coupon with a BBB-rated industrial firm. Other logical counterparties would be thrift institutions or small banks. The BBB-rated firm used existing floating-rate or short-term debt, or it could have sourced its funds from a bank, relying on the floating-rate interest payments from the life firm to service its floating-rate debt.

Since the BBB-rated firm was interested in fixed-rate debt, it was willing to pay a spread of 300 basis points over five-year treasuries at the time. Five-year treasuries were yielding 10.5 percent, making the fixed-rate payment to the life firm 13.5 percent. In exchange the life insurance firm paid over to the BBB-rated firm its floating-rate interest receipts of 0.25 percent over six-month LIBOR (10 percent at the time) of 10.25 percent in the first interest period. Of course, the six-month LIBOR rate will be reset each six months.

As an advantage the life insurance firm received fixed-rate income at a yield reflecting a BBB-rated credit as if it lent the funds to a BBB-rated firm rather than investing them in a bank-issued floating-rate CD. The BBB-rated firm also enjoyed the benefits of obtaining fixed-rate financing at a time when fixed-rate funds were not otherwise accessible and at a cost that reflected no appreciable increase in its cost of debt capital.

Examining the risk profile of the life firm in this example is noteworthy. First, the risk of principal is always that of the issuer of the CD, a bank in this case, since principal is not swapped in a coupon swap. Therefore, the only risk that the insurance firm is exposed to by the BBB-rated firm is the uncertainty of the BBB-rated firm to remit the required fixed rate interest flows. Even then the level of exposure is only the difference between the 13.5 percent fixed-rate and the 10.25 percent and subsequent floating-rate payments. Moreover, this risk is really an opportunity type of risk (i.e., the risk that the insurance firm may have to reinvest its principal at a lower fixed-rate).

Thus, there is no principal risk and only a small coupon risk based on possible reinvestment at lower rates. As we examine the risk to the life insurance firm further, it becomes clear that the reinvestment rate risk is both symmetric and tends to operate in the favor of the life insurance firm. That is, if interest rates were to go down and the reinvestment rates of return decline, a scenario most likely consistent with a period of economic expansion, when the BBB-rated firm would be least likely to fail or default. Similarly, if rates move higher after an economic recovery, any likely loss due to reinvestment risk becomes nil at the same time that the probability of failure of the lower-credit party becomes greater. Nevertheless, this prospect would cause little concern or detriment to the life insurance firm because reinvestment of the principal would produce higher yields under such conditions. Hence, this asset or portfolio coupon swap permits both parties to obtain the interest characteristics that they prefer, at rates that are mutually attractive and without undue risk to the swapping investor.

In a diametrically opposite application another life insurance company at another time used a coupon swap to exchange some of its illiquid, private placement, fixed-rate assets for floating-rate assets. In this case the counterparty was a bank. Evidently the life insurance company, for asset management reasons, preferred to move into floating-rate assets, or perhaps it engaged in the swap because its view on total floating-rate interest receipts exceeded the fixed-rate receipts, which it gave up. In any event its position regarding the illiquidity of its assets remained unchanged because the portfolio of the life insurance company still carried the illiquid assets. That is, only the interest payments and not the principal were swapped.

These examples illustrate typical applications for fixed- versus floating-rate coupon swaps. They also illustrate that different firms often have opposite asset or liability management motives, each for a good reason. Such diverse preferences both foster and are facilitated by an active market in coupon swaps. In Chapter 14 we examine a number of developments and extensions of the fixed- versus floating-rate coupon swap concept and attempt to identify the size and direction of the coupon swap market.

Footnotes

[1]See unpublished article, "Interest Rate Swaps," Goldman, Sachs & Co., 1982.

Development of the Market for Coupon Cover

INTRODUCTION

When it became apparent that the application of the swap concept developed in connection with long-date currency cover could be readily used to exploit the huge market anomaly that existed between the fixed- and floating-rate debt markets, the volume of coupon swaps exploded. For some time in late 1982, every Eurobond placement by a European or Far-Eastern bank seemed to be linked to a coupon swap. Some observers have estimated that over $10 billion in coupon swaps were done in 1982, with a somewhat larger volume written in 1983.

As a result of this extensive borrowing of fixed-rate dollars by the large international banks, the Eurobond market became less hospitable to bank issuers, and the interest spread vis-à-vis lower-rated credits declined noticeably. Moreover, as the recession came to an end, weaker U.S. credits were able to borrow at rates far closer to those of top-grade borrowers, thus lessening their desire to resort to coupon swaps for fixed-rate funds. Evidence of the decline in credit risk spreads in the U.S. domestic bond market is shown in Table 14–1.

Table 14-1 Interest rates on domestic issues of corporate Aaa and Baa dollar bonds*

Period	Aaa (%)	Baa (%)	Basis Point Spread
September 1982	12.94	15.63	269
December 1982	11.83	14.14	231
March 1983	11.73	13.61	188
June 1983	11.74	13.37	163
August 1983	12.51	13.64	113

Source: U.S. Financial Data, Federal Reserve Bank of St. Louis, September 23, 1983.
*Monthly averages of daily rates.

The decreased attractiveness of the use of coupon swaps to arbitrage the shrinking credit risk premium differential between the fixed- and floating-rate debt markets was, in part, the result of the voluminous use of coupon swaps to arbitrage that anomaly. Although less attractive than in their original application, the interest in coupon swaps has not disappeared. Instead, the flexibility that they afford to liability and asset management, coupled with the nearly complete market productization that has taken place in coupon swaps in their short lifetime, has led to new and innovative developments for their use.

In this chapter we consider the characteristics of the market for coupon swaps as it has developed through the rapid buildup of demand for a rather homogeneous product. Then we examine techniques that link coupon swaps and currency swaps together to access fixed- or floating-rate funds in various currencies. This is followed by an introduction to the use of floating- versus floating-rate coupon swaps. Further extensions of the coupon swap concept are then suggested. The chapter concludes with an evaluation of the liquidity of the coupon swap market and some of its prospects for the future.

CHARACTERISTICS OF THE MARKET FOR COUPON SWAPS

The relative homogeneity of the components of a coupon swap has led to a much more rapid degree of standardization and productization than has occurred in currency swaps. We saw in Chapter 13 how coupon swap pricing has been standardized. This standardization was necessary to focus on the essential pricing elements of an instrument used to exchange fixed-rate coupon obligations for floating-rate obligations. Each side of a coupon swap has a standard index or basis for pricing (i.e., they are normally quoted in terms of spreads over term treasuries and spreads over London Interbank Offer Rate [LIBOR]). On the floating-rate side, this basis may vary, leading the way to standardized pricing of floating- versus floating-rate coupon swaps.

Size

Productization of coupon swaps has gone much farther than standardized units of pricing. Although swap size has not been totally standardized, coupon swaps can be readily obtained in units of $10 million, with the largest swap exceeding $200 million. The importance of swap size should not be overemphasized for two reasons. First, although desirable, it is not always necessary to offset a coupon risk position with full precision. If a player can manage the bulk of its unwanted coupon risk with a coupon swap of available size, perhaps it can bear the balance of the risk or seek to minimize it in other ways. Second, syndication is underway in the coupon swap market whereby an intermediary attempts to package coupon swaps into larger or smaller blocks to accommodate the size requirements of one side or another. Moreover, an intermediary's taking a portion of the swap on its own position book to round out a deal is not unusual. This practice is done in much the same way that an investment banker takes a portion of a large secondary security transaction on its own book with the expectation of laying it off in the market at a later point.

Trading

The carrying of coupon swaps in inventory by financial intermediaries represents another characteristic of the coupon swap market that reflects its rapid progress toward a mature market. Actually, the willingness of intermediaries to carry a coupon swap inventory now goes beyond simply rounding out a deal. Within the first two years of their development, coupon swaps had already been transacted on a trading basis. This transaction has been possible because intermediaries are aware that a counterparty can be found at a price or rate for either side. The volume of supply of fixed- and floating-rate funds has now prompted a number of investment banking and commercial banking firms to act as principals in the marketing of standardized coupon swaps.

The dramatic increase in volume and resulting market liquidity that facilitated taking open positions has also resulted in a reduction in the size of fees charged by arranging banks. The shaving of fees provides additional evidence of the forces of competition in a maturing market. Reduced fees have also provided some thrust behind the willingness of progressive bankers to openly trade coupon swap positions. In this way they can increase their volume and offset the impact of a diminished fee rate on total revenue. The fact that coupon swap deals are being done on a trading basis suggests that pricing of swaps could be handled on a bid–ask basis and, in due course, be carried on a continuously updated quotation device.

The willingness of progressive bankers to assume exposed positions is not justified by market volume alone or by their expected ability to lay off the position in short order. In addition, coupon swap market makers can now nearly neutralize their risk exposure by doing offsetting operations in the treasuries cash, or treasuries futures markets. The risk to holders of open coupon swap positions is that interest rates may change and losses occur. This exposure exists primarily on the fixed-rate side of the open position. Floating-rate payments and receipts will tend to match off the floating-rate side even if interest rates change. Some basis risk may exist if floating-rate payments and receipts are indexed to different bases. The size of this exposure can be very significant and should be managed by holding to as uniform a basis as possible.

However, the fixed-rate side of an open coupon swap is analogous to a term bond position. Receivers of fixed-rate funds are essentially long in bonds, and if interest rates rise, they face a risk of loss of market value. This risk can be easily offset by shorting equivalent treasuries or by selling an appropriate number of treasury bill or bond futures contracts to obtain the needed offset position. If, on the other hand, the intermediary's open position is on the paying side of fixed-rate coupons, it is essentially short in term treasuries and faces risk in that its position will be adversely affected if interest rates fall. This exposure may also be offset by going long in term treasuries or by buying the proper ratio of treasury futures contracts. Thus, the normal asset and liability management techniques used by banks to manage their coupon risk exposure can also be employed by market makers in coupon swaps to enable them to offer quoted rates for their product.

Note that a measurable reinvestment risk on the profit obtained from the disposal of the treasuries used to hedge an open coupon swap exists if rates go down. An opposite favorable reinvestment prospect would occur if rates rise and profits are taken from disposal of the hedged short positions. Over time, however, these reinvestment rate risks should balance out, making open coupon swap positions reasonably hedgable. The increase in the number of intermediaries offering to assume market risk on coupon swaps is testimony to the effectiveness of the hedging operation.

Having seen the rapid development of a standardized, productized market in coupon swaps, we next examine the deployment of standard fixed-to floating-rate coupon swaps to related transactions designed to provide more flexible cover of currency and coupon risk. We look first at a combination with currency swaps and then to a modification that provides for floating- versus floating-rate swaps. Moreover, as our discussion develops, we will continue to focus on the underlying rationale and financial applications of each of these concepts.

COMBINED CURRENCY AND COUPON SWAPS

We have seen that the sizable demand that large international money market banks have placed on the Eurodollar bond market to obtain fixed-rate term funds for coupon swaps has caused bank term paper to trade down in price. This condition reflected the higher interest rates required by investors as the market became saturated. As a result, some of the large bank players sought in other markets nondollar fixed-rate funds, which could first be swapped for fixed-rate dollars using a currency swap and subsequently or simultaneously swapped for floating-rate dollars using a coupon swap.

Proxy Fixed-Rate Currencies

The problem of an adequate source of fixed-rate funds has been faced by both dollar- and nondollar-based banks. As Eurodollar term lenders became less hospitable to the large international banks, the banks sought to acquire fixed-rate currencies wherever they were available. This strategy enabled the banks to diversify the currency of their liabilities or, if they chose, to swap nondollar fixed-rate currencies for fixed-rate dollars to match the currency of their Eurodollar assets.

A popular proxy currency for acquiring floating-rate dollars was the Swiss franc. Both dollar- and nondollar-based banks have floated substantial amounts of fixed-rate Swiss francs to source floating-rate U.S. dollars ultimately. In addition sterling-based banks have swapped fixed-rate sterling for floating-rate sterling, and Canadian banks have used the coupon swap market in a similar way to source floating rate Canadian dollars. Others have done cross-currency swaps of fixed-rate sterling for floating-rate dollars. This practice follows the natural availability of fixed-rate sterling to U.K. banks. A similar practice has occurred in West Germany and Japan where indigenous banks borrowed fixed-rate home currencies with the intention of ultimately swapping for floating-rate dollars to match their floating-rate Eurodollar loan portfolio.

Sourcing fixed-rate funds outside the Eurodollar market for ultimate exchange to floating-rate dollars has encountered resistance in some countries. As we might expect, certain central banks have been reluctant to permit their capital markets to be used to finance the rest of the world because of the potential adverse effect on their own exchange rates. In one example of this posture, the Bundesbank initiated controls to prevent the export of capital from West Germany. Such controls involved a prohibition of swaps that involve capital market transactions in West Germany. Hence, only seasoned issues could be used to seek permission for either currency or currency–coupon swap participation. On the other hand the active private placement term loan market in West Germany has provided an opportunity to swap floating-rate dollars for fixed-rate marks for investment in Germany to the mutual advantage of the players.

At times Japanese monetary officials have been rather paranoid about the export of capital. The high Japanese savings rate has generated large volumes of capital, but tradition has been to control its deployment. Consequently, the ministry of finance had established a queue for coupon swaps involving fixed-rate yen. Participating banks had to get permission from the ministry of finance before a swap could be arranged. The initial allocation arrangement permitted the four large Japanese banks to do one coupon swap per calendar quarter, with smaller city banks having access to the coupon swap market only once every nine to twelve months.

Similar determent has not occurred in all fixed-rate capital markets. For example, the Swiss franc market has been amenable to fixed-rate placements. Moreover, as long as supranational agencies have been interested in swapping dollars for francs to get a low nominal interest cost, this market has provided an ongoing supply of fixed-rate funds to swap for floating-rate dollars. And, of course, the Eurocurrency markets, of which the Eurodollar segment has been dominant, has been available to supply fixed-rate funds at market rates without controls from domestic monetary authorities.

Sourcing fixed-rate funds outside the Eurodollar market has had other advantages to banks. Not only did this procedure provide incremental finance without going to a dollar lender, but it also kept the bank's name out of the often overextended Eurodollar market. This form of borrowing in absentia has frequently provided a strong motive for currency and combined currency coupon swaps.

Proxy Floating-Rate Currencies

Despite the concern over where and in what currency the fixed-rate side of a combined currency coupon swap would be sourced, the question of the currency of the floating-rate side does not matter in a material way for any actively traded currency. If there is an active short-term forward market in a currency, any floating interest rate currency can be readily converted to any other floating interest rate currency. To see why this is so, assume that we own a floating-rate asset that is repriced every six months in a given currency, say sterling, and wish to swap it for fixed-rate dollars. We again assume that dollar interest rates exceed sterling rates, and sterling is selling at a forward premium.

To convert this floating-rate sterling asset to a floating-rate dollar asset, all we do is borrow floating-rate dollars in the Eurodollar market (with six-month interest repricing) and sell the next six-month sterling interest receipt forward for dollars. This forward sale of sterling would have to be repeated each six months for the life of the floating-rate obligation. If the short-term forward market is in equilibrium, the forward premium on the sale of the sterling interest receipt would be just sufficient to augment the sterling interest and provide the proper amount of funds to service the floating-rate dollar debt each half year. Thus, we would end up with the economic equivalent of floating-rate dollars in place of our former position in floating-rate sterling.

The economic equivalent of floating-rate obligations can be produced for any pair of currencies for which efficient short-term forward markets exist. This is an important concept in the structuring of combined currency coupon swaps because it eliminates much of the concern over the availability and/or risk of the currency in which the floating-rate funds are sourced. However, a few minor concerns about this procedure warrant attention. First, a small transaction cost is incurred in borrowing the desired currency and, again, in selling the undesired currency forward. Second, the procedure relies on the fact that covered interest arbitrage is effective and that the forward discount/premium just equals the interest rate differential between offshore or Eurodeposit transactions in the respective currencies. Studies have shown that forward markets are generally dominated by arbitrageurs rather than by speculators; hence, the second problem should not be an overriding concern.[1]

Obtaining the loan in the desired currency in the offshore Eurocurrency market is important because the equilibrium between the forward discount/premium and the interest differential may be disrupted by imposing domestic currency controls in either currency. The possibility of currency controls by the governments of either country introduces an element of risk that can only be managed in this simulation of floating-rate funds in alternative currencies by using offshore, Eurocurrency markets. If such markets are not available and if the risk of possible currency controls is not bearable, the floating-rate funds should be sourced *only* in the currency desired.

Configurations of Combined Currency Coupon Swaps

Combined currency coupon (CCC) swaps may take on a number of different configurations to achieve the desired end result in terms of the currency and coupon of each party's ultimate cash flow receipt or obligation. CCC swaps can involve two, three, or four principal parties, in addition to the arranging and credit-assuming intermediaries. We begin with the four-party swap to illustrate the interconnection of each currency and coupon flow more easily. The number of parties decreases when one of them fulfills the currency and coupon preferences of two of the parties in a four-party swap. The minimum number of parties, of course, is two. Note that the difficulty of arranging swaps goes up exponentially as the number of parties increases.

Four-Party Swaps

In a four-party CCC swap, each party fulfills only one of the four currency and coupon functions necessary to implement the swap. To illustrate we use British sterling and the U.S. dollar as representative currencies. In a hypothetical four-party CCC swap, party A is a natural fixed-rate payer of sterling that is forced to borrow floating-rate money because it lacks access to the sterling fixed-rate market, which had been dominated by the Bank of England for years. Avoiding the risk of fluctuating, and perhaps markedly higher, floating sterling interest rates represents a welcome opportunity for A, which has been denied access to fixed-rate funds.

Party B is a strong-credit U.K. bank that is a natural floating-rate payer of sterling but has obtained access to the fixed-rate sterling market. Because it also has fixed-rate dollar assets, B prefers to hedge its position by swapping fixed-rate sterling for fixed-rate dollars.

Party C is a strong U.S. credit that is a natural floating-rate payer of dollars and has access to fixed-rate dollar finance. Perhaps C is a large international bank or a multinational manufacturing firm that prefers to finance a portion of its assets with floating-rate funds because of the flexibility this avails or because of its view on the course of interest rates. C may also have a subsidiary in the U.K. with the need to finance sterling assets, giving it a preference for sterling liabilities.

Finally, party D is a weaker U.S. domestic credit that is a natural payer of fixed-rate dollar interest in order to lock-in an acceptable spread on its fixed and current assets. It has, however, been discriminated against by the fixed-rate market because of its risk posture. Alternatively, D can borrow floating-rate dollars from banks who provide careful surveillance over its activities.

Given the players for each of the parts, we can now construct a flow-diagram for a four-party CCC swap where each player plays only a single part. For simplicity, we eliminate credit intermediaries at this stage. The currency flows and players associated with a hypothetical four-party combined currency coupon swap are presented in Figure 14–1.

Figure 14–1 Currency flows associated with a hypothetical four-party combined currency coupon swap

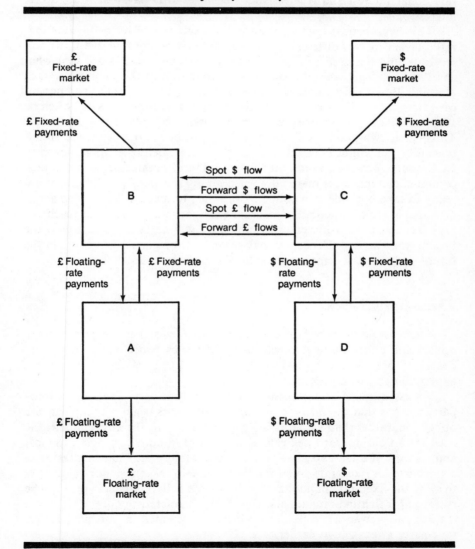

Implicit in Figure 14–1 is a sterling fixed- for floating-rate coupon swap between A and B, a sterling–dollar currency swap between B and C, and a fixed- for floating-rate dollar coupon swap betweeen C and D. Credit intermediary banks could be placed between each pair of players as deemed necessary. As a result of the three swaps, each player pays and receives the form of currency flows that it prefers (i.e., A pays fixed-rate sterling interest, B pays floating-rate sterling interest and receives spot dollars, C pays floating-rate dollar interest and receives spot sterling, and D pays fixed-rate dollar interest).

This hypothetical four-party swap links two sets of fixed- for floating-rate players in two different currencies in such a way that the fixed-rate receivers find the need to also swap their currency flows. While somewhat contrived and, perhaps, not likely to be found all at the same time, such plausible flows and applications illustrate each of the essential component cash flows of a CCC swap. In practice one or two of the flows can often be short-circuited by the parties, resulting in three- and two-party CCC swaps. Three- and two-party CCC swaps are less difficult to orchestrate simultaneously and will be covered in the next sections. Before leaving four-party CCC swaps, however, note that the feasibility of organizing such complex combinations increases materially when an intermediary is willing to stand ready to take one side of a coupon swap (i.e., to make a market and act as principal in the transaction). Because the coupon swap market has reached a high degree of maturity, enterprising banks will be likely to step into the breach when needed. Hence, we may see more four-party CCC swaps in the future with a bank temporarily filling one of the roles.

Three-Party Swaps

The most popular form of a three-party CCC swap has occurred between dollars and either sterling, marks, or Swiss francs. Since many three-party deals have been done in Swiss francs, we will shift to Swiss francs and dollars as our illustrative currencies.

An essential difference between a typical three-party swap and a four-party swap is that the flows in one of the currencies begin with a fixed-rate obligation, rather than with a floating-rate borrowing, thereby removing the need for a floating- for fixed-rate coupon swap in both currencies. In most applications of three-party swaps, a nondollar fixed-rate financing serves as a surrogate for fixed-rate dollar funding. In these cases the major objective is to swap the fixed-rate nondollars for fixed-rate dollars, which in turn will be swapped for floating-rate dollars. Hence, the characteristics of the players in a three-party swap are different from those presented in our hypothetical four-party swap shown earlier.

The currency flows associated with an actual three-party swap are shown in Figure 14–2. In this scenario party E represents a natural floating-

Figure 14–2   Debt service currency flows associated with a three-party combined currency coupon swap

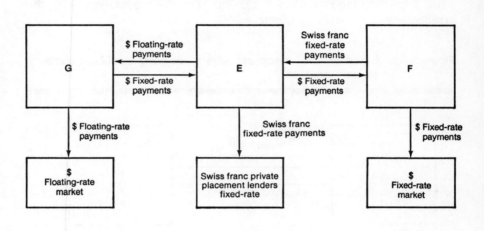

rate dollar borrower, that has access to the fixed-rate Swiss franc market as a surrogate for fixed-rate dollar funds. E obtains these term funds from the active private placement market fed by bank trust funds and private investors in Zurich and other Swiss money centers. Preferring dollars rather than francs, E uses a currency swap to exchange the fixed-rate francs for fixed-rate dollars with party F, which has a strong preference for low nominal interest costs (perhaps a supranational institution like the World Bank). This swap provides E with a flow of francs to service the fixed-rate franc term loan and a fixed-rate dollar obligation. Still preferring to obtain floating-rate dollar finance, E simultaneously swaps its fixed-rate dollar obligation for floating-rate dollars with party G, a weaker U.S. credit that has access to floating-rate funds but a preference for fixed-rate funds.

As before, credit intermediaries may be placed between the parties as deemed necessary by any of them. Again, each player was able to obtain the type of cash flows that it desired; E wound up with a net obligation to make floating-rate dollar payments for its finance, F obtained a fixed-rate Swiss franc obligation, and G secured fixed-rate dollar funding.

Two-Party Swaps

Two-party CCC swaps are simpler still. They require one party to exchange a fixed-rate obligation in one currency for a floating-rate liability in another currency, and vice versa. Continuing with our Swiss franc–dollar currency combination, we can illustrate a two-party swap by having party **H** borrow fixed-rate Swiss francs and use a CCC swap to exchange them with party **I** for floating-rate dollars. The currency flows associated with this arrangement are shown in Figure 14–3.

Figure 14–3 Currency flows associated with a two-party combined currency coupon swap

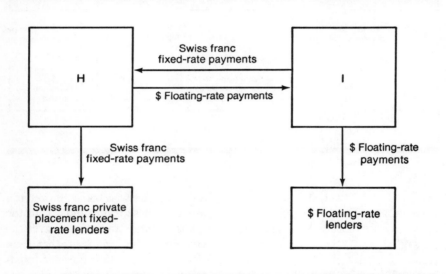

Again, credit intermediation may be inserted if desired, and each party obtained the type of payments it desired. Party H, perhaps a Eurobank, tapped the Swiss franc fixed-rate debt market as a surrogate for its desired floating-rate dollar interest payments, and party I, perhaps a weaker-credit U.S. multinational firm, used its access to the dollar floating-rate market to establish a Swiss franc liability, which could be used to balance the net asset position of its Swiss subsidiary.

Irregular Cash Flows

When a currency swap is combined with coupon swap, the possibility of irregular cash flows associated with the currency agreement must be considered. The potential irregular nature of the periodic cash flows is the result of possible changes in spot exchange rates from the initiation of the swap until the time of the actual cash flow. This matter was discussed in Chapter 3, and the impact of a change in exchange rates on the periodic flow was presented in Equation (3-1).

As we indicated in Chapters 2 and 3, a currency swap may be put together using a series of fees that flow from the party with the low-interest currency to the party with the high-interest currency. These fees are used to reflect the interest differentials between the currencies. This point was illustrated in Equation (3-1). Currency swaps may also be constructed by omitting the periodic flows and employing a single forward premium or discount as was shown in Equation (3-2). When a currency swap is combined with a coupon swap, a problem may occur because of the irregular flows that result from the appreciation (depreciation) of the currency trading at a forward premium (discount). Since CCC swaps have been applied in both Swiss francs and marks, which trade at a forward premium, finding counterparties for the periodic payments when the dollar value of the required cash flow increases over time has sometimes been difficult. The solution to this problem is to set up a currency swap where the cash flows are uniform in the currency in which a coupon swap is appended (e.g., dollars). When this is done, balancing off the over- or underpaid periodic premium into a premium on the principal exchange at the end of the swap may be necessary.

Another possible solution, of course, is to drop the periodic cash flows on the currency swap and build the entire forward premium or discount into the terminal exchange rate on the principal in accordance with Equation (3-2). If this procedure were followed, there would be no periodic cash flows between the parties, and each would have to service its own debt in its undesired currency and coupon configuration. Although the final desired effect could be reconstituted in the premium or discount at maturity, the cash flow objectives of the swap would not be realized in each period under this method. This approach is not likely to be acceptable to any of the parties. Hence, an arrangement that provides for a uniform periodic payment in dollars with some adjustment in the premium or discount at maturity might be more appropriate. A more basic approach, where appropriate, would be for the parties to exchange each other's interest obligations and make the necessary fixed- or floating-rate interest payments in the swapped currency of choice.

Combined Currency and Coupon Swap Applications

Most of the important applications of CCC swaps have already been disclosed in illustrating the various CCC swap combinations. A few remain, however; they will be helpful in describing the breadth of applications of CCC swaps in most of the major currencies. A number of Swiss franc–dollar applications were described earlier; hence, we focus on other currencies in these examples.

Sterling–dollar applications include a case of a U.S. firm that was long in sterling assets and faced floating interest rates that were lower in the United Kingdom than in the United States. Hence, it borrowed floating-rate sterling to obtain both a lower cost of funds and reduce its foreign exchange risk. Moreover, it was able to obtain another reduction in cost of nearly 100 basis points by swapping the floating-rate sterling for fixed-rate sterling with a financial institution whose view on interest rates was that floating-rate funds would turn out to be less costly than fixed-rate funds. This provided low-fixed-rate sterling, which was then swapped for fixed-rate dollars with another U.S. firm with a net sterling asset exposure to obtain very attractive fixed-rate dollar financing.

Mark–dollar CCC swaps have also been done in numerous instances. This case illustrates a portfolio- or asset-motivated CCC swap. Here a U.S. institution borrowed floating-rate dollars in the commercial paper market and swapped the floating-rate dollars for fixed-rate German marks for investment in the active private placement market in West Germany. The German borrower of fixed-rate marks was pleased to get this finance without taking its name to the public fixed-rate market or submitting to the queues and approval process inherent in public issues in West Germany. The German payer of floating-rate dollars was a German Eurobank with Euro-dollar floating-rate assets. The strategy employed in this CCC swap was neutral to the export of capital from West Germany because no principal flows crossed national boundaries. All that occurred was an agreement to service fixed-rate mark interest in exchange for the service of floating-rate dollar interest. In a more direct use of mark–dollar CCC swaps, West German banks have approached the Bundesbank for approval to swap unseasoned issues to enable them to borrow fixed-rate marks and swap to floating-rate Eurodollars for deployment in the Eurodollar market.

An example of a French franc–dollar CCC swap also illustrates a *multiparticipant* or *syndicated swap*. In this case financial intermediaries offered minimum subscriptions of $10 million each to a number of principal players. The CCC swap was for five years. It involved a French utility that needed fixed-rate French francs to service its fixed-rate French franc debt. The French utility could borrow floating-rate dollars at LIBOR but was having difficulty sourcing French francs to service its existing French franc debt. Hence, it offered to swap floating-rate dollars for fixed-rate French francs. Counterparties to the French utility would receive floating-rate dollars at LIBOR plus 0.5 percent plus an exchange of principal at maturity at the same exchange rate that existed on day one. In exchange the counterparties incurred a fixed-rate French franc obligation. This application was of interest to U.S. dollar-based firms that had a net asset position in France and were generating sufficient French franc cash flows to enable them to participate in the minimum subscription that the banker was offering.

Other applications have become apparent and could be documented; however, those shown illustrate most of the salient points in combined currency and coupon swaps. We turn now to another refinement of swap methodology, that of floating- for floating-rate coupon swaps.

FLOATING- VERSUS FLOATING-RATE COUPON SWAPS

As we saw in our discussion of the characteristics of coupon swap participants, floating-rate receipts or obligations interest certain parties because of their underlying floating-rate cash flows characteristics. In many cases the primary underlying floating-rate basis was LIBOR, and the first generation of fixed- for floating-rate swaps was based on LIBOR as the floating-rate index. As the concept of fixed- for floating-rate swaps became more accepted, other indices soon became desirable as the basis for the floating-rate side. Thus, the floating-rate side of fixed- for floating-rate coupon swaps began to be priced in terms of a spread over or under treasuries, prime, certificate of deposit, or commercial paper rates.

As alternative floating-rate bases became appropriate for different players depending on the basis for their own cash flows, interested players soon found floating- versus floating-rates coupon swaps also quite fitting in the management of their particular cash flow configurations. To date various combinations of floating- versus floating-rate coupon swaps have been done. In the examples that follow, the characteristics of the underlying cash flows that drive each of them are emphasized.

Applications

We have seen how natural U.S. fixed-rate payers can further arbitrage the floating-rate interest spread between the Eurodollar market based on

LIBOR and the U.S. commercial paper market. That is, by funding its floating-rate debt in the commercial paper market at rates 75 to 100 basis points less than the LIBOR it receives, a floating-rate receiver can further reduce the cost of its fixed-rate debt by this amount.

This nonformalized application of arbitrage is the equivalent of a floating-versus floating-rate coupon swap. Both sides of the informal swap are conducted by the same party; hence, there is no need for formal documentation. If different parties took each side, the same arbitrage application could be accommodated by a LIBOR versus commercial paper floating- versus floating-rate coupon swap. Similar combinations could be instituted using treasury bills, prime, certificate of deposit, or other floating-rate indices as appropriate to the cash flows or arbitrage opportunities available to the players.

A rather typical floating- versus floating-rate coupon swap application involved a U.S. bank that had a Nassau offshore branch, which had access to LIBOR-priced funds and the assets of which were primarily based on prime. This bank would be a natural counterparty for a prime versus LIBOR floating- versus floating-rate coupon swap in which the bank paid a floating-rate indexed to prime and received a floating-rate indexed to LIBOR. In this way it could hedge any change in the basis or difference between its cost of funds and return on assets. Logical counterparties may be London branches of U.S. banks that have assets, the yields of which are tied to LIBOR but which are partly financed with U.S. certificates of deposit, the cost of which is more closely correlated to prime than to LIBOR.

Another source of LIBOR for prime swaps occurred in large volumes in 1983 as a result of the restructuring of bank credits to the less-developed countries (LDC). This application involved a one-time option available to the banks involved in negotiating the LDC debt restructuring to index the interest payments to U.S. prime or LIBOR. At the outset, non-U.S. banks were inclined to choose LIBOR because their funding was on a LIBOR basis. They were uncomfortable about the basis risk between prime receipts and LIBOR funding. U.S. banks, on the other hand, were quite willing to choose prime because it was a higher rate and their funding base was attuned to prime receipts.

The reluctance of non-U.S. banks to select prime-indexed receipts continued until they "discovered" that they could swap the prime interest receipts for a LIBOR-based income stream. That is, they could use a floating- versus floating-rate coupon swap to convert a prime-based asset into a LIBOR-based asset with which they were more comfortable. The result was a series of prime for LIBOR floating- versus floating-rate coupon swaps traded against U.S. banks with LIBOR-based funds and prime-based assets. In addition, the supply of prime for LIBOR swaps filled the LIBOR funding requirements of many U.S. regional banks (with approximately $5 billion in assets) that felt competitive pressures to grant LIBOR-priced loans but did not have normal access to LIBOR-based funds. Typical pricing saw the regional bank receive prime less 75 basis points and pay three-month LIBOR with zero premium. Sources have estimated that a volume of approximately $1 billion was done in this type of application.

Another application of a floating- versus floating-rate coupon swap combines it with a fixed- versus floating-rate coupon swap into a three-party example. This case involved a U.S. industrial borrower that was a natural fixed-rate payer and wanted to convert floating-rate dollars to five-year fixed-rate dollars (i.e., it wished to swap its floating-rate prime interest obligation for a fixed-rate commitment). The natural fixed-rate payer was willing to pay 175 basis points over five-year governments and receive prime to service its floating-rate borrowing. However, it could find no one willing to pay prime on a fixed- versus floating-rate coupon swap.

In searching for counterparties an intermediary found a number of European and Japanese banks willing to receive 100 basis points over five-year treasuries and pay LIBOR. These players could be coupled with a U.S. bank that needed LIBOR-based funding because of its cash flow characteristics and was willing to pay interest pegged to prime. The pricing terms of a typical LIBOR for prime floating- versus floating-rate coupon swap were six-month LIBOR plus zero premium and prime less 75 basis points. When both the floating- versus floating-rate coupon swap and the fixed- versus floating-rate coupon swap were put together, each party received and paid interest flows that had the characteristics that it desired. These transactions are shown in flowchart form on Figure 14-4.

In this example the U.S. bank paid prime less 75 basis points and received six-month LIBOR to service its LIBOR-based floating-rate debt; the Japanese or European bank paid six-month LIBOR and received fixed-rate interest at 100 basis points over five-year treasuries with which to service its fixed-rate debt; and the U.S. industrial firm netted out at a fixed-rate payment of 175 basis points over five-year treasuries after it paid its lenders at prime. As in earlier examples, executing both swaps simultaneously is desirable. Moreover, placing a bank between the U.S. industrial firm and the Japanese or European bank, if this is desired by the parties, may ease the transactions.

We have now covered most of the important ramifications of coupon swaps. A few extensions of the concept remain to be mentioned for completeness. To date none of these has been implemented with any regularity. They are covered briefly in the next section with the prospect that some may prove to be meaningful applications.

241

Figure 14–4 Currency flows associated with a three-party combined fixed-versus floating-rate and floating- versus floating-rate dollar coupon swap

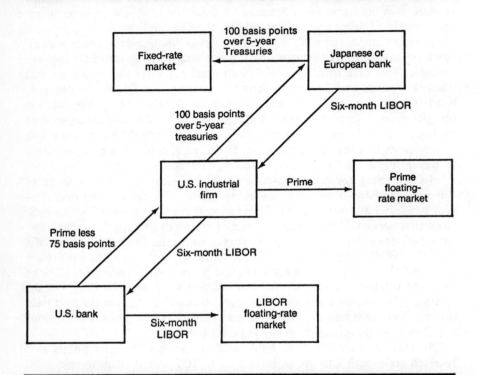

EXTENSIONS OF THE COUPON SWAP

The swap concept that was originally developed and refined to facilitate the management of long-date currency exposures found ready application in the management of coupon risk as well. A few additional extensions of the concept have been tried, and others, perhaps, remain undiscovered. Those extensions in the area of coupon risk for which a few swaps have been put into place include the swap of forward sterling for Eurosterling and forward dollars for Eurodollars. A detailed description of an application of the former set of cash flows was presented under the heading of confidentiality in Chapter 9. Other potentially swappable cash flows include taxable for tax-free fixed-rate coupons, and fixed-rate or floating-rate coupons for zero coupon bonds. Actually, almost any pair or combination of cash flows could be swapped provided economically motivated parties can be found for both sides of the transaction. The possibility of an arbitrage opportunity due to market anomalies helps to encourage the parties to participate. The volume of interested parties and the degree of financial motivation also depends, in part, upon the liquidity and transactions volume in related markets.

In Chapter 11 we saw the liquidity and volume prospects for currency swaps. We turn next to an examination of the liquidity of the coupon swap market and a crude estimate of its prospective volume.

COUPON SWAP MARKET LIQUIDITY

The coupon swap product deals with cash flows in a single currency; hence, it does not have to contend with the risk considerations of changes in exchange rates. In addition, the risk inherent in an open coupon swap position can be mitigated in the cash or futures markets with reasonable ease. As a result of these features, the market for coupon swaps has matured quickly, and trading in swaps with standardized terms by creditworthy parties can now take place on very short notice.

The degree of liquidity achieved in the market for coupon swaps is now sufficient to sustain itself, which is a desirable characteristic of any market. Adequate liquidity or market depth to enable the unwinding of a position, if the circumstances that prompted the position change, reduces resistance to undertaking initial transactions and provides comfort to uneasy decision makers. The presence of an after-market is derived from adequate liquidity and provides the liquidity necessary to unwind positions when necessary. The coupon swap market has demonstrated commensurate liquidity to enable new players to modify their interest cash flows to better fit their expected operating flows or to reverse prior positions if circumstances warrant a change. In this section we examine some of the factors that have led to coupon swap market liquidity.

Market Participants

Coupon swap market liquidity is the result of a plenteous number of players that desire to participate in coupon swaps to alter the shape of their financial cash flows. A number of factors have jointly contributed to the rapid increase in the number of assenting players. Because market participants are normally apprehensive about new financial products, a full understanding of the nature of the coupon swap product should head the list of factors contributing to its market acceptance. Knowledge of the nature of the credit risk involved, including the fact that the principal is not at risk and only the differential in interest payments may be lost or suffer a reinvestment rate risk, has been a positive factor in the acceptance of the coupon swap as a useful instrument in financial management.

The willingness of commercial banks to intermediate credit risk and the more recent willingness of investment banks to assume market risk as principals has overcome much of the discontinuity involved in finding counterparties and has fostered the flow of transactions. A willingness to assume market risk also reflects a better understanding of financial futures markets where the coupon swap open positions can be hedged. A coupon swap of nearly any size and maturity can be simulated by a proper combination of treasury bill and ten-year treasury note futures contracts. Some basis risk remains because of imperfect simulation, but the magnitude of this risk is readily manageable.

Recent growth in the term certificates of deposit (CD) market has also fostered the desire to do coupon swaps. Insurance companies have become more interested recently in investing in term CDs, thereby providing sizable amounts of fixed-rate funds to the banks. Acceptance by the issuing banks that coupon swaps represent a viable way of converting the fixed-rate term CD funds to floating-rate money has facilitated the desired cash flow configurations of each of the parties and contributed to the liquidity of the coupon swap market. Non-U.S. banks are also issuers of term instruments and acquire large quantities of fixed-rate funds, which they may wish to convert to floating-rate money using coupon swaps.

Flexibility

Some of the refinements of the coupon swap market have also stimulated the use of coupon swaps. For instance the growth of the floating- versus floating-rate swap market activity has led to opportunities to do a so-called *double swap* to obtain the contour of interest flows that the parties desire. Therefore, a bank might be more willing to do a coupon swap using LIBOR as an index if it knows it can shift the basis to U.S. treasuries. Treasury rates are more attractive to U.S. banks as a basis for their interest cost because, when rates go up, the spread between LIBOR and treasuries widens, and a treasuries cost basis results in a lower cost of funds to the bank. Hence, if a bank is offered a fixed- for floating-rate coupon swap tied to LIBOR, it may be willing to take it as an intermediate step in moving to a treasury bill cost base using a second floating- versus floating-rate swap.

Volume of Currency Swaps

Growth of volume in currency swaps has also helped quicken the coupon swap market. This growth can be seen in the rapid increase in the use of nondollar fixed-rate funds to obtain floating-rate dollars using a combined currency coupon swap. This strategy has been prompted by the fact that the Eurodollar bond market has been sated by bank demand for fixed-rate money by non-U.S. banks to be swapped for floating-rate dollars. Other examples include the resistance of U.S. floating-rate lenders to offer funds to Canadian banks because of the overhang effect of the banking difficulties in Canada. Again, financial swaps provide the solution: The Canadian bank can borrow fixed-rate Swiss francs and use a currency swap to convert to fixed-rate U.S. dollars and a coupon swap to shift to floating-rate U.S. dollars to fund its LIBOR-based loan portfolio. Thus, the availability of currency swaps has also helped to bolster the development of the coupon swap market.

Nondollar Coupon Swaps

While coupon swaps are obviously not solely a dollar instrument, little has been said about their development in other currencies. Actually, Canada and the United Kingdom have experienced considerable growth in indigenous coupon swaps within their own currencies to facilitate the desired cash flow configurations of the parties. Moreover, indigenous coupon swaps have been done in West Germany and Switzerland in their domestic currencies. Such parallel development of coupon swaps is helpful to market liquidity because it provides synergism for cross-currency coupon swaps. Combined currency coupon swaps are nurtured by the availability of coupon swaps in multiple currencies and, in turn, foster the liquidity of the coupon swap market in each participating currency. The proven capability to do coupon swaps in other major currencies supplies synergism to enhance the liquidity of the dollar coupon swap market as well.

Alternative Views

A final development that has helped enlarge the liquidity of the coupon swap market is the emergence of high-quality credits on the natural fixed-rate paying side. The preference of borrowers rated AA or better to borrow floating-rate money and swap it for fixed-rate (i.e., pay fixed-rate interest and receive floating-rate interest) reflects a complete shift in the attributes of these swap parties from the attributes of the same parties at the early stage of coupon swaps. In the early days coupon swaps were done by strong bank credits borrowing fixed-rate funds and swapping with weaker corporate credits that borrowed floating-rate funds and swapped for fixed-rate obligations. More recently both strong bank and corporate credits have borrowed floating-rate money with the intention of swapping it for a fixed-rate obligation (i.e., these players wish to be fixed-rate payers).

This revised strategy has been motivated by the arbitrage opportunity available in using the floating-rate receipts that are indexed to LIBOR to service commercial paper sourcing of the floating-rate funds and obtain an approximate 75 basis point cost saving. This saving can then be used to reduce the effective cost of the fixed-rate loan. The other side of many of these swaps would be international money market banks and others that have access to fixed-rate funds but that wish to pay floating-rate and receive fixed-rate payments. Included in this group of counterparties would be U.S. banks that extend term CDs to institutional investors; the Student Loan Marketing Association (Sally Mae), which has acted as floating-rate payer in more than $1.8 billion of coupon swaps[2]; and other quasigovernment or government-guaranteed agencies that can tap fixed-rate funds but normally have floating-rate receipts.

Another source of fixed-rate funds is strong U.S. corporate credits that can borrow fixed-rate funds but prefer to increase their floating-rate obligations. There has not been much corporate swapping of fixed- for floating-rate coupons because the strong credits can also issue commercial paper at attractive rates. Nevertheless, some demand exists for floating-rate funds in exchange for fixed-rate obligations from those firms that view fixed-rates as being too high and believe floating-rates represent a cheaper cost of capital or from firms that have already borrowed more floating-rate funds than the market is willing to accommodate.

SIZE OF THE COUPON SWAP MARKET

All of the foregoing factors have given rise to a liquid coupon swap market in which reversing out or unwinding prior deals is now possible if circumstances change. In dealing with the overall size of the coupon swap market, it is not possible to categorize all of the elements of the underlying supply and demand. However, to provide some perspective to the potential volume, attempting to estimate the volume of one of the sides of a coupon swap transaction as a rough measure of potential annual volume may be helpful. In doing so we consider an estimate of the supply of funds with fixed-rate dollar interest obligations to the coupon swap market, which seeks to exchange this obligation for a promise to make floating-rate payments instead.

A crude approximation of the supply of fixed-rate funds to the dollar coupon swap market for 1984 is shown in Table 14–2. These estimates are not based on exhaustive surveys, but on limited discussion with market participants. The $11 billion estimate of supply of fixed-rate funds to the

Table 14–2 Estimated supply of fixed-rate funds to the dollar coupon swap market for 1984

$ Billion	Source of Supply of Fixed-Rate Funds
$ 3.0	Japanese banks
3.0	Other non-U.S. banks
1.0	U.S. banks
2.0	Sally Mae and government agencies
1.0	Term CDs at U.S. banks
0.5	Reversals and unwinds
0.5	U.S. corporations
$11.0	Total

dollar coupon swap market for 1984 is only slightly higher than the estimated volume of $10 billion for 1983. Whether it is realized depends, in part, on the supply of floating-rate funds. The supply of floating-rate funds depends on the prevailing level of interest rates. Obviously, fewer players wish to lock-in high interest rates, and many have indicated that they would be more willing to take on a fixed-rate obligation in place of a floating-rate stream of interest payments if rates were to fall. Hence, there undoubtedly is a large shadow calendar of offerings to swap floating- for fixed-rate payments if rates come down and lower fixed-rates can be locked-in.

There are other factors that will affect the volume of dollar coupon swaps. Among them is the volume of surrogate dollar fixed-rate borrowing that is done in other currencies. If the World Bank were to find proxy borrowers of fixed-rate Swiss francs that would prefer to pay floating-rate dollars to the World Bank in exchange for the bank's servicing the fixed-rate Swiss franc debt, we would probably see a flood of combined currency coupon swaps absorbing floating-rate dollars. The World Bank, of course, could use these floating-rate dollar receipts to service its short-term discount note debt.

From all of this, the coupon swap market will, by all appearances, remain very dynamic with a volume that oscillates between $10 billion and $15 billion in the next few years unless some dramatic event occurs to tip the balance of supply and demand for coupon cover. In Chapter 15 we consider some of the possible forces that might radically change the complexion of the coupon swap market and innovations that could give rise to far-reaching extensions to the financial swap concept.

Footnotes

[1]See J. L. Hilley, C. R. Beidleman, and J. A. Greenleaf, "Does Covered Interest Arbitrage Dominate in Foreign Exchange Markets?" *The Columbia Journal of World Business* (Winter, 1979), vol. 14, no. 4, pp. 99-107.

[2]See B. McGoldrick, "The Interest Rate Swap Comes of Age," *Institutional Investor* (August, 1983), vol. 17, no. 8, p. 90.

Innovations, New Dimensions, and Outlook for Financial Swaps

INTRODUCTION

We have covered a great deal of ground since our initial discussion of the fundamental characteristics of cash flows in Chapter 1. We have trekked through the persistence of market anomalies, the development of various types of swaplike instruments, and the identification of numerous applications of currency and coupon cover. All of this has led to refinements in the use of the financial swap concept for covering long-date currency and coupon risk, while extracting an element of profit, where possible, from the presence of market anomalies and making financial markets more efficient in the process. As we covered this ground, there have been frequent references to the nature of the markets for long-date cover and to improvements and refinements as these markets have developed. Little can be added in the way of subtleties to what has already been covered regarding market operation and efficiency.

Along the way we have seen an evolution of instruments used to accommodate the need or desire to exchange cash flows with one configuration for cash flows of another contour. Although some of the more rudimentary instruments are still being used because of special features, their simplicity and advantages clearly make the financial swap or long-date forward contract the most advanced forms of long-date currency or coupon cover to date. As instruments have become more polished and better understood, new applications for them have been found. This, in turn, widened the usage of financial swaps and long-date forward contracts and contributed to sizable improvements in market liquidity.

INNOVATIONS IN FINANCE

Innovation in finance has proceeded at a varying pace since the inception of finance as a field of endeavor. As in most other professions, improvements and new developments in finance have occurred in fits and starts, and the most significant advances are the result of attempts to find solutions to former impediments to the smooth flow of financing. The period since 1980 has reportedly been a golden age of financial inventiveness, as evidenced by the promulgation of new products and concepts including original issue discount bonds, zero coupon bonds, stripping of coupons from principal, defeasance, partly paid bonds, options on almost anything, coupon swaps, dual currency issues and adjustable rate preferred stocks.

Note that many of these innovative concepts have been in response to the problems imposed on financial managers by the high level and variability of both inflation and interest rates that have surfaced in recent years. The high and volatile rates of inflation across countries have caused wide fluctuations in interest rates, and, together, high and fluctuating inflation and interest rates have contributed to significant movements in exchange rates. These modulations have been facilitated by the movement from fixed to floating exchange rates in many of the developed countries in 1973 and, in the United States, at least, by the change in fixation of the monetary authority from an emphasis on interest rates to monetary aggregates as targets of monetary policy.

In this final chapter we do not evaluate the merits of many of the more-or-less minor innovations in swap instruments, applications, or markets. We have already dealt with most of these. Instead, we focus on a few significant possibilities that, if adopted, could have massive impacts on the market for financial swaps. The chapter ends with a summary of the importance of swaplike instruments to the contemporary financial mind-set, and vice versa, with a gentle reminder that if we are to enjoy the advantages of innovations in finance, we must be prepared to evaluate and deploy them wherever appropriate.

SOME SLEEPING GIANTS

Large blocks of debt still exist in the world where the characteristics of the interest payments are not well-synchronized with the cash flow expectations of the debtors. This imbalance may occur with either natural floating-rate payers that have previously locked-in high fixed rates of interest or natural fixed-rate payers that cannot afford abnormally high floating-rate debt service.

A finite duration of call protection on high coupon fixed-rate debt places a limit on the period of imbalance to most natural floating-rate payers. An exception to this is found in issuers of original issue discount or zero coupon debt. However, these players should have sufficiently high assured rates of profitability to cover their known high debt cost or should have avoided such exotic debt arrangements that lock-in high interest rates over long periods. In contrast, many natural fixed-rate payers that have recently faced exceedingly high floating rates have incurred the most acute problems.

The most massive class of borrowers that have had difficulty servicing high secular floating rates of interest has been the less-developed countries (LDCs). The world recession in the early 1980s reduced the demand for their export products at the same time that interest rates peaked and much of their debt came due. Since both the public and private sectors of the LDCs borrowed heavily from the international banks, the LDCs had much of their debt denominated in dollars and priced at London Interbank Offer Rate (LIBOR) plus some risk premium. This resulted in very high debt service in dollars at a time when hard currency was extremely scarce.

Many of the LDCs have managed to reschedule their debt and/or obtain swing financing from supranational or other lenders. Nevertheless, at some time when interest rates are reasonable, many of them would be likely to choose to convert the bulk of their floating-rate debt to fixed-rate payments if this were possible. Countries like Mexico, Indonesia, Malaysia, the Philippines, Italy, Greece, and Spain would probably be interested in restructuring the shape of their interest payments from floating rate to fixed rate. Not all LDCs would be so inclined, however. Some countries with very high inflation rates have adopted a kind of floating-rate mentality to which fixed-rate debt at high current rates may not be acceptable or compatible.

A limitation to the success of a wave of floating- for fixed-rate coupon swaps for the LDCs may be the question of who will take the credit risk on the coupon swaps. The international banks have been both chastised for and encouraged in providing continuous support to the LDCs. Their response appears to be to carefully limit any increase in exposure. Hence, international agencies may be called upon to take any incremental credit risk associated with coupon swaps for LDCs. Since the principal is not at risk in a coupon swap and only the differential in interest payments is exposed, perhaps an international agency may be willing to guarantee this risk in an attempt to reduce the overall risk to the debtor LDC. An alternative might be to seek an insurance type of underwriter for the incremental credit risk or to apply hard currency deposits or other liquid assets within the debtor country as security for the credit risk.

Other large potential users of coupon swaps would be government agencies with large amounts of short-term or floating-rate debt and municipal governments or agencies wishing to convert floating-rate to fixed-rate debt.

The driving force for large-scale conversion of floating- to fixed-rate debt would be a reduction in interest rates to a reasonable level coupled with an expectation or fear that they may rise again to very high levels. If a similar sequence of events were to occur in the currency area, we might find a run on currency swaps as well. That is, if the forces that cause exchange rates to fluctuate become rampant in either direction, parties with net asset or net liability positions or exposed currency flows will move quickly to secure cover. In Chapter 6 we saw the size of potentially exposed positions, many of which could be offset against one another through a currency swap. And another sleeping giant may awaken.

RATE VOLATILITY

A key factor or motive behind the use and currency and coupon swaps is the expectation or fear that exchange rates or interest rates will move unchecked to a disadvantage. If exchange rates and interest rates remain quite stable, concern over currency or coupon risk exposure would be unnecessary and currency or coupon swaps would be unnecessary for risk management purposes. They would still find application in exploiting arbitrage opportunities, but their volume would be significantly diminished. Despite the desire for stability in both exchange and interest rates, given the current world environment, the acceptance of freely floating exchange rates, the role of monetary policy in combatting inflation, the wave of deregulation of dollar interest rates, the prospect of cost-push shocks to inflation, and the recent inflation experience, exchange rates, interest rates, and inflation rates clearly will continue to fluctuate with some degree of volatility. Currency swaps and coupon swaps have been developed to enable financial managers to address the problems of fluctuations in exchange rates and interest rates. In the next section we briefly examine an application of the swap concept to hedging a party's exposure to the risk of inflation.

INFLATION SWAPS

If inflation rates can be held stable or within a creeping range of, say, 2 to 4 percent per year, their impact on the real outcome of commercial operations can be readily managed or tolerated without great aggravation. For one thing, the expected rate of inflation is built into the nominal rate of interest and, if stable, is paid by borrowers and recovered by lenders so that each is able to preserve its real position unimpaired. However, when inflation rates rise to beyond 6 or 7 percent, and certainly when they fluctuate in a double-digit range, the operating and investment performance of many parties can be seriously affected. The impact of inflation on an entity's results depends upon the responsiveness of its various components of revenue and cost to the inflationary process.

Our objective at this juncture is to suggest an innovative application for financial swaps to hedge inflation or price-level risk. We will not attempt to develop a thoroughly complete framework for the supply and demand for cover of inflation-induced exposure. Nevertheless, a few rudimentary concepts may help to characterize those players affected by each side of the inflation process and suggest a means to alleviate the impact of inflation on their financial performance.

Consider first the extreme case where the impact of the inflationary process is uniformly distributed across a player's entire spectrum of revenue and cost functions. That is, all of the entity's revenue *(R)* increases at a uniform inflation rate *(h)* in each year *(t)*. Then the effect of inflation on the player's total revenue is to cause it to increase in accordance with Equation (15–1):

$$R_t = R_{t-1} (1+h) \qquad (15–1)$$

Similarly, suppose all cost *(C)* are equally responsive to inflation and will increase in accordance with Equation (15–2):

$$C_t = C_{t-1} (1+h) \qquad (15–2)$$

Since the profit *(P)* of the entity is the residual difference between all revenue and all cost, profit is calculated in accordance with Equation (15–3):

$$P_t = R_t - C_t \qquad (15–3)$$

Substituting Equations (15–1) and (15–2) into (15–3), we see that in this case of uniform inflationary outcomes, profits are also fully responsive to the rate of inflation as shown in Equation (15–4):

$$P_t = R_{t-1} (1+h) - C_{t-1} (1+h)$$

$$P_t = (R_{t-1} - C_{t-1})(1+h)$$

$$P_t = P_{t-1} (1+h) \qquad (15–4)$$

Thus, in this extreme case where all revenue and costs are fully responsive to a uniform rate of inflation, nominal profits are also fully responsive to the inflationary process and real operating results are unaffected.

Inflation-induced risk to a player's real operating results occurs when revenue and cost responsiveness are not uniform. This situation becomes readily apparent to *both* the borrower and the lender in a fixed-rate term loan agreement when the rate of inflation changes tangibly sometime after the agreement is consummated. Since the interest payments are fixed, they are nonresponsive to the rate of inflation. Thus, if inflation were to increase after day one of the loan agreement, the lender would receive fixed interest and principal payments with diminished real value and be an unintended victim of the inflationary process. The borrower would continue to pay the fixed dollar interest payments and be a fortuitous beneficiary of inflation because it would be repaying both interest and principal in currency units of lower real value.

While seen more directly in terms of the debtor–creditor relationship where the cash flows are nonresponsive to the incidence of a change in the rate of inflation, inflation can also produce asymmetric effects on a player's real operating results for other reasons as well. Prices and/or costs could be differentially responsive to inflationary forces, causing an inflation-induced advantage or disadvantage to real operating results. For example, product prices may be frozen or sticky due to controls, regulations, or rigorous competition, while variable factor costs rise with the general wave of inflation. This set of circumstances would lead to an erosion of real operating income, an exposure that risk-averse operating managers would like to protect themselves against if possible.

Conversely, prices may be responsive to inflationary pressures while certain costs remain sticky or even fixed. This result may occur when factor costs for materials or labor are contractually fixed across multiple reporting periods. It also occurs with some regularity when costs of prepaid assets are fixed by accounting practice, the most common of which is depreciation of fixed assets. And those firms that have maintained a first-in, first-out inventory valuation method regularly mix holding profits, resulting from the inflationary process only, together with operating profits in an inflationary environment. As a result, they report inflation-induced profts in their income statements. Opposite outcomes could occur if inflation rates were to fall or turn negative.

Players whose reported income tends to benefit from an inflationary environment may be willing to swap some portion of these benefits with others whose operating results are debased by inflation. This could occur for reasons of more accurate reporting, or, more likely, to protect themselves against deviations in the forthcoming rate of inflation from an agreed upon expected inflation norm. An appropriate mechanism for this process could be a swaplike instrument where the dollar impact of an experienced differential from some negotiated nominal rate of inflation on a fixed-rate term security would be paid and received by the parties. If structured properly, the demand for and supply of such inflation cover could be significant in any period of dynamic inflationary prospects. That is, an annual payment would be received or paid to restore the real value of the term instrument to its original real value to offset any erosion or gain in value due to differences in the actual inflation rates from the negotiated nominal rate.

It may be argued that both currency and coupon swaps find applications in hedging the risk of future inflationary consequences. Moreover, observed inflation and inflationary expectations influence both exchange rates and interest rates. But the forces that link inflation rates to exchange rates and interest rates are not always direct, proportional, or rapid. Moreover, in the case of currency swaps, only the differential in inflation rates between the countries is hedged; and, in the case of coupon swaps, no protection is provided against the inflationary erosion of the real value of the principal of either party. Hence, a more unique instrument would be desirable to obtain full cover of the exposure on either side of a dynamic inflationary experience. Given proper development, this cover could be obtained by using an inflation swap. Because various parties are differentially affected by the inflationary process, an adequate supply of counterparties should be forthcoming.

CONTEMPORARY FINANCIAL MIND-SET

Considering such ideas as converting large amounts of LDC floating- to fixed-rate debt at a propitious level of interest rates or hedging the risk of unknown inflationary outcomes in excess of an agreed-upon standard or normal rate requires a thorough knowledge of available instruments and an open willingness to use them. The same financial mind-set is necessary to implement financial swaps by potential players. Potential users must overcome the inertia of past resistance to financial innovation and acquire an understanding and confidence in what can be done with swaps and swaplike instruments.

People who have already used financial swaps agree that they are complex and require an initial investment in time and effort to develop the necessary proficiency and insight. However, after having developed a basic understanding and confidence in the underlying concept of financial swaps, initial users usually become repeat users. They take delight in their newly found ability to manage more effectively much of the currency and coupon risk that was formerly inherent in their balance sheet and/or income statement.

The potential to apply portfolio management concepts to liabilities places a responsibility on uninformed financial managers to acquire the skills necessary to deploy new financial concepts and tools. Despite the expenditure of time and effort necessary to obtain the needed skills, the advantages in terms of improved control and less vulnerability to the ravages of risk have been the pleasant rewards to finance managers who have become proficient enough to deploy these contemporary financial tools. The flexibility provided by financial swaps as a means to hedge various kinds of risk, exploit advantages inherent in market anomalies, or simply to make changes in a balance sheet in response to revised circumstances make them a very useful device easily accessible to informed financial managers. Their continued use and growth is largely a function of their acceptance by managers of finance. I hope that this volume increases the understanding of financial swaps and reduces the fear and apprehension formerly attached to swaps by many financial managers, among others. If this can be accomplished, applications will continue to expand, liquidity will increase further, and financial management will be carried out more efficiently and expediently.

Appendix–Potential Worldwide Currency Exposure Supplemental Data

Table A-1 U.S. direct investment position abroad at year-end 1982 ($ billions)

Area	Petroleum	Manufacturing	Trade	Banking	Finance (nonbanking)	Other	Total
Canada	$ 8.7	$19.7	$ 4.1	$0.4	$ 7.1	$ 4.5	$ 44.5
Europe	23.0	44.1	14.8	3.7	10.5	3.8	99.9
Japan	1.7	3.5	1.1	0.3	0.3	—	6.9
Australia, New Zealand South Africa	2.5	4.1	1.8	0.1	1.1	2.2	11.8
Developing countries	16.0	19.3	5.5	5.1	0.5	6.7	53.1
Other	3.8	—	—	—	—	1.3	5.1
Total	$55.7	$90.7	$27.3	$9.6	$19.5	$18.5	$221.3

Source: *Survey of Current Business*, August 1983, Table 12, p. 24.

Table A-2 U.S. direct investment position abroad at year-end by area ($ billions)

Area	1977	1978	1979	1980	1981	1982	Trend Rate of Growth*(%)
Canada	$ 35.1	$ 36.4	$ 40.7	$ 45.1	$ 45.1	$ 44.5	5.5
Europe	62.6	70.6	83.1	96.3	101.5	99.9	10.2
Other developed countries	12.5	14.2	15.8	16.8	18.8	18.7	8.3
Latin America	27.5	31.8	35.2	38.8	38.9	33.0	4.6
Other	8.3	9.7	13.1	18.4	22.1	25.2	23.9
Total	$146.0	$162.7	$187.9	$215.4	$226.4	$221.3	9.2

Source: *Survey of Current Business*, August 1983, Table 10, p.22.

*The trend rate of growth is obtained from a time series regression of the natural logarithms of the growth series using observations for each year of the data span.

Table A-3 U.S. direct investment position abroad at year-end by Industry ($ billions)

Industry	1977	1978	1979	1980	1981	1982	Trend Rate of Growth* (%)
Petroleum	$ 28.0	$ 30.5	$ 39.1	$ 47.6	$ 51.2	$ 55.7	14.8
Manufacturing	62.0	69.7	79.0	89.3	92.4	90.7	8.2
Other	56.0	62.5	69.8	78.5	82.8	74.9	6.9
Total	$146.0	$162.7	$187.9	$215.4	$226.4	$221.3	9.2

Source: *Survey of Current Business*, August 1983, Table 10, p. 22.

*The trend rate of growth is obtained from a time series regression of the natural logarithms of the growth series using observations for each year of the data span.

Table A–4 U.S. long-term foreign securities position abroad at year-end 1982 ($ billions)

Area	Bonds	Corporate Stock	Total
Western Europe	$10.4	$ 7.2	$17.6
Canada	31.6	8.9	40.5
Japan	2.3	1.7	4.0
Other Western Hemisphere countries	1.0	0.5	1.5
Other foreign countries	6.9	0.3	7.2
International organizations	4.5	—	4.5
Total	$56.7	$18.6	$75.3

Source: *Survey of Current Business*, August 1983, Table 3, p. 44.

Table A-5 U.S. long-term foreign securities position abroad at year-end by type ($ billions)

Type	1977	1978	1979	1980	1981	1982	Trend Rate of Growth* (%)
Bonds	$39.3	$42.2	$42.0	$43.5	$45.8	$56.7	6.0
Corporate stocks	10.1	11.2	14.8	19.0	17.3	18.6	13.2
Total	$49.4	$53.4	$56.8	$62.5	$63.1	$75.3	7.7

Source: Survey of Current Business, August 1983, Table 3, p. 44.

*The trend rate of growth is obtained from a time series regression of the natural logarithms of the growth series using observations for each year of the data span.

Table A-6 Income* on U.S. direct investment abroad at year-end 1982 ($ billions)

Area	Petroleum	Manufacturing	Trade	Banking	Finance (nonbanking)	Other	Total
Canada	$ 1.1	$0.9	$0.2	$ —	$0.6	$0.1	$ 2.9
Europe	3.3	3.0	1.3	0.7	0.6	0.3	9.2
Japan	0.3	0.4	—	—	—	—	0.7
Australia, New Zealand							
South Africa	0.3	—	0.1	—	0.1	0.3	0.8
Developing countries	4.6	0.9	0.4	2.0	0.3	0.4	8.6
Other	0.7	—	—	—	—	—	0.7
Total	$10.3	$5.2	$2.0	$2.7	$1.6	$1.1	$22.9

Source: *Survey of Current Business*, August 1983, Table 18, p. 30.

*Income consists of U.S. affiliate's earning plus interest (net of withholding tax) less U.S. withholding tax on dividends. Alternatively, it is the sum of interest, dividends, and earnings of unincorporated affiliates and reinvested earnings on incorporated affiliates.

Table A-7 Income on U.S. direct investment abroad by year by Industry ($ billions)

Industry	1977	1978	1979	1980	1981	1982	Trend Rate of Growth* (%)
Petroleum	$ 5.3	$ 6.0	$13.3	$13.2	$13.3	$10.3	16.3
Manufacturing	6.7	10.0	13.1	11.1	8.2	5.2	(5.8)
Other	7.7	9.5	11.8	12.8	10.9	7.4	0.8
Total	$17.7	$25.5	$38.2	$37.1	$32.4	$22.9	4.1

Source: *Survey of Current Business*, August 1983, Table 10, p. 22.

*The trend rate of growth is obtained from a time series regression of the natural logarithms of the growth series using observations for each year of the data span.

Table A-8 U.S. fees and royalties earned abroad by year by Industry ($ billions)

Industry	1977	1978	1979	1980	1981	1982	Trend Rates of Growth* (%)
Petroleum	$ —	$0.2	$0.3	$0.2	$0.2	$0.3	4.1
Manufacturing	2.8	3.0	3.5	4.1	4.0	3.7	6.9
Other	1.1	1.5	1.2	1.5	1.6	1.6	6.5
Total	$3.9	$4.7	$5.0	$5.8	$5.8	$5.6	7.4

Source: *Survey of Current Business*, August 1983, Table 10, p. 22.

*The trend rate of growth is obtained from a time series regression of the natural logarithms of the growth series using observations for each year of the data span.

Table A–9 Recurrent international cash-flow on U.S. investment abroad ($ billions)

Cash-Flow Item	1977	1978	1979	1980	1981	1982	Trend Rate of Growth* (%)
Interest	$ 0.8	$ 0.9	$ 0.8	$ 0.6	$ 0.2	$(1.7)	NMF†
Dividends	6.5	7.1	9.1	10.8	9.6	10.7	10.2
Fees and royalties	3.9	4.7	5.0	5.8	5.8	5.6	7.4
Earnings of nonincorporated affiliates	5.5	5.7	9.5	8.8	9.2	8.6	10.3
Total	$16.7	$18.4	$24.4	$26.0	$24.8	$23.2	7.4

Source: *Survey of Current Business*, various issues.

*The trend rate of growth is obtained from a time series regression of the natural logarithms of the growth series using observations for each year of the data span.

†NMF—not meaningful.

Table A–10 Foreign direct investment position in United States year-end 1982 ($ billions)

Area	Petroleum	Manufacturing	Trade	Banking	Insurance	Other	Total
Canada	$ 1.3	$ 3.6	$ 1.4	$0.5	$0.4	$ 2.6	$ 9.8
Europe	17.3	23.9	11.9	5.1	5.2	5.1	68.5
Japan	0.1	1.5	5.3	1.3	0.2	0.3	8.7
Latin America	1.8	2.7	1.5	1.1	0.6	1.5	9.2
Middle East	—	0.1	0.1	0.4	—	3.9	4.5
Other	—	0.4	0.4	—	—	0.3	1.1
Total	$20.5	$32.2	$20.6	$8.4	$6.4	$13.7	$101.8

Source: *Survey of Current Business*, August 1983, Table 10, p. 36.

Table A–11 Foreign direct investment position in United States at year-end by area ($ billions)

Area	1977	1978	1979	1980	1981	1982	Trend Rate of Growth* (%)
Canada	$ 5.7	$ 6.2	$ 7.2	$10.1	$ 9.9	$ 9.8	12.7
Europe	23.8	29.2	37.4	45.7	60.5	68.5	21.9
Japan	1.8	2.7	3.5	4.2	7.0	8.7	31.2
Other	3.3	4.4	6.4	8.4	13.0	14.8	31.5
Total	$34.6	$42.5	$54.5	$68.4	$90.4	$101.8	22.5

Source: *Survey of Current Business*, August 1983, Table 8, p. 35.

*The trend rate of growth is obtained from a time series regression of the natural logarithms of the growth series using observations for each year of the data span.

Table A-12 Foreign direct Investment position In United States at year-end by Industry ($ billions)

Industry	1977	1978	1979	1980	1981	1982	Trend Rate of Growth* (%)
Petroleum	$ 6.6	$ 7.8	$ 9.9	$12.4	$18.0	$ 20.5	24.0
Manufacturing	14.0	17.2	20.9	25.2	30.0	32.2	17.2
Trade	7.2	9.2	11.6	14.3	17.6	20.6	21.2
Insurance	2.3	2.8	4.1	5.4	5.9	6.4	21.8
Other	4.5	5.5	8.0	11.1	18.9	22.1	34.3
Total	$34.6	$42.5	$54.5	$68.4	$90.4	$101.8	22.5

Source: *Survey of Current Business*, August 1983, Table 8, p. 35.

*The trend rate of growth is obtained from a time series regression of the natural logarithms of the growth series using observations for each year of the data span.

Table A-13 Foreign holdings of long-term U.S. securities at year-end 1982 ($ billions)

Area	Bonds	Corporate Stock	Total
Western Europe	$12.8	$53.6	$66.4
Canada	1.3	13.3	14.6
Japan	0.7	1.0	1.7
Other Western Hemisphere countries	0.8	4.9	5.7
Other foreign countries	0.6	3.4	4.0
International organizations	0.3	0.6	0.9
Total	$16.5	$76.8	$93.3

Source: *Survey of Current Business*, August 1983, Table 3, p. 44.

Table A-14 Foreign holdings of long-term U.S. securities at year-end by type ($ billions)

Type	1977	1978	1979	1980	1981	1982	Trend Rate of Growth* (%)
Bonds	$11.4	$11.5	$10.3	$ 9.5	$10.7	$16.5	4.4
Corporate Stocks	39.8	42.1	48.3	64.6	64.6	76.8	13.9
Total	$51.2	$53.6	$58.6	$74.1	$75.3	$93.3	12.2

Source: *Survey of Current Business*, August 1983, Table 3, p. 44.

*The trend rate of growth is obtained from a time series regression of the natural logarithms of the growth series using observations for each year of the data span.

Table A-15 Income on foreign direct investment in the United States by year by area ($ billions)

Area	1977	1978	1979	1980	1981	1982	Trend Rate of Growth* (%)†
Canada	$0.3	$0.4	$0.6	$1.8	$0.1	$(0.2)	(6.9)†
Europe	1.9	3.0	4.4	5.8	5.4	3.8	15.7
Japan	0.2	0.3	0.6	0.7	0.8	0.4	18.7
Other	0.4	0.5	0.8	1.2	1.2	0.8	18.6
Total	$2.8	$4.2	$6.4	$9.5	$7.5	$4.8	13.8

Source: *Survey of Current Business*, August 1983, Table 8, p. 35.

*The trend rate of growth is obtained from a time series regression of the natural logarithms of the growth series using observations for each year of the data span.

†Canada's trend rate of growth is for 1977–81.

Table A-16 Income* (loss) on foreign direct investment in United States at year-end 1982 ($ billions)

Area	Petroleum	Manufacturing	Trade	Finance	Insurance	Other	Total
Canada	$(0.1)	$(0.1)	$ —	$0.1	$ —	$(0.1)	$(0.2)
Europe	2.7	0.1	0.5	0.3	0.4	(0.2)	3.8
Japan	—	(0.1)	0.2	0.3	—	—	0.4
Latin America	0.2	0.1	—	0.2	0.1	(0.1)	0.5
Middle East	—	—	—	—	—	0.2	0.2
Other	—	—	0.1	—	—	—	0.1
Total	$ 2.8	$ —	$0.8	$0.9	$0.5	$(0.2)	$ 4.8

Source: *Survey of Current Business*, August 1983, Table 16, p. 40.

*Income consists of U.S. affiliate's earning plus interest (net of withholding tax) less U.S. withholding tax on dividends. Alternatively, it is the sum of interest, dividends, and earnings of unincorporated affiliates and reinvested earnings on incorporated affiliates.

Table A-17 Income on foreign direct investment in the United States by year by Industry ($ billions)

Industry	1977	1978	1979	1980	1981	1982	Trend Rate of Growth* (%)
Petroleum	$0.8	$1.2	$2.0	$3.5	$3.4	$2.8	28.4
Manufacturing	0.9	1.1	1.7	2.4	1.0	—	(54.5) †
Trade	0.7	0.8	1.1	1.4	1.5	0.8	8.0
Insurance	0.1	0.4	0.6	0.8	0.2	0.4	14.7
Other	0.3	0.7	1.0	1.4	1.4	0.8	20.9
Total	$2.8	$4.2	$6.4	$9.5	$7.5	$4.8	13.8

Source: *Survey of Current Business*, August 1983, Table 8, p. 35.

*The trend rate of growth is obtained from a time series regression of the natural logarithms of the growth series using observations for each year of the data span.

† The trend rate of growth for manufacturing is for the period 1977–81.

Table A-18 Foreign fees and royalties earned in the United States by year ($ billions)

	1977	1978	1979	1980	1981	1982	Trend Rate of Growth* (%)
Total fees and royalties	$0.2	$0.4	$0.5	$0.5	$0.4	—	(24.7) †

Source: *Survey of Current Business*, August 1983, Table 8, p. 35.

*The trend rate of growth is obtained from a time series regression of the natural logarithms of the growth series using observations for each year of the data span.

†The trend rate of growth for fees and royalties includes $.042 billion in 1982.

275

Table A–19 Recurrent International cash flow on foreign investment in the United States ($ billions)

Cash Flow Item	1977	1978	1979	1980	1981	1982	Trend Rate of Growth* (%)
Interest	$0.1	$0.3	$0.6	$0.9	$1.1	$2.1	55.8
Dividends	0.8	0.8	1.0	1.4	1.9	2.3	23.5
Fee and royalties	0.2	0.4	0.5	0.5	0.4	—	(24.7)†
Earnings of unincorporated affiliates	0.3	0.5	0.8	1.0	0.7	0.7	15.6
Total	$1.4	$2.0	$2.9	$3.8	$4.1	$5.1	25.4

Source: *Survey of Current Business,* various issues.

*The trend rate of growth is obtained from a time series regression of the natural logarithms of the growth series using observations for each year of the data span.

† The trend rate of growth for fees and royalties includes $0.042 billion in 1982.

Table A-20 New International bond issue by type of issue ($ billions)

Type of Issue	1977	1978	1979	1980	1981	1982	Trend Rate of Growth* (%)
Eurobonds	$17.8	$14.1	$18.7	$24.0	$31.6	$50.3	22.5
Foreign bonds outside U.S.	8.8	14.4	17.7	14.5	13.8	19.9	10.7
Foreign bonds inside U.S.	7.4	5.8	4.5	3.4	7.6	5.9	(1.7)
Total	$34.0	$34.3	$40.9	$41.9	$53.0	$76.1	15.3

Source: "World Financial Markets," Morgan Guaranty Trust Company.

*The trend rate of growth is obtained from a time series regression of the natural logarithms of the growth series using observations for each year of the data span.

Table A-21 New Eurobond Issues by category of borrower ($ billions)

Borrower	1977	1978	1979	1980	1981	1982	Trend Rate of Growth* (%)
U.S. companies	$ 1.1	$ 1.1	$ 2.9	$ 4.1	$ 6.2	$12.6	50.6
Foreign companies	7.4	4.6	7.2	9.1	12.9	13.2	17.8
State enterprises	4.7	3.3	4.5	5.8	7.5	13.5	22.8
Governments	2.9	3.6	2.4	3.1	2.6	7.6	11.7
International organizations	1.7	1.5	1.7	1.9	2.4	3.4	14.2
Total	$17.8	$14.1	$18.7	$24.0	$31.6	$50.3	22.5

Source: "World Financial Markets," Morgan Guaranty Trust company.

*The trend rate of growth is obtained from a time series regression of the natural logarithms of the growth series using observations of each year of the data span.

Table A-22 New Eurobond Issues by currency of denomination ($ billions)

Currency of Denomination	1977	1978	1979	1980	1981	1982	Trend Rate of Growth* (%)
U.S. dollar	$11.6	$ 7.3	$12.6	$16.4	$26.9	$42.9	30.6
West German mark	4.1	5.3	3.6	3.6	1.3	2.5	(19.1)
Dutch guilder	0.5	0.4	0.5	1.1	0.5	0.6	(6.8)
Canadian dollar	0.7	—	0.4	0.3	0.6	1.2	14.8
ECU	—	0.2	0.3	0.1	0.3	1.8	43.9
Other	0.9	0.9	1.3	2.5	2.0	1.3	14.0
Total	$17.8	$14.1	$18.7	$24.0	$31.6	$50.3	22.5

Source: "World Financial Markets," Morgan Guaranty Trust Company.

*The trend rate of growth is obtained from a time series regression of the natural logarithms of the growth series using observations for each year of the data span.

Table–23 New foreign bond issues outside the United States by category of borrower ($ billions)

Borrower	1977	1978	1979	1980	1981	1982	Trend Rate of Growth* (%)
U.S. companies	$0.1	$ 0.2	$ 0.2	$ 0.3	$ 0.6	$ 2.0	53.4
Foreign companies	1.4	2.1	3.5	3.2	3.4	4.2	19.6
State enterprises	2.4	3.2	3.3	2.8	3.7	5.4	12.4
Governments	2.1	5.8	7.6	4.1	2.7	3.5	(1.0)
International organizations	2.8	3.1	3.1	4.1	3.4	4.8	9.3
Total	$8.8	$14.4	$17.7	$14.5	$13.8	$19.9	10.7

Source: "World Financial Markets," Morgan Guaranty Trust Company.

*The trend rate of growth is obtained from a time series regression of the natural logarithms of the growth series using observations for each year of the data span.

Table A–24 New foreign bond issues outside the United States by currency of denomination ($ billions)

Currency of Denomination	1977	1978	1979	1980	1981	1982	Trend Rate of Growth* (%)
West German mark	$2.2	$ 3.8	$ 5.4	$ 4.8	$ 1.3	$ 2.8	(6.1)
Swiss franc	5.0	5.7	9.7	7.6	8.3	11.1	13.9
Dutch guilder	0.2	0.4	0.1	0.3	0.5	1.0	28.0
Japanese yen	1.3	3.8	1.8	1.1	2.4	3.4	8.4
Other	0.1	0.7	0.7	0.7	1.3	1.6	44.9
Total	$8.8	$14.4	$17.7	$14.5	$13.8	$19.9	10.7

Source: "World Financial Markets," Morgan Guaranty Trust Company.

*The trend rate of growth is obtained from a time series regression of the natural logarithms of the growth series using observations for each year of the data span.

Table A-25 New foreign bond issues in the United States by category of borrower ($ billions)

Borrower	1977	1978	1979	1980	1981	1982	Trend Rate of Growth* (%)
Canadian entities	$3.0	$3.1	$2.2	$2.1	$4.6	$3.2	4.2
International organizations	1.9	0.5	1.1	0.6	1.4	1.7	5.5
Other	2.5	2.2	1.2	0.7	1.6	1.0	(17.4)
Total	$7.4	$5.8	$4.5	$3.4	$7.6	$5.9	(1.7)

Source: "World Financial Markets," Morgan Guaranty Trust Company.

*The trend rate of growth is obtained from a time series regression of the natural logarithms of the growth series using observations for each year of the data span.

Table A-26 Long-term and medium-term export financing authorized during year ($ billions)

Country	1980	1981
Belgium	$ 1.1	$ 0.8
Canada	0.7	1.3
France	10.6	11.7
West Germany	1.6	1.8
Italy	3.6	4.3
Japan	4.1	7.4
United Kingdom	N/A*	N/A*
United States	5.4	3.5
Total	$27.1	$30.8

Source: Report to the U.S. Congress on Export Credit Competition and the Export–Import Bank of the United States, December 1982.

*N/A—Not available.

Table A-27 Percent of total exports that receive official support

Country	1980 %	1981 %
Belgium	N/A*	N/A*
Canada	6.4	N/A*
France	34.0	32.0
West Germany	N/A*	9.2
Italy	7.1	6.0
Japan	43.0	55.0
United Kingdom	30.5	30.8
United States	8.1	5.3

Source: Report to the U.S. Congress on Export Credit Competition and the Export–Import Bank of the United States, December 1982.

*N/A—Not available.

Bibliography

Antl, B., ed. *Swap Financing Techniques.* London, Great Britain: Euromoney Publications Limited, 1983.

————, and A.C. Henry, "The Case for a Coordinated Hedge." *Euromoney*, May 1980, pp. 109–19.

Battersby, M.E. "Avoiding Risks by 'Parallel Lending'." *Finance Magazine*, September–October 1975, pp. 56–57.

Beidleman, C.R.; J.L. Hilley; and J.A. Greenleaf. "Alternatives in Hedging Long-Date Contractual Foreign Exchange Exposure." *Sloan Management Review*, Summer 1983, pp. 45–54.

Benedict, N.P., Vice President-Salomon Brothers Inc., "Currency Swaps and Back-to-Back Loans," Speech presented before the International Institute on Tax and Business Planning: *Surviving in a Floating Currency World*, New York City, October 19, 1978.

Berger, A., ed. "1983 International Tax Summaries." *Coopers and Lybrand International Tax Network.* New York: John Wiley & Sons, 1983.

Brittain, B. and V. Gadkari. "An Introduction to Currency Options." Salomon Brothers, Inc., Bond Market Research, October 1983.

Burn, A.L. "Buttressing the Lender's Legal Position." *The Banker*, January 1979, pp. 89–93.

Cooper, J.C.B. "The Foreign Exchange Market." *Management Accounting*, May 1981, pp. 18–23.

Dempsey, J.R. "The Mexican Back To Back Loan." *Euromoney*, May 1978, pp. 69–75.

Dinur, D.D. "Tax Consequences in Settlement of Currency Futures Unclear Despite Recent Decisions." *Taxation of International Trade*, November 1979, pp. 282–90.

Dranginis, E.M. "Taxation of Foreign Currency Transactions." *Corporation Law Review*, Spring 1983, pp. 156–61.

Eiteman, D.K., and A.I. Stonehill. *Multinational Business Finance.* 3d ed. Reading, Mass.: Addison Wesley Publishing Company, 1982.

"Evolution and Growth of the United States Foreign Exchange Market." *Federal Reserve Bank of New York Quarterly Review*, Autumn 1981, p. 33.

Federal Reserve Bank of New York. "Summary of Results of U.S. Foreign Exchange Market Turnover Survey Conducted in April 1983," and Press Release No. 1550 dated September 7, 1983.

Gelardin, J.P., and D. Swensen. "The Changing World of Swaps." *Euromoney,* June 1983, pp. 33–35.

Giannotti, J.B., and D.P. Walker. "How the New FAS 8 Will Change Exposure Management." *Euromoney,* November 1980, pp. 111–18.

Giddy, I.H. "Foreign Exchange Options." *Journal of Futures Markets.* Summer 1983, pp. 143–66.

————. "An Integrated Theory of Exchange Rate Equilibrium." *Journal of Financial and Quantitative Analysis.* December 1976, pp. 883–92.

————, and G. Duffy. "The Random Behavior of Flexible Exchange Rates." *Journal of International Business Studies,* Spring 1975, pp. 1–32.

Hanna, J.; B. Brittain; and G.M. Parente. "The Case for Currency-Hedged Bonds." Salomon Brothers, Inc., Bond Market Research, November 1983.

Hekman, C.R. "Measuring Foreign Exchange Exposure: A Practical Theory and Its Application." *Financial Analyst Journal,* September/October 1983, pp. 59–65.

Henderson, S.K. "Termination Provisions of Swap Agreements." *International Financial Law Review,* September 1983, pp. 22–27.

Hill, J., and T. Schneeweis. "Forecasting and Hedging Effectiveness of Pound and Mark Forward and Futures Markets." *Management International Review,* 1982, pp. 43–52.

Hilley, J.L.; C.R. Beidleman; and J.A. Greenleaf. "Does Covered Interest Arbitrage Dominate in Foreign Exchange Markets?" *The Columbia Journal of World Business,* Winter 1979, pp. 99–107.

————. "Why There is No 'Long' Forward Market in Foreign Exchange." *Euromoney,* January 1981.

Holmes, A.R., and S.E. Pardee. "Treasury and Federal Reserve Foreign Exchange Operations." *Federal Reserve Bank of New York.* Spring 1978, pp. 54–70.

"Interest Rate Swaps," Goldman, Sachs & Co., 1982.

"Interest Rate Swaps: An Innovative Asset-Liability Tool for the Thrift Industry." Salomon Brothers, Inc., Interest Rate Swap Group, Fall 1983.

Jack, J.E., and J.F. Hughes. "Treasurer's Challenge: Position Firm for Growth in a High Interest Rate Environment." *Cash Flow,* November 1981, pp. 33–34.

Jacque, L.L. "Why Hedgers Are Not Speculators." *Columbia Journal of World Business,* Winter 1979, pp. 108–16.

Kahnamouyipour, H. "Forward Exchange: Hedge, Speculation, or Swap?" *Accountancy,* October 1980, pp. 52, 54–55.

Kemp, D.S. "Hedging a Long-Term Financing." *Euromoney,* February 1981, pp. 102–05.

Leader, S. "International Borrowing in the 1980's." *Institutional Investor,* November 1979, pp. 203–06.

Logue, D.E.; R.J. Sweeney; and T.D. Willett. "The Speculative Behavior of Exchange Rates During the Current Float." *Journal of Business Research,* May 1978, pp. 159–74.

MacBride Price, J.A.; J. Keller; and M. Neilson. "The Delicate Art of Swaps." *Euromoney,* April 1983, pp. 118–25.

Mathur, I. "Attitudes of Financial Executives Toward Foreign Exchange Issues." *Financial Executive,* October 1980, pp. 20–26.

McGoldrick, B. "The Interest Rate Swap Comes of Age." *Institutional Investor,* August 1983, pp. 83–86, 90.

————. "New Life for Interest Rate Swaps." *Institutional Investor International Edition,* August 1983, pp. 91–94.

————. "The Great Debate About Debit-Equity Swaps." *Institutional Investor,* October 1982, pp. 197–204.

Naidu, G.N. "How to Reduce Transaction Exposure in International Lending." *Journal of Commercial Bank Lending,* June 1981, pp. 39–45.

Peckron, H.S. "Tax Consequences of Currency Futures after Hoover." *International Tax Journal,* 1980, pp. 165–77.

Perham, J.C. "The Mysterious Market in Blocked Accounts." *Dun's Review,* October 1976, pp. 93–135.

Piteo, T.A. "Forward Contracts-Free Market Financial Tools." *Journal of Accountancy,* August 1982, pp. 72–82.

Reier, S. "The Boom in Long-Dated Forwards." *Institutional Investor,* October 1983, pp. 353–54.

————. "The Rise of Interest Rate Swaps." *Institutional Investor International Edition,* October 1982, pp. 95–96.

————. "The Enduring Appeal of Currency Swaps." *Institutional Investor,* April 1981, pp. 261–62.

Richelson, S. "Appreciated Foreign Currency Contracts Can Be Used to Fund Private Foundations." *Journal of Taxation,* October 1978, pp. 202–04.

Samuels, L.B. "Federal Income Tax Consequences of Back-to-Back Loans and Currency Exchanges." *Tax Lawyer,* Spring 1980, pp. 847–80.

Shank, J.K.; J.F. Dillard; and R.J. Murdock. "FASB No. 8 and the Decision-Makers." *Financial Executive,* February 1980, pp. 18–23.

Shapiro, A.C. "Executive Summary: The Impact of Taxation on the Currency-of-Denomination Decision for Long-Term Foreign Borrowing." Unpublished paper, *International Business Education and Research,* University of Southern California.

Strauss, P. "The New Foreign Policy of U.S. Companies." *Institutional Investor,* April 1979, pp. 135–42.

Suhar, V.V., and D.D. Lyons. "Choosing Between a Parallel Loan and a Swap." *Euromoney,* March 1979, pp. 114–16.

Teck, A. "Treasurer's Dilemma: How to Resolve Conflicting Domestic, International Cash Management Objectives." *Cash Flow,* January–February 1982, pp. 34–38.

Waldner, S.C. "How to Borrow in a Foreign Currency." *Euromoney,* June 1980, pp. 96–103.

Wallich, C.I. "The World Bank's Currency Swaps." *Finance and Development,* June 1984, pp. 15–19.

Wolf, K. "The Impact of Rate Fluctuations on the Profitability of Swap Transactions." *Euromoney,* November 1974, pp. 26–29.

"World Bank Annual Report." The World Bank, Washington, D.C., 1982.

Index